THE
HITLER
BLOOD
LINE

About the author

David Gardner is a bestselling author and journalist who is an editor with *Newsweek*. He worked for the *Daily Mail* as a crime writer and senior foreign correspondent, filing dispatches from war-torn Beirut, covering the first Gulf War – he was the first British print journalist into Baghdad – and travelling around the world on assignments for the award-winning newspaper. He moved to California as the *Mail*'s Los Angeles correspondent, which saw him cover four presidential elections and all the biggest US stories of the past two decades, and worked until recently as the London *Evening Standard*'s US correspondent. His 2021 book, *9/11: The Conspiracy Theories*, issued by John Blake Publishing to mark the twentieth anniversary of the terrorist attacks on New York and Washington, D.C., was a *Sunday Times* bestseller. His other books include *The Tom Hanks Enigma* (John Blake Publishing, 2007) and *Legends: Murder, Lies and Cover-Ups* (John Blake Publishing, 2016), in which he investigated some of the most famous celebrity deaths in recent history, including those of President John F. Kennedy, Marilyn Monroe and Diana, Princess of Wales. His most recent book for John Blake Publishing is *COVID-19: The Conspiracy Theories* (2022), and he has also written two novels. He divides his time between the UK and LA.

THE HITLER BLOOD LINE

UNCOVERING THE FÜHRER'S SECRET FAMILY

DAVID GARDNER

First published in the UK by John Blake Publishing
An imprint of The Zaffre Publishing Group
A Bonnier Books UK company
4th Floor, Victoria House
Bloomsbury Square,
London, WC1B 4DA
England

Owned by Bonnier Books
Sveavägen 56, Stockholm, Sweden

www.facebook.com/johnblakebooks
twitter.com/jblakebooks

First published in hardback in the UK, as *The Last of the Hitlers*, in 2001 by BMM
This revised and updated edition first published in paperback in 2023 by John Blake Publishing

Paperback ISBN: 978-1-78946-668-3
Ebook ISBN: 978-1-78946-674-4
Audiobook ISBN: 978-1-78946-675-1

British Library Cataloguing-in-Publication Data:
A CIP catalogue record for this book is available from the British Library.

Design by www.envydesign.co.uk

Printed and bound in Great Britain by Clays Ltd, Elcograf S.p.A

1 3 5 7 9 10 8 6 4 2

John Blake Publishing is an imprint of Bonnier Books UK
www.bonnierbooks.co.uk

CONTENTS

FOREWORD

In 1976, Mike Unger, then editor of the *Liverpool Daily Post*, told me of the existence of a journal written by a woman calling herself Brigid Hitler, who claimed not only that Adolf Hitler was her brother-in-law but that he had visited Liverpool in 1912. Brigid, a genteel Irish girl, had met the dashing Alois, half-brother to Adolf, in Dublin in 1909 and promptly eloped with him to England, where they married and set up home in rented accommodation in Upper Stanhope Street, the Toxteth area of the city. Her journal, written long after Alois had deserted her, is deposited in the New York Public Library. That she was indeed married to Hitler's half-brother is proven, but most of what she wrote in her journal, possibly with the help of journalists and gossip columnists, could have been culled from any newspaper of the 1930s. She recalled a visit to Berchtesgaden; a meeting with Angela Raubal and Goebbels – but what rings true, by reason of its mundane content, its very naivety of expression, is her account of Adolf's arrival in Liverpool.

Alois, having gone into the business of promoting safety razors, had decided to employ his sister Angela as his agent in Germany. To this end he sent her money for the fare to England. Accordingly, he and his wife went to Lime Street Station to meet her off the train. Brigid, holding in her arms their infant son, William Patrick, records, prosaically enough, how, instead of Angela, young Adolf Hitler stepped down onto the platform. Later, she describes how their unwelcome guest slept a lot, was nice to the baby, and showed no inclination to earn his keep.

Mike Unger wrote an excellent book based on the journal, and sometime later I wrote a fictional account of this supposed event, one wholly inspired by that first encounter at Lime Street Station. Just imagine the scene – the belch of steam as the train drew in, and out of the swirling mist the emergence of Adolf, shabby, twenty-three years old, and yet to make his bloody boot-print on history.

What you are about to read is an extraordinary account of a search for the descendants of that Liverpool-born William Patrick who, by an accident of birth, was related to the Fuehrer. This is not a book written to expose or give notoriety to those who bear that infamous name; merely an exploration into the subsequent fate of the last of the Hitlers.

DAME BERYL BAINBRIDGE, DBE (1932–2010)

'Of family and history, I have no idea. In this respect I am completely ignorant. Before I did not know that I had relatives. Only when I became Reich Chancellor I learned this. I am a totally unfamilial creature. That does not suit me. I belong only to my people.'

ADOLF HITLER, *MONOLOGUES*, 1942

'I am the only living descendant of the Hitler family bearing that name and I expect shortly to enter the United States Navy.'

WILLIAM PATRICK HITLER, 1944

'Let sleeping dogs lie. There has been enough trouble with this name.'

PHYLLIS HITLER, 1998

The Hitler Bloodline
From the Führer's grandparents to his great-nephews

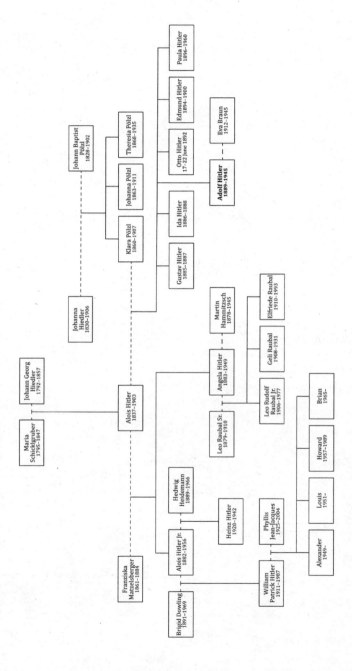

INTRODUCTION

When I first wrote about the extraordinary story of the last living descendants of Adolf Hitler, I was told by an impeccable source that the three surviving Hitler brothers, all living in a New York suburb, had agreed never to marry or have children to ensure the Hitler gene died out with them. There are other members of the extended family, but these are the last in the paternal line – literally the last of the Hitlers.

They, of course, have no idea if evil is passed down through the genes, although their experience would tend to suggest otherwise. All three have lived decent, quiet, unassuming lives. Other than their names – which they have hidden for nearly three-quarters of a century under an assumed surname – they have nothing in common with one of the most hated men in history.

The idea that the brothers had a pact, however, continues to fascinate, as does the remarkable life of their father, William Patrick Hitler, who, until this book's original publication, was dismissed as the Führer's 'loathsome' nephew. His immediate family insist the truth was quite the opposite, and that he was a brave man who dared to speak out against his uncle in the face of considerable personal danger.

The eldest brother has suggested that my description of an agreement between them not to father a new generation of Hitlers was an exaggeration, but I stand by the story and by my source, whom I agreed not to name. It is certainly true that as a young man, one of the younger brothers hoped to marry a Jewish girlfriend, but their engagement ended after she learned of his harrowing family history. This, I am told, was just one of the reasons for the decision to end the Hitler line and save any future generations from the considerable burden it carried. All of them, and I hope they will forgive me for saying this, are now in their twilight years. More than two decades on from my initial contact with them, all three remained unmarried and without children. In the intervening years, I have spoken to the Hitler family numerous times. They are always politely steadfast in their decision not to talk openly about a family connection that has cast a vast shadow across their lives even though they have done nothing to deserve it. I have filled in the gaps as best I can, and I have tried my best to respect their wishes, withholding the name the family chose to replace Hitler, the town where they grew up in Long Island and the towns where they live now. I was even able to pass on to the brothers a copy of a diary I uncovered that their father wrote while he was living in Hitler's Germany in the 1930s that they had never previously seen.

Nearly eighty years after Adolf Hitler's death in 1945, the name throws a darker shadow still than more contemporary genocidal leaders such as Pol Pot, Osama bin Laden and Vladimir

Putin. William Patrick saw at first-hand how his uncle rose to power as head of the National Socialist German Workers' Party through a campaign of brutality and intimidation and provoked the Second World War on 1 September 1939 with the invasion of Poland. Like the rest of the world, William Patrick didn't learn of the Holocaust, Hitler's persecution of the Jews that cost 6 million lives, until after the Second World War, the deadliest conflict in history with an estimated 70 to 85 million fatalities.

With such a trail of death and devastation left in Hitler's wake, it was no surprise that his English nephew dropped out of sight soon after the end of the 1939–1945 war. Living under an assumed name, he raised his own family in a small town a far cry from the tumult of his youth. After a search that took me four years and halfway around the world, I was finally able to tell their extraordinary story for the first time. In this book, I have included new details without, I hope, impinging any further on the surviving brothers' privacy.

This book is not just a history of the family – the American Hitlers – it is also the story of my dedicated research.

It was just a grave, little different from so many of the others lying back to back across the well-tended lawns of the rural cemetery in the backwoods of New York's Long Island. A freshly watered geranium was propped against the marble headstone and a small American flag seemed to have taken root in the soil still soft from an autumn rainstorm.

There was nothing to mark out the grave from its neighbours, nothing to suggest that the lives it commemorated were worth more than a second glance from a stranger.

Only when I saw the words engraved on the headstone did I know for certain it held the key to one of the untold mysteries of the Second World War. Inscribed in bold capitals was a manufactured double-barrelled surname that had served to hide the truth from scores of historians and academics for more than five decades. Underneath was the inscription that, while offering no clues to the drama of their lives, contained the vital information for which I had spent four years searching and had flown 3,000 miles to find.

Rest in Peace

7-3-91 Brigid Elizabeth 11-18-69

3-12-11 William Patrick 7-14-87

The downpour had left me the only person in the graveyard, and I knelt to pull the flowers away from the marble to check the dates of birth. I knew them for sure, but still I needed to check in my notebook to remove any doubt.

William Patrick, born in Liverpool on 12 March 1911, died at his home in Long Island at the age of seventy-six. Sharing the grave was his mother Brigid Elizabeth, born in Dublin, Ireland, on 3 July 1891, and died on 18 November 1969, aged seventy-eight.

There was a surname in the notebook, but it was not the one carved on the headstone. The surname in the notebook was the unwanted legacy the mother had handed to her son: the name William Patrick had been born with but spent more than half of his life trying to escape. It was the reason for my search.

I do not intend to reveal the name on the headstone, but it should have read Hitler.

As the nephew of Adolf Hitler, there was a time William

Patrick called arguably the greatest tyrant of the twentieth century 'Uncle Adolf'.

William Patrick was, in turn, said to have been described by his uncle as 'my loathsome nephew'.

The English-born Hitler had toured the USA and Canada lecturing about the evils of the German leader and had joined the US Navy to fight with the Allies towards the end of the Second World War. But he could never cast off the role appointed him by Nazi historians and Hitler biographers as the Führer's 'black sheep nephew' – just a shady conman. That might explain why he had chosen to disappear and live the rest of his life in obscurity in an anonymous corner of the United States.

History had hardly been kinder to his mother, widely accused of attempting to profit from her position as Hitler's sister-in-law by the accident of an unhappy marriage to his older half-brother, Alois. She, too, chose anonymity in preference to a life as Mrs Hitler.

My excitement at finally finding the grave of the man I believed to be the last to bear the name of the infamous dictator was tempered by the tinge of disappointment at the realisation that William Patrick Hitler had achieved his wish of taking his secret with him to the grave. It may seem fanciful, but I also felt a sinister sense that history was crowding in on me in the deserted garden of remembrance, although I was an ocean and half a century away from the horrors of Adolf Hitler. It was a sensation of being watched – if not by the living, then perhaps by the dead.

For William Patrick, much of his life must have been like this; fearing the memory of a man who had died in a Berlin bunker in 1945 but lived on still in the nightmares of so many. Every day brought with it the possibility of discovery. He had succeeded in hiding his secret from the world, but the reality of his uncle's bloodline was something he could not escape.

I turned to see a figure approaching from the direction of the mausoleum, and for an irrational second or so I justified myself for being spooked with the thought that I was after all being watched.

'I am sorry to drag you away from a loved one,' the man said with a practised politeness. 'I'm the superintendent here and I'm about to close the gates, so I'm afraid I'll have to ask you to leave in a few minutes. I saw you standing out here in the rain. Must have meant a lot to you,' he added. 'I'm sorry for your loss.'

Mumbling my thanks, I took a last look at the headstone and walked back across the sodden grass to my hire car. Just three days earlier, I had been sitting in my office in Newport Beach, California, ready at last to give up my obsession with the English Hitler. During my five years in the United States, working as a freelance journalist on the East and West coasts for British newspapers, I kept going back to the story, exhausting inquiries and giving up yet again. It seemed I would end up being thwarted just like others who had tried before to uncover William Patrick's story.

But on that afternoon three days earlier I made a chance discovery leading to what I thought would be the long-lost nephew's grave. Now I knew it was.

Driving back to the small town that William Patrick chose all those years ago as his retreat from the past, I wondered about my next move. It was especially ironic that while Adolf Hitler went to such great lengths to disown his family, even turning the

Austrian countryside where he grew up into an artillery range, I finally had evidence that his nephew was just as paranoid about his past and had taken extraordinary steps to disguise it.

If it was so important to Adolf Hitler to keep his family and his ancestry from the public eye, was it possible that by learning more about the life of William Patrick, the nephew he allegedly described as one of his 'most repulsive relatives', we could help unlock the puzzle of Hitler's own evil mind?

One question had been answered in the deserted cemetery, but many more remained. Was William Patrick the last of the Hitlers? Or did he have heirs who carried the name he had made up?

I was to discover that William Patrick had carried on his uncle's bloodline; that he had sired four sons – one of whom died in a traffic accident – and that the surviving brothers had decided together in a remarkable pact not to have children in order that Adolf Hitler's genes would die with them.

The eldest of these sons holds an even more remarkable secret: he was named after his despotic uncle. So, an Adolf Hitler lives on to this day in a forgotten corner of America. Although he has lived most of his life shielded by the alias assumed by his parents, William Patrick's firstborn son was named Alexander Adolf Hitler.

Just why a man who spent more than half his life trying to distance himself from the name Hitler should pass on the most despised name in history to his son is one of the many contradictions in this fascinating saga of a family cursed by its birthright.

It was equally strange that William Patrick should choose

part of the name of a pro-Hitler English writer as his adopted identity. The writer's background is explored later in this book. As a member of the family told me: 'There are many pieces to this puzzle – and they don't all necessarily fit nice and neatly together.'

Deep in the American heartland, Hitler's great-nephews still keep his secrets. They had never spoken before and remain fiercely protective of their hard-won anonymity. Yet their determined disappearance means that now, after all these years, they can offer new perspectives – and new details – of the twisted enigma that was Adolf Hitler.

Historians have wondered for years whether Hitler's well-documented admiration for England was borne out of a visit to the country. The alleged visit is much disputed. Almost to a man, historians have discounted the possibility. But the version that Brigid passed on to William Patrick and that he, in turn, passed on to his sons was that Adolf Hitler not only visited Liverpool and London, but he also travelled to Ireland.

Many of those same Hitler experts have long maintained that a manuscript purporting to have been written by William Patrick's mother was a fake. The surviving Hitlers have tried their best to further that impression, insisting to me that the unique memoir, currently held at New York's Public Library, was a 'fantasy'.

The reason is they know all too well that to confirm the facts from the book would only stir up more interest in themselves and further risk of being publicly outed. The truth, according to a family member, is that the memoir, which includes details of Hitler's England visit, was essentially factual and was written jointly by William Patrick and his mother.

INTRODUCTION

'I just wish you could have met him. I know you would have liked him,' I was told about William Patrick. Sadly, my journey started too late for that. But with the gracious, if not all-embracing, help of some of his surviving family, his mother's memoir, a never-before-seen pre-war diary, previously unpublished FBI and intelligence files and a myriad other sources, I believe I have done what Hitler went to such great lengths to avoid when he was alive. I have given his family a human face.

It has been over two decades since I visited that graveyard and discovered what happened to Hitler's long-lost relative and his children, the last living members of the paternal Hitler line. In that time, the fascination with the family's story has, if anything, grown, as have the requests for the surviving members to sit down and talk about their past. They have firmly rebuffed any requests, even after Phyllis, William Patrick's widow, passed away in 2004. When I first wrote about the American Hitlers, Oprah Winfrey's producers were among those who asked me to forward a request on her behalf for them to appear on her top-rated show and discuss their unsettling heritage with the queen of US television. They weren't interested.

'When I was a kid, I'd ask my father,' Alex told me during one visit to his Long Island home. He said William Patrick replied: '"Why? What do you want to know for? It's not going to do anything to help you." He didn't really talk about it. When he came to the United States, he said that life is over; this is my new life.'

He was able to do just that, creating a new, quieter life for himself and his family, with Nazi Germany a dark and distant memory. It hasn't been so easy for his children.

Are people born evil? Being born a Hitler undoubtedly carried immense challenges. As you will read, it has been a burden for the American Hitlers. It has cast a long shadow over their lives. But William Patrick's children have lived long, decent lives. They have gone out of their way to make a positive difference in the lives of their family and friends. They just want to leave the past behind, as their father did.

I interviewed a survivor of Auschwitz, who lived a few towns away from the Hitlers in Long Island, New York, and I was interested in knowing how he felt about having the only surviving Hitlers as his neighbours. Interestingly, he felt no enmity towards them at all. He didn't even blame Hitler and his henchmen for the horrors they wrought in the Holocaust. To him, the German people were to blame for allowing it to happen.

From the BBC to CNN and HBO and every publication from the *New York Times* to the *Daily Mail,* the *Daily Telegraph*, *Paris Match* and *Bild* there has been avid interest over the years in telling their full story, but this book remains the only account of the fascinating, unique history of the last of the Hitlers.

CHAPTER ONE

INTERVIEW WITH THE FBI

30 MARCH 1942. NEW YORK CITY

Although William Patrick had arrived in the USA in March 1939, some six months before the German invasion of Poland, the FBI did not take an interest in him for three years and then only after he had written to President Franklin D. Roosevelt about the possibility of enlisting in the US Army. The inquiry was entrusted to Special Agent T. B. White who was to interview William Patrick Hitler at the New York Field Division headquarters of the Federal Bureau of Investigation in Foley Square.

The inquiry into the case of the Führer's British relative had been launched a little over two weeks earlier when a top-secret White House memo landed on the desk of FBI Director J. Edgar Hoover in Washington, D.C. Dated 14 March 1942, it read:

CONFIDENTIAL MEMORANDUM FOR: Hon. J. Edgar Hoover, Director, Federal Bureau of Investigation

Dear Edgar

This letter comes from Hitler's nephew who apparently is on a lecture tour of the United States. I thought it might be well to look into the matter as he is now writing to the President asking that he be allowed to join the United States Army. Sincerely,

EDWIN M. WATSON, Secretary to the President

The accompanying letter to the President, dated 3 March 1942, was now on White's desk together with an order from the FBI chief demanding an 'expeditious' investigation into the young Hitler's background.

The letter read:

His Excellency Franklin D. Roosevelt,
President of the United States of America,
The White House,
Washington D.C.

Dear Mr President:

May I take the liberty of encroaching on your valuable time and that of your staff at the White House? Mindful of the critical days the nation is now passing through, I do so only because the prerogative of your high office alone can decide my difficult and singular situation.

Permit me to outline as briefly as possible the circumstances of my position, the solution of which I feel could be so easily achieved should you feel moved to give your kind intercession and decision.

I am the nephew and only descendant of the ill-famed Chancellor and Leader of Germany who today so despotically seeks to enslave the free and Christian peoples of the globe.

Under your masterful leadership men of all creeds and nationalities are waging desperate war to determine, in the last anyalsis [sic], whether they shall finally serve and live in an ethical society under God or become enslaved by a devilish and pagan regime.

Everybody in the world today must answer to himself which cause they serve. To free people of deep religious feeling there can be but one answer and one choice, that will sustain them always and to the bitter end.

I am one of many, but I can render service to this great cause and I have a life to give that it may, with the help of all, triumph in the end.

All my relatives and friends soon will be marching for freedom and decency under the Stars and Stripes. For this reason, Mr President, I am respectfully submitting this petition to you to enquire as to whether I may be allowed to join them in their struggle against tyranny and oppression? At present this is denied to me because when I fled the Reich in 1939, I was a British subject. I came to America with my Irish mother principally to rejoin my relatives here. At the same time, I was offered a contract to write and lecture in the United States, the pressure of which did not allow me the time to apply for admission under the quota. I had, therefore, to come as a visitor.

My mother, having been rendered stateless by the

Austrian authorities, left me with no British kith or kin and all my relatives are Americans.

I have attempted to join the British forces, but my success as a lecturer made me probably one of the best attended political speakers, with police frequently having to control the crowds clamouring for admission in Boston, Chicago and other cities. This elicited from British officials the rather negative invitation to carry on.

The British are an insular people and while they are kind and courteous, it is my impression, rightly or wrongly, that they could not in the long run feel overly cordial or sympathetic towards an individual bearing the name I do. The great expense the English legal proceedure [sic] demands in changing my name, is only a possible solution not within my financial means at present. At the same time, I have not been successful in determining whether the Canadian Army would facilitate my entrance into the armed forces or whether I am acceptable to them. As things are at present, and lacking any official guidance, I find that to attempt to enlist as a nephew of Hitler is something that requires a strange sort of courage that I am unable to muster, bereft as I am of any classification or official support from any quarter.

As to my integrity, Mr President, I can only say that it is a matter of record and it compares somewhat to the foresighted spirit with which you, by every ingenuity known to statecraft, wrested from the American Congress those weapons which are today the Nation's great defense in this crisis. I can also reflect that in a time of great complacency and ignorance I tried to do those things which as a Christian I knew to be right. As a fugitive from the Gestapo, I warned France through the press that Hitler would invade her that year. The people of England I warned by the same means that the so-called 'solution' of Munich was a myth that would bring terrible consequences. On my arrival in America I at once informed the press that Hitler would lose his Frankenstein on civilisation that year. Although nobody paid any attention to what I said, I continued to lecture and write in America. Now the time for writing and talking has passed and I am mindful only of the great debt my mother and I owe to the United States. More than anything else I would like to see active combat as soon as possible and thereby be accepted by my friends and comrades as one of them in this great struggle for liberty.

Your favourable decision on my appeal alone would ensure that continued benevolent spirit on the part of the American people, which today I feel so much a part of. I most respectfully assure you, Mr President, that as in the past I would do my utmost in the future to be worthy of the great honour I am seeking through your kind aid, in the sure knowledge that my endeavours on behalf of the great principles of Democracy will at least bear favourable comparison to the activities of many individuals who for so long have been unworthy of the fine privelege [sic] of calling themselves Americans. May I therefore venture to hope, Mr President, that in the turmoil of this vast conflict you will not be moved to reject my appeal for reasons for which I am in no way responsible?

For me today there could be no greater honour, Mr President, to have lived and to have been allowed to serve you, the deliverer of the American people from want, and no greater privelege [sic] than to have striven and had a small part in establishing the title you once will bear in posterity as the great Emancipator of suffering mankind in political history.

I would be most happy to give any additional information that might be required and I take the liberty of enclosing a circular containing details about myself.

Permit me, Mr President, to express my heartfelt good wishes for your future health and happiness, coupled with the hope that you may soon lead all men who believe in decency everywhere onward and upward to a glorious victory.

I am,

Very respectfully yours,

Patrick Hitler

After Roosevelt's secretary Major General Edwin Watson passed the letter on to the FBI, Agent White had spoken to several of William Patrick Hitler's associates and was quickly building up a considerable dossier on the subject of the high-priority White House inquiry. Hoover had insisted on an experienced agent to determine the letter writer's 'background, activities, associates and loyalties' and included a suggestion that the British Embassy in Washington had already deemed that 'Mr Hitler was OK'. In the same letter to P. E. Foxworth, assistant director of the FBI's New York Field Division, Hoover asked that Patrick Hitler be 'discreetly thoroughly interviewed'.

Hitler attended at the FBI office, hoping to be allowed to go to war against his uncle. He showed White his draft card, registered under his full name of William Patrick Hitler and giving his address as 4315 45th Street, Sunnyside, Queens, New York.

As Agent White made notes, Hitler, sporting a thin pencil moustache, offered his personal details.

Name: WILLIAM PATRICK HITLER

Age: 31

Born: March 12, 1911, Liverpool, England

Height: 6' 1"

Weight: 175 lbs

Build: Medium

Eyes: Blue

Hair: Black

Complexion: Ruddy

Nationality: British

It was three years to the day since William Patrick Hitler had sought a new life in the United States, an escape from the burden of his name. Apart from having relatives living in Brooklyn and the Bronx, William Patrick had hoped a man called Hitler might survive, and even prosper, three thousand miles from the conflict and chaos of a divided Europe. He told Agent White that both he and his mother, Brigid Hitler, had been dismissed from jobs in London because of their relationship with the German dictator and, rather than travel as the son of Adolf Hitler's half-brother, Alois, William Patrick took the pseudonym of Carter Stevens to cross the Atlantic in 1939 on board the French liner SS *Normandie*.

In his classified report on the case, FBI File number 100-21611, White added that William Patrick also used the aliases William Patrick Dowling and Patrick Dowling.

Shortly after being assigned the Hitler case, White had phoned Brigid at the New York home she shared with her son, only to be told that William Patrick was in Pennsylvania visiting a friend and was not expected back until the end of the month. By the time the special agent had completed his interview with the Hitler nephew and spoken to other informants, Hoover was becoming impatient to see the report and telexed his New York office to have it sent to him 'without further delay'.

When writing his report on 1 April 1942, White noted that several New York newspapers had carried stories about William Patrick and his mother. Included among them was an article in the 30 January 1941 edition of the *Herald Tribune* saying that William Patrick was about to leave the United States to join the Canadian Air Force. It mentioned his mother was active in the British War Relief Society. Another *Herald Tribune* story, dated 1 April 1939, stated that after William Patrick had arrived in America he stayed at the Buckingham Hotel on Sixth Avenue, confined to his bed with influenza.

White's report was careful to record William Patrick's own version of his life.

INTERNAL SECURITY – G SPECIAL INQUIRY – WHITE HOUSE
Subject Hitler advised that he was born in Liverpool,

England on March 12, 1911 and was educated at St Marcy College at Liverpool and Ashford College, Middlesex. Hitler advised that he studied accountancy and left college at 17, at which time he went to work for Benhan & Son Ltd. of Whitmore Street, London, England. He and his mother were both employed by this concern until March 1932, at which time both he and his mother were discharged because of the name which they bore. Hitler advised that he first went to Germany for a two week summer vacation in 1928 to visit his father, Alois Hitler, who was in Berlin at that time. Subject Hitler reported that he had had some correspondence with his father and that it was upon his suggestion that he went to Germany. At this time his father was employed in the restaurant and wine business in Berlin. Subject Hitler said that in the summer of 1929 he again visited his father, at which time they went to the Nuremberg Congress of the Nazi Party and that they remained for about five days at this Nazi rally. It was at this time, Hitler said, that he met his uncle, Adolf Hitler.

On October 20, 1933, subject Hitler advised, he arrived in Germany of his own volition to fill a position with the Defaka Department Store, Berlin, where he took a job at 250 marks a month. Subject advised that he obtained this position through a friend in England and that when he reached Germany it was necessary for him to obtain necessary labor papers subject to the approval of Adolf Hitler. He said that Koerner, the economic czar of Germany, called on him and advised him that Adolf Hitler would not allow a relative to take a clerk's job in a department store. He was then advised to get in contact with Adolf Hitler's half sister and when he did so she denied the story that there was any relationship on her part, or on the part of Adolf Hitler, to William Patrick Hitler. Subject advised that he then produced documents which were taken by Adolf Hitler's half sister to the Fuehrer and that he, William Patrick Hitler, was then summoned before the Fuehrer and given 500 marks and Adolf Hitler was extremely courteous to him. He stated that the Fuehrer advised him that this 500 marks was being given to him in order to help him subsist until such a time that he was able to find a position.

At the termination of this interview with Adolf Hitler, subject advised that the Fuehrer then introduced him to Rudolph Hess and advised Hess that William Patrick Hitler was under his supervision and that he was to find him a suitable position. Subject Hitler, continuing, said that Hess promptly delegated this assignment to one of his subordinates by the name of Bowler and that Bowler did absolutely nothing in regard to finding him a position. Subject Hitler said that upon realizing that no position was to be provided him he secured a position with a bank at approximately $35 a month and remained in this position for approximately 10 months. He stated that he quit his job with the bank in view of the fact that he was unable to provide any money for his mother who was at that time in England. Subject Hitler advised that he then secured a position with the Opel Automobile Works and that he had received the necessary O.K. from the Nazi government in order for him to fill this position . . .

He said, continuing, that he worked as a mechanic in the automobile factory until February, 1935, at which time he secured a transfer to the sales department, at which time he took up his duties as an automobile salesman. He advised that as one of his assignments he was given a list of names of prospective buyers and that upon contacting one of these prospective buyers he learned that it was a Nazi party newspaper. Upon introducing himself as William Patrick Hitler, the representative of the party newspaper inquired as to his relationship with the Fuehrer and subject Hitler informed that it was true, he was a nephew of Adolf Hitler, at which time the party newspaper representative excused himself and telephoned the local police, who in turn contacted the office of Adolf Hitler. Subject Hitler was then ordered before one of Adolf Hitler's adjutants who threatened him with arrest and advised him the Fuehrer's wrath had been incurred in view of the fact that subject Hitler had publicly claimed relationship with the Fuehrer in order to sell automobiles for the Opel Works. At this time the subject informed the adjutant that he had committed no crime and that he had taken the position with Opel Automobile Works with the O.K. of the Nazi government and that the Fuehrer was acquainted with the fact that he had taken such a position. He further advised the adjutant that if he were arrested he intended to take the matter up with the British Ambassador.

The subject then advised that he was called before

Adolf Hitler, who was extremely cordial to him, but that he later received notice to the effect that he had been suspended from duty by Adolf Hitler from the Opel Automobile Works.

Hitler then advised that he then returned to England for approximately six months in order to straighten out the affairs of his mother and that after this was completed he returned to Germany on March 30, 1938. Hitler advised that he had written his father previous to his return to Germany and requested that he advance him sufficient money for him to live in Germany until such a time that he was able to secure another job.

The subject advised that his real purpose for returning to Germany was in order to see a girl whom he had become extremely fond of. Continuing, he advised that Scholz Klink, known in Germany as the Perfect German Mother, or the head of German womanhood, took a personal interest in him and secured for him a job with a brewer in Berlin. He advised that this woman invited him to various social functions and that on one occasion he attended a White Russian charity drive and that while at this function he was seen in the company of Prince Ashwiln and an aide of Ribbentrop had made this fact known to Adolf Hitler. The subject advised that Hitler then requested him to appear before him and after a violent argument on the part of Adolf Hitler the subject was advised to either become a German citizen or leave Germany; that the subject had continually embarrassed the Fuehrer and it was no longer believed advisable for him to remain in Germany in view of the fact that the Fuehrer never did believe he would be a good German. Subject Hitler said that for this reason on February 1, 1939 he left Germany, being driven to the Dutch border by a friend, and from there returning to England. Continuing, he advised that before he left Germany his mother had been contacted by the German Ambassador's office in England and had been requested to sign a document that she was voluntarily returning to Germany and that all of her expenses were being paid. He said that his mother refused to sign the document and nothing further was heard in regard to the German government desiring her return to Germany.

During the 'blood purge' of 1934 in Germany, the subject advised, he was arrested by the Gestapo and held for two days and in his opinion the only reason he was released was because a friend of his in whose presence he had been arrested contacted the British Consulate, who intervened and caused the release of subject Hitler. He further advised that all of the time he was employed in Germany his various employers were required to submit monthly reports as to his activities and the type of work which he was doing.

Subject Hitler advised that one of his reasons for leaving Germany was in view of the fact that he was a devout Catholic and he observed with horror Hitler's persecution of the Catholic Church and, further, that he never subscribed to the Nazi doctrines.

Subject advised that he arrived in the United States on

a visitor's visa March 30, 1939 on the *S.S.* Normandie and that he had come to this country at the instigation of the William Morris Theatrical Agency; that since he had been in this country he has supported his mother by conducting numerous lectures in regard to his experiences in Germany and had also written an article for the July or August, 1939 issue of Look magazine. He stated that he had also consulted with Confidential Informant #2 concerning a book which was to be entitled My Uncle Adolf but which book had never been written, and that he had consulted with Mr Eugene Lyon of the American Mercury magazine in regard to the publication of this book. However, he had been advised that if it were published at this time it would probably not be as successful as it would have been had it been published before the start of the war.

In regard to the publicity which subject Hitler had received concerning numerous newspaper articles which referred to his joining the Canadian forces in Canada, he advised that he had never gone to Canada to consult the Canadian authorities. However, he said that he had written to the British Consul and had received a rather negative answer in regard to his enlistment in the Canadian forces. He said that British authorities had more or less advised him to continue his lectures. As to his plans for the future, Hitler informed that he had written to the President of the United States for intercession in assisting him in gaining admission to the armed forces of this country. He further advised that he had also written that he was desirous of becoming an

American citizen, if possible. The subject advised that all of his relatives were American citizens and that he had very few associates, and that the few that he did have he became acquainted with through his lectures.

The subject exhibited his draft card which indicated that he had registered under the name of William Patrick Hitler, giving as his address 4315 45th Street, Sunnyside, Queens, New York, on October 16, 1940 and precinct 12, ward 2 of Queens, New York.

Special Agent P. J. Martin on checking the files of the Credit Bureau of Greater New York advised that there was no credit record in regard to William Patrick Hitler.

White's report was approved by Foxworth and sent to Hoover in Washington, D.C. on 20 April 1942. Hoover's potted synopsis of the report was forwarded by special messenger to the President's Secretary, Major General Watson, at the White House.

'No information was developed to indicate that he was engaged in any activities of a subversive nature,' wrote Hoover, although he added: 'At this time efforts are being made to ascertain whether Hitler, while in England, was engaged in any activities which might be of interest, and if anything deemed pertinent is developed in this connection, this information will immediately be brought to your attention.'

In his confidential letter, the FBI Director also mentioned that 'contact was had with other individuals who have been associated with him since his arrival in this country'.

CHAPTER TWO

STARTING THE SEARCH

19 APRIL 1995. NEW YORK

'My name is David Gardner. I'm a British journalist and I've got a rather unusual question to ask you.' I took a deep breath and plunged in: 'Is there any way that your husband could be related to Adolf Hitler?'

The blank look on the face of the portly woman peering from behind her screen door suggested she was wondering what I was trying to sell. 'I don't need anything, and my husband is at work . . . but he'll be back very soon,' she added quickly as she stepped back to close the front door.

'Please, if you could just bear with me a minute, I'd like to explain,' I said, keeping a metaphorical foot in the door by talking fast without taking a breath. 'I know it must be really strange for you to have an Englishman turn up out of the blue like this, but I'm not trying to sell you anything. I just want to ask if you can help with an article I am writing about a relative of Adolf Hitler.'

'Adolf who?'

'Adolf Hitler. You know, the German leader in World War Two.'

'I don't know him.'

'No, I know. I'm sorry, let me tell you some of the background and then it will make a little more sense.'

'I told you I don't want to buy anything. Not today.'

'I know you don't want to buy anything. I'm a reporter. I work for a newspaper.'

'We already get the *New York Post*. We get it delivered every day.'

'I'm from a British newspaper . . .'

'We don't want one of those.'

'Please, I am not selling newspapers. I just want your help with a story I am writing. I write articles for a British newspaper called the London *Mail*. I'm a journalist. I have got the right house, haven't I? Is your name Dowling?'

Now looking totally perplexed, the woman adjusted her hair, tugged at her patterned blouse, and turned around to yell: 'Will you behave, Vinnie! Stop crying and watch the TV. And leave your sister alone.' She looked back at me, hesitated for a moment, and took the monumental leap of opening the screen door. 'Yes, my name is Dowling, but what's that got to do with Hitler? This is Queens. You must have the wrong place. There's no Hitlers here.'

'I'm sure you're right,' I said. 'But if you can spare me a couple more minutes, I'd like to tell you more about why I'm here.'

'Are you from England? I knew a guy from England once. He stayed with his sister up the road. He lived where the Beatles came from. Same town.'

'Liverpool?'

'No, I think it was Manchester. Somewhere near London anyway.'

'Really,' I said, happy to have at least struck up a rapport with the woman. 'Have you ever been to England?'

'Me? No. But that Englishman was a nice man. Name of Swift. Do you know the Swifts from Manchester?'

I shook my head, and the woman went on: 'He talked funny, too. My husband thought he was from Australia. Well, thank you for calling, but I've gotta feed my son and my daughter and pick up my other kids from school. Sorry I can't help you.'

I soldiered on: 'If you could just spare me a fraction more of your time. You see, Adolf Hitler had a nephew who grew up in England and came out to the US before the war and fought in the navy. Then he pretty much disappeared, and no one has ever heard from him since. He's supposed to be living in the New York area somewhere and I'm trying to find out what happened to him.'

'And what's that got to do with me?'

'His real name is William Patrick Hitler, but I can't find any Hitlers living in America. It's not a particularly popular name.' I looked up expecting a smile but got the same blank stare.

'Anyway, as his mother's name was Dowling, it seems there is a very good chance he changed his name from Hitler to Dowling after the war. And your husband was the only William Patrick Dowling I could find in New York. The only other one was a W. P. Dowling in Far Rockaway, and he turned out to be Walter Peter Dowling.'

'So, you are saying that my husband could be related to Adolf Hitler?'

'That's what I was wondering.'

'But he's at work. He never mentioned anything about it to me.'

'Do you think there's any possibility that he maybe just wanted to keep it a secret? He had a mother called Brigid from Ireland. I hope you don't think me rude, but have you been married for long?'

'Twenty-seven years. We lived with his mother for ten of those years. But she wasn't Irish. She was Polish. Hardly spoke English. Her name was Anna. His dad was Irish though. He was Bill, too. Drank like a fish.'

'So, you don't think there's any way your husband came over here from England then?' I said, knowing the answer. 'He doesn't have a little bogbrush moustache?'

'Bogbrush? What's that?'

'Sorry, a little Hitler moustache. Like the one Adolf Hitler had.'

'No, no moustache. He had a beard once but shaved it off because it itched so much. I don't think he's hardly ever left Queens. Except we go down to the New Jersey shore most years for a week in the summer. Bill was born in the Bronx and he's lived here all his life and I don't think he knows any Germans. Not unless he knows any at the bar he uses after work. The one up the road under the subway.'

'Well, thanks ever so much. I'm sorry to have troubled you,' I said, eager now to leave. 'I'll be going then. I don't want to keep you any further.'

I was well into my second week working on the story and

doors were slamming on every line of inquiry to try and learn the fate of Adolf Hitler's mysterious English nephew.

I had tried everyone in America with the various names Adolf Hitler's family had used through the years, from Hiller to Hiedler to Heidler and the original, Schicklgruber. There were William Hillers in Frewsburg, Niagara Falls, Rochester and Westfield, all in New York and all no relation. There was a William Hillermeier in Smallwood and a William Hillery in New Jersey. Again, no relation.

Then there were the William Dowlings in the Bronx, Brooklyn, Coxsackie, Flushing, Garden City, Jamaica, Morides, Peckskill, Saratoga Springs and Staten Island. There was even another William Patrick Dowling in Islip. None of them had the faintest idea what I was talking about when I contacted them to ask if they were relatives of Adolf Hitler.

The call that started this had come through the previous Monday at the New York office of US News and Features, the agency I had set up in 1993 with partner Tim Miles to cater for the needs of British newspapers seeking stories from North America. We had chosen the office at 220 Lafayette Street because of its film noir feel. With its smoked-glass door and views of the Soho rooftops, the small corner office was just waiting for Sam Spade. It backed onto Mulberry Street and Little Italy, boasting a Godfather cliche on every corner, and opened out onto trendy Soho and all its wild variety of restaurants, vintage boutiques, tattooed millionaires and impossibly tall models.

On the line was Paul Palmer, a former colleague from Fleet Street and someone I had always had a lot of time for, not least because he paid promptly for the stories he ordered. Palmer had a typically off-the-wall idea for a story for the *Mail* in London.

'Dave, can you do a job for us?' he said, using the newspaper executive's favourite Catch 22 question that will certainly result in a payday but could also mean committing to a job you do not really want to do. I knew I would not find out what the story was unless I agreed to take it on, so I decided to sound enthusiastic.

'Of course, what's up?'

'It could be a really good one,' he said. 'It might need some more digging, but we're looking for a piece to mark the fiftieth anniversary of Adolf Hitler's death in a couple of weeks, and I found these ancient cuttings that look really interesting. There is a chance some long-lost relative may be tucked away somewhere over on your patch. His name is William Patrick Hitler and he's Adolf's British-born nephew. I've got a birth date here, 12 March 1911, and there's a few names in the library stuff worth chasing.

'I've got conference in a moment, but I can fax the cuts and you can let me know what you think. Is that okay?'

'Sure, Paul, but how long have we got?' I replied, fully expecting to be told the story had to be researched, written and illustrated by yesterday.

'The anniversary's two weeks away, so you've got a fair bit of time. I've got to go. I'll call tomorrow.'

Alone in the office, I waited for the laborious, one-year-old and already outdated fax to churn out several inky pages before grabbing my coat with the intention of reading the old pre-war cuttings on the subway home.

Now, more than a week later, I was no nearer to tracking down the elusive William Patrick Hitler.

Driving back from Queens on the car park New Yorkers called the Long Island Expressway, I headed through the Midtown Tunnel towards Les Halles, the late Anthony Bourdain's now shuttered Park Avenue bistro which, following the closure of Costello's – a loud, lively Irish bar on the East Side – had become a regular meeting place for the British and Australian journalists working in Manhattan.

It was a good time to be a freelance in New York, I thought, as I sought out my partner, Tim Miles. Leaving my coat with the maître d' opposite the ranks of meat carcasses hanging over the counter, I pushed my way through the crowded bar to make my apologies and gladly accept my first drink of the day.

Tim asked for an update on the Hitler story. 'I really thought we had the right one this morning, but it was another complete blow-out. The guy's wife thought I was a nutcase.'

Taking a seat in the still-busy restaurant, I told my friend the latest hiccup in the Hitler saga. We had struck up a strong rapport in the years we had worked together in Manhattan. My more cautious approach was a perfect match for his world-weary tenacity.

Both of us had taken risks to join forces in New York. I left a good job with the *Daily Mail* in London, where I was a senior reporter with some measure of respect and a decent salary. I was the first English newspaper journalist to get into Baghdad at the outset of the Gulf Conflict; spent two years as a crime correspondent, covered big stories around the world; and worked with some of the nicest people in the business, but the two-hour daily commute to Kensington, West London, was getting me down and the lure of America was, in the end, simply too strong to resist.

My wife, Michelle, quit her job at Coutts, the late Queen's bank, in London, and we uprooted our two young children, Mickey, then four, and ten-month-old Jazmin, from semi-detached suburbia in Essex to New York's commuter belt in leafy Rutherford, New Jersey, in the spirit of adventure. Our third child, Savannah, was born soon after we settled in America.

When Tim had left London some years before, he was generally regarded as one of the best, if not the best, reporter in Britain. He was half of a formidable media couple with wife, Wendy, who had been promoted by proprietor Rupert Murdoch to the helm of the *News of the World*, making history as the first woman editor in Fleet Street. She went on to edit the *Sunday People*, and when she was headhunted for a top job in Florida, Tim set up as a freelance in Boca Raton, a faceless coastal town north of Fort Lauderdale.

But while carving out a profitable niche, it was never a good fit for a restless man who craved the excitement and challenge of a city like New York, where he had worked some years before as the *Daily Mail*'s US correspondent. So, when a mutual friend and former colleague, *Mail* Chief Reporter David Williams, told Tim that I was considering a move to the United States, he relocated with Wendy to his spiritual home in Midtown Manhattan and started looking for a suitable office.

I handed in my notice to Paul Dacre, the *Mail* Editor-in-Chief who first employed me at the paper when he was News Editor, and embarked on a series of farewell parties. We also recruited Steve Douglass, one of the *Mail*'s top photographers. Several weeks later, US News and Features was in business.

'Let's look again at what we've got,' said Tim. 'We've got a date of birth and we've got names for William Patrick and for his mother, but there's an outstanding chance that the name has been changed. We'll just have to keep checking out all the possible combinations and hope something comes up.'

I spread out the cuttings on the table just as our steaks arrived. As well as those faxed by Paul Palmer, I'd tracked down a couple more from the *New York Times* and the *Daily News* and one from the library of the *Toronto Star* in Canada. We went quiet as we tried to ingest both the cuttings and the seared rare New York strips. The shanks hanging from hooks by the bar attested to the freshness of the meat. But, apart from one barely readable one from the seventies, the most recent newspaper cutting was dated 13 May 1944.

One fading story particularly fascinated me, as it described Adolf Hitler as his nephew's 'idol' and seemed to contradict later accounts of William Patrick dramatically denouncing his uncle. The headline in the 22 November 1937 edition of the *Daily Express* read: 'Hitler's English Nephew Is Here – Visiting His Mother'.

By-lined by Constance Forbes, it continued:

As William Patrick Hitler said to me, 'I am the only legal descendant of the Hitler family,' he crossed his arms in characteristic Fuehrer fashion and added, 'That gesture must be in the blood. I find myself doing it more and more.'

The 26-year-old son of Alois Hitler, the Fuehrer's

innkeeper brother, is in England for a short holiday after nearly five years in Germany. He talked to me in the little back sitting room of a modest six-roomed house where his mother lives in Highgate.

'I came back because I felt homesick for England.' He stumbled for a word.

'I find it difficult speaking English again after so long, although, of course, it is my native language.'

Occasionally there is a trace of German accent. William Hitler bears a strong resemblance to the uncle, who is his idol. The moustache is copied almost to a hair, the same parting but in black hair which is sleek not unruly. He has the same height and build. 'My uncle the Fuehrer gave instructions that I was to be given every facility to go anywhere,' he told me.

'I worked in banks studying finance, and I have worked through the great Opel car factory and other industrial concerns. In Germany they say no one can manage finance like the English.

'In Germany I am a private individual and in England I am a private individual. I have no authority to make any political statement and I would not say anything to embarrass my uncle.

'Germany is good for Germans and England for the English. The German people admire the English and their stability of temperament.

'My mother is Irish and a good Catholic and I find it very difficult to convert her to National Socialism. There are some things she feels very bitter about.

'She lost her British nationality when she married my father and became Austrian. Recently, the Austrian consulate refused to renew her papers, so that now she has no country.

'I was born in Liverpool. In 1914, we were in London. My father had a razor business. He left England to join the Austrian Army and I was sent to Liverpool to live with my Irish grandparents.'

There is hushed reverence in his voice as he speaks of his uncle. 'Since the Fuehrer has been in power Germany has improved enormously,' he said.

A second cutting, this time from the *New York Daily News* and dated 31 March 1939, had the words: 'Where is he now – alive or dead? Wife? Children?' scrawled in the margin. It helped explain why the *Mail* was looking to the United States for answers to the mystery.

The article read:

Hitler's Irish nephew, a tall, well-built young man with a trim moustache, plenty of dignity and bristling with authority, stepped from the liner Normandie yesterday and divested himself of a lot of uncomplimentary remarks about Uncle Adolf.

The young man announced he was William Patrick Hitler, nephew of the Fuehrer, here with his mother on a lecture tour about the Reich. He was born in Liverpool, son of Hitler's half-brother, Alois Hitler, who now runs a tearoom in Berlin.'

'It's obviously not going to be easy, but it would still be a bloody great tale if we could track him down,' I said to Tim. 'He'd be in his eighties, but he could still be alive. It's got to be worth digging about for.'

'That bastard cop who pulled me over the other day for having the dog on my lap in the jeep was a right little Hitler. It was probably him,' said Tim, grinning as he took a sip of his Dewars and water. 'Or that guy who had a go at Michelle for parking outside his house. The world is full of little Hitlers.'

'That's probably why the real ones are keeping out of sight,' I said.

Tim's phone rang as I held another ageing cutting to my eyes in an attempt to read the tiny print so badly fudged by the fax that it was almost impossible to decipher. So poor was the light in the restaurant that in order to see what it said my face was almost on the table.

It was the one post-war article that was particularly poorly reproduced but contained the only real clues we had to William Patrick's fate after he arrived in New York in 1939. Tim was still speaking on the phone, struggling to get any kind of reception. He had just bought the brick-shaped flip phone and it was still something of a novelty. Oblivious to the curious looks from neighbouring tables, I pulled out of my bag a magnifying glass I bought earlier that day at a stamp store to make out the story word by word.

Headlined 'Tracks of Hitler's Nephew Lead to America', from *The Times* of 10 August 1972 and written by Peter Hopkirk, it read:

William Patrick Hitler, the Fuehrer's English nephew, may be living somewhere in America today under the name Dowling.

Dr Werner Maser, Hitler's biographer, had until yesterday believed that William died in America immediately after the Second World War. But now a London family who were once the Hitlers' neighbours have come up with evidence to prove that he was alive and well in 1948 and living at 505 West 142nd Street, New York (our New York Correspondent reported last night that he was not now living at that address).

The evidence is a photograph of William, his young wife, Phyllis, and their baby. It was sent to their former British neighbours by Mrs Bridget Hitler, William's mother. In a letter she told them they had changed their name to Dowling, her own maiden name.

After that the correspondence ceased, possibly because the Hitlers wanted to start a new life under their new name.

The last letter informed the British family, who prefer to remain anonymous, that William Hitler had found himself a good job in a hospital urology department after three years on the United States Navy medical corps.

Investigation in London shows that the Hitlers lived at 26 Priory Gardens, Highgate, from 1930 to 1939, when they left for America. Previously, William had spent a year in Germany, but had returned to Britain because he was afraid he might be 'liquidated' or so he told a former neighbour, today a London businessman.

One of the reasons for his uncle's wrath was an article he wrote for the magazine 'Look' on January 4, 1939, entitled 'Why I Hate My Uncle.'

The last that was heard of Mrs Hitler in London was on January 19, 1939, when she was summoned for non-payment of rates. The Hitlers were good and friendly neighbours, according to people living in Highgate who still remember them.

Dr Maser, who is trying to trace Hitler's nephew if he is still living, previously believed him to have been born in Northern Ireland, but his American Navy discharge papers show him to have been born in Liverpool.

His father, Hitler's half-brother, Alois, married William's mother in Ireland in 1910, deserting her four years later. He was arrested for bigamy when he returned to Germany, where he later ran a restaurant in Berlin.

Although I had read through the article many times since it was faxed over from London and had earmarked some of the clues it offered, this was the first time I was able to make out the entire piece and there were a couple of additional facts I wanted to discuss with Tim. But my partner's steak was forgotten, and he was busily scribbling on a bill he was using as a makeshift notebook. 'Well, my friend, it looks like we are in business,' he said after hanging up.

'Good news?'

'Definitely. It looks like we've got our man. That was a contact of mine who was helping look for our Mr Hitler. He's got a William Patrick Dowling, born March 12, 1911 – right name, right birth date – and he served in the US Navy just as it said in that *Times* cutting. He's married with a son and lives in Connecticut. It all fits perfectly. It's got to be him. There's just one problem.'

'What's that?' I asked.

'He's dead. Died in April 1989, according to my friend, which is a bit of a pisser.'

'Yes, but if he had a son then we've still got a Hitler alive and well and living in the US,' I said, delighted that the story was finally moving along. 'It's about bloody time we got some luck on this one. I've spent the best part of two weeks chasing around on it, asking absolute strangers if they had an Uncle Adolf. Do you want to head up there now?'

'No. he's still trying to dig out an address for the widow,' said Tim. 'He said he'd call back this evening, so we might as well go up tomorrow morning. He'll charge us the same so we might as well let him find the address. They weren't desperate for the *Mirror* story I was looking at, so I'll put it off for a day and bring the cameras. We might even be able to get some video and sell it to *Hard Copy* or *American Journal*. This could be a really good one. If all these Hitler biographers and historians have been trying to find out what happened to William Patrick for all these years, then there should certainly be some good sales for the story after it's been in the *Mail*. Germany and France and even Australia. They're going to be interested, especially if we can get some good pictures.'

'They'll probably be paranoid in case it's another *Hitler Diaries* and think it's all a big scam,' I said.

'Not if it has already appeared in the *Mail*. The *Mail* trusts us and if we show them it's genuine, they'll run with it. You can be certain of that. It's a great story. Once it's been in the *Mail*, the others will take it, no problem.'

After pushing my way out of the packed restaurant, I said: 'I was thinking of heading up to that address in Harlem that's mentioned in the Hitler cutting from *The Times* before heading home. You know, the one at 505 West 142nd Street. Do you want to come?'

'Don't bother,' said Tim. 'I forgot to tell you that I popped up there this morning. Total waste of time. I didn't get to the Hitler part. I spoke to a nice old couple who'd been living in the area for quite a while, but they said the neighbourhood had changed so much in the last ten or twenty years. They said none of the old families are left. I don't think there's a lot of point going all the way over there again. They probably only lived there for a little while and now it looks like we've pinned them down to Connecticut, we can always have another scout around there if the family is helpful and gives us some more details of their history. I've got to pick up my car from the office and then pick up Wendy. Do you need a lift?'

'No thanks. I'm going the other way. I've got my car. I'll drop you at the office and go home through the Holland Tunnel. If you let me know the address tonight, we can meet up there tomorrow.'

Tim was waiting the following morning at the Dunkin' Donuts just outside Middletown, Connecticut. 'I've spoken to Palmer,' I said. 'It should work out perfectly. Hitler died on April 30, 1945, so they can run our piece on Sunday. I just hope the widow talks to us. They've kept this whole thing secret for a heck of a long time.'

'Even if she doesn't, we should still be able to put a piece together,' said Tim. 'We don't have to give the new name or where they live; in fact, it could sound better if we say we know their identity but we don't want to disrupt their lives and all that bullshit. That may be a good way to bring the widow around if she won't co-operate. But hopefully, she'll welcome us in and tell us what a relief it is to finally get it all off her chest.'

'Yeah, and pigs might fly,' I said.

'We'll soon see. You can do the talking and I'll take the cameras. Do you want to jump in my jeep?'

We drove slowly through the light early-morning traffic, finding the Dowling house in a leafy neighbourhood a couple of blocks from the high street.

'Looks like he did all right for himself,' I said, as we stopped a little way up from the house. 'Might as well knock on the door. You coming?'

'Why not? Give me a second to get the camera gear in a bag. I'll never get used to this stuff. I know now why they used to call photographers monkeys – you need the strength of an ape to carry all this stuff around everywhere.'

Walking up the gravel drive, an inquisitive neighbour lifted her curtain next-door but there was no sign of life in the white Cape Cod-style house. We banged on the door several times and waited.

'She's probably at work. Let's try in the back,' I said. 'You know it's going to end up like every other job we do, sitting on a doorstep waiting for someone to get themselves home. It would be so nice if, just for once, somebody opened the door and invited us in without any delays or unpleasantness.'

'In your dreams,' said Tim just as a woman approached behind us and asked: 'Can I help you?'

'Oh! Hello, Mrs Dowling? I'm sorry to bother you like this but—'

'I'm not Mrs Dowling,' she said curtly. 'She's not here at the moment. Can I help?'

'I'm not sure really,' I continued, trying to work out how much to tell a stranger. 'We're actually from a British newspaper and we're writing a story about Mrs Dowling's husband, William.'

'But he's dead. He died some years ago,' she said.

'Yes, we know. But there was a particular reason we wanted to write about him. It's all to do with the war. I'm sure Mrs Dowling will be happy to talk to us about it.'

'That remains to be seen. She's out at the moment. I think she was going to visit one of her sons.'

'Are you a friend of hers?'

'Yes, she's a friend. I happened to see you going around the back and it seemed a little suspicious.'

'Did you know Mr Dowling?' asked Tim. 'Do you remember if he had an English accent or talked about the war at all?'

'Vietnam?'

'No, the Second World War.'

'He was a bus driver, I think, before he retired. I recall he did have a big funeral. He was a member of the Ancient Order of Hibernians and I think he was in the navy in the war. Why do you want to know all this?'

'Did he ever say anything about Hitler?'

'What on earth do you want to know that for? Are you some kind of salesmen? I think you had better go before I call the police. Mrs Dowling will be back later and if you give me your number, I'll make sure she gets it.'

We had walked back to the front of the house, and I saw a middle-aged man standing in the street taking down the jeep number plate.

'Who's that man?' said Tim.

'That's my husband,' said the neighbour. 'I told him to keep an eye on me when I came over. Unless you want to tell me what you are really doing, I think you should leave.'

'It's nothing sinister,' I blustered. 'It's just a slightly sensitive matter that we want to talk to Mrs Dowling about. We don't want to tell everybody her private business.'

'Very well, I shall have to ask you to leave.'

'We have every right to sit in a public street if we want to. There's no law against that,' said Tim, his hackles rising.

'She's an elderly lady. She doesn't want any surprises.'

'We will be very polite. We shall wait outside until Mrs Dowling comes back.'

The woman frowned and marched back to her house, where she stood whispering angrily to her husband, before disappearing inside. Every few minutes, the blinds in the front room crinkled up as the couple peered out across the road to where we were still sitting.

'Well, that was a bit awkward,' I said. 'But it sounds good. The Hibernians are a Celtic set-up, so that could relate back to the Irish heritage, I suppose. The navy bit fits in and we've got the birth date. It's got to be him. I'm not sure where the bus driver bit fits in.'

'I don't see why Hitler's nephew shouldn't be driving a

bus. Everyone's got to make a living,' said Tim, noticing on his mobile phone that he had missed two calls, which was no great surprise with the technology of the time. One was from Paul Palmer wondering how it was going. 'I'm holding a couple of pages open and keeping my fingers crossed,' he said. 'Call me when you know.' The other call was from Tim's contact, saying there was an obituary for William Patrick Dowling in the local library, but that he could not get it until the following day.

'The old dear isn't going to be back for a while,' said Tim. 'Let's find the library and look up the obit ourselves. I've got his death date. Maybe then the neighbours can get a life for a while.'

At Middletown's Russell Library, we were shown into the reference room where a researcher gave us a reel of microfiche containing copies of the local newspaper for 1989. Trawling through copies for April, the month he died, I spotted the name we were looking for. 'Tim, stop! There it is. William P. Dowling.'

But when we read through the obituary, our hearts sank.

'Born in Middletown,' read Tim. 'The son of the late Michael and Hannah. A lifelong resident of Middletown. A brother and a sister. Shit! I don't believe it. It's the wrong guy.'

'It can't be,' I said.

'Look, it's even got the mother's maiden name. It's not Dowling, it's Fitzpatrick. And his wife was Helen, not Phyllis.'

It was two very different reporters who returned to sit outside the house later that morning. There was little conversation and the still-swishing curtains up the street went unnoticed. A police patrol car drove slowly past soon after lunch, but we carried on reading our newspapers and ignored him.

At a little after 3 p.m., an elderly lady parked in the driveway and searched in her handbag for the front door key. We lurched out of the car and called politely from the street to ask if she could spare us a moment. We had something we wanted to ask her. Tim didn't bother taking the camera.

'I'm terribly sorry to bother you,' I said, standing by the woman's car, 'but we work for a British newspaper, and we have rather an unusual question to ask.'

'Yes?' she said, looking worried.

'I realise this is going to sound very strange, but were you or your late husband in any way related to Adolf Hitler?'

'I haven't got the faintest idea what you are talking about,' she said, and hurried inside.

CHAPTER THREE

J. EDGAR HOOVER'S REPORT

1 APRIL 1942. NEW YORK CITY

Although J. Edgar Hoover was in a hurry for White's report on William Patrick Hitler, the case was not as straightforward as the subject of the inquiry would have led him to believe at the interview two days earlier. While William Patrick had given every impression that he was vehemently opposed to Adolf Hitler and everything his regime stood for, two of his former associates suggested to Agent White that William Patrick was simply bitter that his uncle had not offered him a more lucrative position within the Third Reich.

One man, a writer described by White in his report as 'Confidential Informant number 2', had spent three or four months with William Patrick for a possible collaboration on a book about the Briton's experiences in Germany. According to White, the informant said, 'It was necessary for him to obtain from subject Hitler his entire life's history and also all information concerning his contacts and relationships with Adolf Hitler.'

The FBI agent continued:

Hitler was put up at the Buckingham Hotel at Sixth Avenue and 57th Street, New York City, where he received a great deal of publicity and every attention possible. The informant informed that evidently the William Morris Agency did not consider Hitler as big an attraction as they thought he would be and the plans that the agency had for him were discontinued. Continuing, the informant stated that Hitler then, during the winter of 1939 and 1940, became affiliated with the Harold R. Peat Agency Inc., located at 2 West 45th Street, New York City, and through this agency Hitler made quite a few lectures regarding his experiences with his uncle, Adolf Hitler, Himmler, Rudolph Hess and other associates of Adolf Hitler. It may be noted that William Patrick Hitler is now conducting his lectures through William B. Feakins Inc, lecture bureau, at 500 Fifth Avenue, New York City.

The informant informed that subject Hitler took up his foreign connections with Adolf Hitler in 1929, at which time he met the Fuehrer on numerous occasions and also Himmler, Hess, Goebbels, Goering and other close associates of Hitler. He stated that subject Hitler also met the dancer with whom Adolf Hitler was infatuated and who later killed herself.

The informant stated that the impressions he gained from talking with subject Hitler was that he, the subject, had tried to use a mild form of blackmail against Adolf Hitler in order to secure for himself a position of importance with little work attached to the position. He continued that subject Hitler had intimated to him that this threat was to the effect that he, subject Hitler, might reveal that his father, Alois Hitler, had deserted his wife, Brigid Elizabeth Dowling Hitler, and had left her to shift for herself; further that in the meantime, Alois Hitler had married again without obtaining a divorce from Brigid Hitler. The informant stated that this blackmail had evidently succeeded in a mild way in view of the fact that subject Hitler was given a few minor jobs as a bookkeeper. However, he secured a position with the Opel Automobile Works which is a subsidiary of the General Motors Corporation.

The informant advised that the Gestapo took up with Adolf Hitler the fact that William Patrick Hitler was using his name in securing sales for these automobiles and was advised by the Gestapo to discontinue these practices. He stated further that subject Hitler was in a position to obtain rather important positions because of his name and his relationship to Adolf Hitler. However, Adolf Hitler would not allow the subject to secure a job in this manner, and also saw to it that he obtained a job which would fit his qualifications, which qualifications were that of a bookkeeper and accountant, and for this reason, the informant stated, subject was opposed to the Fuehrer.

The informant said that subject Hitler was an exceedingly lazy individual, had no initiative and constantly sought a position which paid well with little work. In his opinion, if Adolf Hitler had secured for the subject an important position which paid well, the subject would have been an ardent Nazi and a supporter of

Adolf Hitler. However, on the other hand, the informant said that Adolf Hitler refused to place his nephew in an important position for which he felt he was not qualified and saw to it that he was given lesser jobs in line with his ability and qualifications. Informant 2 informed that undoubtedly this weighed heavily informing the subject's opinion as to Adolf Hitler.

Continuing, he said that subject Hitler was an extremely religious person which was probably due to the influence of his mother. The informant stated that when he first started conferring with the subject in regard to the writing of a book that he, subject Hitler, had told him that his reason for opposing the Fuehrer and the Nazi government was due to the fact that he never subscribed to the Nazi doctrines and that being a devout Catholic he had observed with horror the attacks upon his Church. However, the informant said that his secretary had told him that Hitler had on numerous occasions stopped at her desk to talk to her and had told her, 'Hitler could have given me a good job if he had wanted to.'

To the best of his knowledge, the informant said that Hitler had never gone to Canada in order to attempt to join the Canadian army. He stated that it was his opinion that Hitler's desire to join the Canadian forces was probably motivated by his mother's desire for her son to work at something and not due to Hitler's own sincere patriotism to join the Canadian army. The informant was of the opinion that this might have been a publicity stunt.

The informant informed that at a cocktail party which

he gave some time ago Hitler was present and met a movie actress whose name he recalled as Miss Dot May Goodisky whose present address is in care of Thomas Cook, 9462 Wolshire [sic] Boulevard, Los Angeles, California. He said that the subject became very friendly with Miss Goodisky who later introduced Hitler to Mr Eugene Lyon of the American Mercury Magazine.

The informant stated that Hitler had lectured for some time under the supervision of Harold R. Peat, Inc., a lecture bureau located at 2 West 45th Street, New York City . . . The informant advised that subject Hitler and his mother were residing at the above address under the name of Patrick Dowling and that if the occasion arose to contact the subject at this telephone number or address that the subject preferred that the name Patrick Dowling be used.

In regard to the subject's associates, the informant advised that he was of the opinion that the subject Hitler had very few associates other than those he had made acquaintance with in connection with his various lectures.

Mr Harold R. Peat, of the Harold R. Peat, Inc. lecture bureau at 2 West 45th Street, New York City, was contacted and he informed that subject Hitler was under his supervision for lectures. He further informed that the William Morris Theatrical Bureau had a working agreement with the Harold R. Peat, Inc. lecture bureau in that those persons who they felt they would not be able to use were turned over to the Harold R. Peat Bureau in order that they might be turned in to the lecture field.

Mr Peat advised that he had booked approximately 25 lectures for subject Hitler but that his lectures had not been successful and that it had become necessary that Hitler find another lecture bureau who could make contacts for him. Mr Peat gave substantially the same information in regard to the subject's background as did the confidential informant and was unable to add anything in regard to the subject's background and associates. Mr Peat was of the same opinion that the informant was in regard to Hitler's loyalties; that is, Mr Peat expressed the opinion that the subject in all probability would be loyal to the Nazi government and Adolf Hitler if the Fuehrer had obtained a position for the subject which would have paid him exceedingly well.

Mr Peat further advised that as Hitler's first lecture he had booked him with a club in New York City which is known as the 101 Club and that Hitler made an exceedingly poor showing in view of the fact that in his lecture, he advised that his reason for leaving Germany was not because of Adolf's persecution of the Catholic Church but that he left in view of the fact that his uncle would not obtain a position for him in Germany. Peat advised that he then talked to subject Hitler regarding the advisability of expressing such a reason for leaving Germany. However, he said that in his opinion this was the real reason why the subject had left Germany and that it was not due to the persecution of the Catholic Church and of the fact that subject Hitler did not conform to the ideals and plans of Adolf Hitler.

Peat advised that the subject was now lecturing under the supervision of the William B. Feakins Inc. lecture bureau, located at 500 Fifth Avenue, New York City. Mr Peat furnished a circular regarding advertisement of subject Hitler's lectures and this circular is being made a part of the New York Field Division file in view of the fact that it contains excellent photographs of the subject Hitler.

The FBI file also contained posters advertising William Patrick's lectures.

WILLIAM PATRICK HITLER, NEPHEW OF REICHSFUEHRER ADOLPH HITLER, REVEALS THE SENSATIONAL TRUTH ABOUT THE LEADERS OF NAZI GERMANY TODAY: HEAR HIS DARING EXPOSE OF INTRIGUE AMONG THE ENSLAVERS OF EUROPE

WILLIAM PATRICK HITLER

Born in England to Hitler's half-brother Alois and an Irish mother, he was educated in English schools and did not meet his celebrated uncle until 1929 at the Nuremberg Congress of the Nazi Party. In 1933 William Patrick Hitler went to live in Germany and during the next six years was under the constant surveillance of Hitler himself and such dignitaries as Rudolf Hess and Ernst Wilhelm Bohle, in charge of all Germans living abroad and director of Fifth Column activities.

Jailed during the 'blood purge' of 1934, young Hitler was released through the intervention of British diplomatic officials.

He worked in the Opel automobile plant but was prevented from pursuing an engineering and sales career by a Fuehrer who felt his dignity insulted. Young Hitler was frequently called on the Chancellor's carpet and given unmistakable warning against revelation of Hitler family life, and his freedom to seek employment was curbed at every turn. A devout Catholic, he never subscribed to Nazi doctrines and observed with horror the attacks upon his Church. Finally, in 1939, he was told that he must accept German citizenship, but he slipped out of the Third Reich across to England where he met his mother and with her departed for America.

His story of the Nazi regime is unique, for he brings testimony of the true character of Hitler and his jealous rivals. Constantly threatened with Gestapo reprisal for his indiscretion, William Patrick Hitler has chosen to tell the truth of Hitler's background, his strange assortment of actress and young men friends, the cabals which surround Der Fuehrer, the reaction of the German people to the barbarism of the Nazi party machine.

LECTURES

MY UNCLE ADOLF

Who the Fuehrer really is, how the Fuehrer really lives, what the Fuehrer really says in private and in public.

THE MYSTERY OF RUDOLF HESS

What led this high-ranking Nazi to surrender himself to the English is explained by his former ward.

WHAT ARE THE GERMAN PEOPLE THINKING

How the Nazis have silenced opposition among the German people and how the people prepare their day of revenge.

William Patrick Hitler discusses all topics dealing with Nazi Germany based on his intimate knowledge of its leaders and its peoples.

Comments

'Young Patrick Hitler was so much better than I dared hope . . . We had the largest attendance we've ever had at a Saturday meeting at which he spoke. He received an ovation when he finished . . .' President, Wisconsin Education Association.

'. . . impressed with his fairness in discussing a subject which might easily have shown bias. He was frank and yet pleasing in conducting the Forum following the main address. Even the most critical professors gave him credit for his astuteness and perspicacity in answering the many questions . . .' Superintendent, Public Schools of Monroe County, PA

'We had a very good crowd – some 1,500 people. He made a very dignified presentation and had a very excellent question period. On a day of such atrocious weather, we would have had half so large a crowd with anyone else.' Secretary, Coatesville (PA) Y.M.C.A.

'Almost with his opening remarks, William Patrick

"had" his audience of six hundred. He not only "had" them but continued by popular request way beyond the regular adjournment time.' Executive Secretary, Buffalo (N.Y.) Advertising Club.

'His audience was deeply interested in what he had to say. We were all very impressed with the number of questions addressed to him after his lecture and by the quiet convincing manner in which he answered them.' Horace Bushnell Memorial Hall, Hartford, Conn.

Not all of William Patrick's audiences were so complimentary. Attached to the FBI file were several letters asking the bureau to investigate the speaker, with one complaining about his 'most exorbitant' £150 fee. Another complained that William Patrick 'had spoken favourably toward the German people' in a speech to the Albany Kiwanis in New York.

In the opinion of a Mr Gerald Salisbury, Managing Editor of the *Knickerbocker News*, who was present, 'The speech appeared to be directed at alleviating any sentiment against the German people and that this might be considered clever propaganda looking toward a possible peace movement in the future between Germany and the Allies.'

A woman who attended a round table conference at Milliken Theater, Columbia University, on the subject 'What Shall We Do With the Germans?' phoned the FBI to complain that William Patrick suggested the German people should not be punished severely. He also said that German soldiers were gentlemen. This, she told the agent on duty, she considered to be 'Nazi propaganda'.

But while Special Agent White may have come across some contradictions in his quick character study, he could find no evidence that William Patrick intended to betray his adopted country.

He signed off his report to J. Edgar Hoover with the conclusion: 'Investigation does not reflect that the subject is engaged in subversive activities.'

And the nephew was given hope to believe he might get to go to war against his uncle, after all.

CHAPTER FOUR

BRIGID'S MANUSCRIPT

12 SEPTEMBER 1995. NEW YORK CITY

'If anyone walks into the office now, they're going to think we're from the National Front or the Aryan Brotherhood or whatever they call themselves over here,' said Tim. 'How many more Hitler biographies do you need?'

'I had to get them all out from the library,' I explained. 'I was too embarrassed to sit in there surrounded by Hitler books. I tried it for a while, but people kept looking at me like I was a Nazi. One of my son's teachers even came over to speak to me and I was trying to cover up the bloody great swastikas all over one of them. I tried to explain what I was doing, but I could tell she wasn't really listening. She already thinks I come from another planet because I'm English, so God knows what she thinks of me now.'

'How many have you got?'

'Twelve.'

'You've really got a thing about this story, haven't you? Any luck?'

'Actually, I have found something that may give us a lead. This story is driving me crazy. It's not as if it isn't out there somewhere; we know William Patrick Hitler came over to the States and we know from the cuttings that he was trying to get into the army during the war and then everything stops. It's like he disappeared from the face of the earth. I've gone through every Hitler bio which mentions William Patrick, or his mother, and they all pretty much talk about the same stuff before the war. All the historians have him down as a flake and yet none of them have talked to him. They've all taken the word of Adolf Hitler and gone along with his verdict on his nephew as 'repulsive' and 'loathsome'. But Hitler wasn't exactly the greatest judge of character, was he? I would have thought an insult from Adolf would be a glowing recommendation to the rest of the world.

'As far as I can work out from this mound of books, William Patrick tried to blackmail Hitler out of a few quid by threatening to go to the newspapers with a few facts about the family, fled Germany before the war because he didn't like what was going on over there, went on a lecture tour to tell everyone who would listen what a mean, nasty uncle he had and then tried to sign up to fight against him in the war. And all these things, according to Hitler and his biographers, make HIM the black sheep of the family. His uncle was responsible for the deaths of six million Jews, single-handedly ruled over a barbaric empire built on hatred and fear, and waged war on half the world. And yet William Patrick, the insignificant nephew from Liverpool, was the one being frowned upon. Explain that one to me? It doesn't make any sense, and I would very much like to find Mr Hitler of

Nantucket or New Jersey or wherever he is and ask him what he thinks about it. And that's my rant for the day.'

'Very good. Spoken like a real New Yorker. But what's the lead you mentioned?' said Tim.

'Oh, yeah. One of Hitler's biographers, an American called John Toland, seems to have spoken to our friend William Patrick in the seventies. He mentions it in a footnote on page 383 of his Hitler book. Says William Patrick was living in the New York area and, get this, he says he had a son called Adolf.'

'So, he's saying there could be an Adolf Hitler alive and well and eating bratwurst in Brooklyn. That's a great story if it's true,' said Tim. 'Is Toland still alive?'

'Yes, he lives up in Danbury, Connecticut. I've got a number for him through his publisher. If he can give us William Patrick's name, or at least the town where he was living, then we're home free. Once we've narrowed it down, we'll find him, no problem.'

The fiftieth anniversary of Hitler's death had come and gone without us getting any closer to his long-lost nephew, but I kept plugging away between other jobs, hoping to dig up some tiny clue that might help solve the mystery. Few people other than Hitler historians knew a British-born Hitler ever existed and friends I mentioned it to were fascinated by the search, however fruitless it had been up to now. It became a running joke between me and Tim that I was still refusing to give up on the story.

I had been out to a couple more addresses since the disappointment of finding the wrong William Patrick Dowling five months earlier and was met with the same blank faces each time. One woman with the surname of Hiller even had me thinking for a moment there was a chance her husband fitted the bill when she said his family did, indeed, hail from Liverpool, and added that she was German. But it turned out their respective ancestors were not far behind the *Mayflower* and had lived in small-town Pennsylvania for generations.

Now it seemed we at last had someone who was a direct point of contact to William Patrick in the seventies, the reinvented Hitler we were looking for. But Mr Toland was nothing if not a man of his word. He was eighty-three when I called him up that morning, full of hope that the ageing historian would provide the breakthrough I was seeking. As well as his two-volume tome on Hitler, he had penned a series of books chronicling some of the most tumultuous events of the century and he was not about to give in to the abject pleading of a foreign journalist he had never even met. I could hear Tim lighting up a cigarette at his desk across the office as my entreaties begging the Pulitzer Prize winning biographer for clues became more and more desperate. I knew Tim would have loved to have had a go at persuading Toland to tell us where William Hitler was, but I knew, too, that the old man was not going to give away a confidence he had given his solemn word to keep. In a patient, polite voice, he confirmed that he had traced William Patrick to 'the New York City metropolitan area', but on discovering he did not want to talk about the past, the historian agreed never to divulge either his new identity or his location.

'But how did you manage to find him?' I asked.

'I managed to find some of the family in Hamburg and one of them had a picture of William Patrick holding a baby,' said

Toland. 'On the back of the photograph was a caption giving the baby's name as Adolf. I said, "Do you mean to tell me that William Patrick called his son Adolf?"

'I would like to help you, but I gave my word that I wouldn't tell anyone where he was living.'

Toland graciously gave me the telephone number and address of one of his contacts in Hamburg. 'You could try speaking to some people in Germany. They may decide to help,' he said.

'Is there anywhere else I could look or anything I could do that will put me on the right track?' I persisted, seeing yet another promising lead slip away.

'There is one thing,' he said. 'There's a manuscript on the third floor at the New York Public Library in the Special Collections that I found very interesting. It purports to have been written by William Patrick's mother. You might like to take a look at it.'

A London friend offered to fly to Germany to try and speak to the man mentioned by Toland, but when she arrived in Hamburg the contact steadfastly refused to help put her in touch with any of the people Toland had spoken to and denied knowledge of the photograph of the baby.

There had been references to Brigid's memoirs in some of the other Hitler biographies, in most part questioning its authenticity, and I had made extensive cuttings checks on newspapers from Britain and the US and discovered that Michael Unger, a former Editor of the *Liverpool Daily Post*, had even published them under the title *The Memoirs of Bridget Hitler* in 1979. But the book had long been out of print, and I decided to look at the original manuscript in the hope it would turn up a clue to the missing Hitlers.

The following morning, I was asking a research assistant in the Special Collections department of the New York Public Library on Fifth Avenue if she had a manuscript written by a Brigid or Bridget Hitler.

Moments later, she returned with a well-preserved bound manuscript with the title 'My Brother-in-Law Adolf' on the binding. The typewritten 225-page document bore no date and ended on a comma in the middle of a sentence. A few words had been crossed out and replaced, but otherwise there was no handwriting.

At the start of the book were two pages bearing the stamp: 'EDMOND PAUKER, Capitol Theatre Building, 1639 Broadway, New York', and a handwritten date: 10/6/59. There was also an introductory section, 'The Forward', which read:

This account is the authentic and fascinating story of Mrs Brigid Hitler, sister-in-law of Adolf Hitler.

Mrs Hitler, who, through the courtesy of the State Department, has been enjoying the hospitality of the United States, has up to now chosen to remain in obscurity, hoping that she had succeeded in obliterating every trace that might serve to connect her with the husband who mistreated her and the infamous family into which it had been her misfortune to marry. Recently, however, during an interview requested by the Bureau of Strategic Services in Washington, she was officially urged to set her reticence aside and publish her experiences in order that the American public might be informed of the true facts about the man who has come to be regarded by all decent people throughout the world as the arch enemy of humanity. Feeling that it is her duty to comply to that request, Mrs Hitler, this unwilling occupant of a ringside seat in the arena in which the Hitler family drama has been enacted, discloses her intimate knowledge of Hitler, his family and his past.

When Brigid Dowling, aged 17, eloped from her Dublin home with an Austrian waiter named Alois Hitler, she did not dream that her brother-in-law, Adolf, would one day plunge the world into the bloodiest war in history.

The Alois Hitlers lived together for four years and had one child, William Patrick Hitler.

When Adolf Hitler became the Chancellor of Germany, the English newspapers found a wealth of material on the fact that his sister-in-law and nephew were living in London. No doubt this unwanted publicity initiated the adventure that followed. Its immediate result was that Hitler took steps to lure mother and son to Germany. The Fuehrer's success in this attempt, the ensuing years spent in his shadow and how William Patrick got away to wear the blue uniform of the US Navy, form the substance of this book.

The true story Mrs Hitler tells in this narrative is mainly concerned with her untiring efforts to free her son from Hitler's grasp. It is the poignant account of a mother's fight for her son's life . . . the desperation of a friendless weak woman pitted against the power and cunning of the most ruthless tyrant of modern times.

Mrs Hitler presents a close-up of the German dictator

as she knew him, as only a woman who hates could see the menace threatening the life of her son. She also reveals the intimate details concerning her family which counts it as a curse that its most powerful member, the acting head of the family, should be a man like Adolf Hitler, who has behaved towards its individual members in the same brutal and merciless way suffered by the peoples under his cruel domination.

With the manuscript was a file of documents that appeared to give some credence to the book's veracity. The first was a *New York Times* article, dated 25 June 1941, under the headline: 'Hitler Relative Here. Volunteer British Aide'. The story continued:

The sister-in-law of Adolf Hitler began working yesterday as a volunteer at the headquarters of the British War Relief Society, 730 Fifth Avenue. She is Mrs Brigid Elizabeth Hitler, Irish-born wife of Hitler's half-brother, Alois, reported to have bigamously remarried and to be operating a restaurant now in Berlin.

In a rich Dublin brogue, she acknowledged it was 'a bit ridiculous, but my name is Hitler and I'll work just as hard as anybody, notwithstanding,' when she walked in to offer her services. Then she hastily explained that she hopes to obtain an annulment of her marriage while in this country and would 'dearly love' to become an American citizen but cannot at this time because she's only on a visitor's visa.

Hanging, Mrs Hitler declared, would be too good for her brother-in-law, Adolf.

Her son, William Patrick Hitler, is in Canada on a lecture tour, describing conditions in Germany. Mrs Hitler is 49 years old and lives at 505 West 142nd Street.

With the cutting was a photograph of Alois Hitler; Alois and Brigid's marriage certificate; a British birth certificate that was unreadable but may have been William Patrick's; a postcard from Alois to Cissie, his pet name for Brigid, at a Liverpool address; Alois's birth certificate proving he shared the same father as Adolf; a letter from Dr Frederick Kaltenegger of the British Embassy in Vienna concerning Alois's birth certificate; a post office telegram to B. Hitler telling her to go to the German Embassy in London; a letter from 'Patrick' to Rudolf Hess, which was unreadable but carried the Nazi eagle; a letter in German to Patrick 'inviting' him to the office of Wilhelm Bruckner, Hitler's personal adjutant; a German money order for 100 Reichmarks stamped by the adjutant of the Reichsführer; a letter to Brigid from anti-Nazi writer Rudolf Olden setting up a meeting for 15 September 1937; and a second newspaper article about Brigid's volunteer work for the British War Relief Society.

I thought it an impressive set of documents and certainly very difficult for an outsider to get hold of, or forge. I had my own copies of William Patrick's birth certificate and his mother's marriage certificate, which friends had obtained for me in London, but the rest of the material was new to me. It immediately struck me as strange that Hitler historians who debunked the book never mentioned the existence of these supporting papers. If Brigid herself had not written the book, the author must have had a very detailed knowledge of the family and close access to it. William Patrick would undoubtedly have had contact with the publishing world while on his lecture tours around the United States. Surely he must have had some hand in a book such as this.

Whoever wrote the book, whether it was Brigid, William Patrick or a collaborator, they had a fine turn of phrase, and it must be admitted that neither Brigid nor her son was a professional writer. And comparisons between William Patrick's letter to President Roosevelt and his letters to his mother as quoted in the memoir show a distinct difference in style. But at face value, at least, this was the first and only memoir written by any relation of Adolf Hitler.

The certificates in my pocket gave me the barest bones of William Patrick's early background. His mother was eighteen when she married Alois Hitler, twenty-seven, at Marylebone Register Office on 3 June 1910. Alois was described on the form as an hotel waiter, of 37 Blandford Square, St Marylebone, and son of customs officer Alois Hitler, deceased. Brigid Elizabeth Dowling was listed as a spinster, of 4 Percy Street, St Pancras, daughter of William Dowling, a carpenter.

William Patrick's birth certificate showed he was born at 102 Upper Stanhope Street in the Toxteth Park Central district of Liverpool on 12 March 1911 to parents Bridget Elizabeth Hitler, formerly Dowling, and Alois Hitler.

I was not allowed to take the manuscript from the library, so I settled down in the reading room with a pad and proceeded to fill it with notes and quotations from the unfinished memoir.

And as I read on, the book put flesh on the bones of Brigid's fateful marriage and her son's pre-war adventures.

The first chapter opened in 1909 at the Dublin Horse Show, with the young Brigid on the arm of her father. Resplendent in a hat decorated with ostrich plumes and a white muslin dress 'with flounces and a blue slash' she was taken with a stranger who struck up conversation with her father.

The man was wearing a brown suit, a homburg hat and spats. 'A white ivory walking stick with a gold handle was hooked over his arm with inimitable dash,' the memoir continued. 'In his tie was a pearl pin, and two rings on his left little finger, one a diamond and one a ruby, added just the right note of lavishness. Across his cream-coloured waistcoat a heavy gold chain stretched from one pocket to the other and his moustaches were waxed and curled upright *a la Kaiser*. He introduced himself as Alois Hitler from Austria.'

To an impressionable farm girl, the elegant foreigner was irresistible, and their relationship began with a first date at a Dublin museum. By the end of the night, the book says, Brigid was already head over heels in love and ready to do anything for her Austrian knight.

But her fiercely Catholic family were not so enthusiastic about the boastful stranger who told them he was in the 'hotel business' and on a European tour to study the industry in Britain, France and Belgium. When her father discovered Alois was, in fact, a waiter working at Dublin's Sherbourne Hotel, where he had been sent by a London employment agency, he ordered his daughter to break off the relationship.

Left to choose between her suitor and her family, Brigid

chose to elope to London to marry despite her father's threats to have his unwanted new son-in-law arrested for kidnapping. A baby followed just nine months and nine days after their London wedding, but right from the start, the Hitlers had their differences over baby William Patrick. Brigid chose 'Patrick' because it was Irish, and called her son 'Pat', while her husband thought 'William' sounded German and insisted on calling him 'Willy'.

According to the manuscript, Alois changed jobs four times in their first two years of marriage. He opened a small restaurant in Dale Street, Liverpool, before buying a boarding house on Parliament Street and then a hotel on Mount Pleasant . . . and then going bankrupt. The marriage was very different from the one Brigid had envisioned, and she claimed that she was so short of money at times that she could not afford to buy milk for her baby.

What followed was one of the most astonishing – and disputed – claims in the patchwork history of Adolf Hitler's life. In her memoir, Brigid says that from November 1912 to April 1913 Adolf Hitler was an unwelcome guest in the Liverpool flat where she lived with her husband and baby son.

In his writings and records, Adolf Hitler made no mention of this, but Brigid said it was because his trip to England was to dodge being drafted into the Austrian army.

Whether or not historians chose to believe Brigid's alleged version of events, it seemed to me it was convincing, much like everything else in the book.

The memoir stated that Alois sometimes sent money to his two sisters, Angela and Paula, who were living in Vienna, and, ever the dreamer, after trying his hand as a salesman in the emerging safety razor business, he wanted to persuade Angela's husband, Leo Raubal Sr, to join up with him and branch into Europe. To this end, he supposedly sent money to Vienna so that Angela and Leo could visit him in England. But when Brigid and Alois went to pick up their guests, they found that his half-brother, Adolf, had come instead.

The brothers had endured a difficult upbringing and Brigid claimed they carried their grudges into adulthood. Consequently, Alois was not pleased to see 'good-for-nothing' Adolf.

Their father, Alois Hitler Sr, was, by all accounts, an arrogant man who married three times. The first marriage was childless – Alois Jr and Angela were born to his second wife, and Adolf and Paula were the children of the third marriage.

The memoir quotes Alois as saying that his stepmother – Adolf's mother – made his life a misery. 'When I was only thirteen,' he said, 'my stepmother drove me out of the house. She persuaded my father to send me to Linz without a penny. I was apprenticed to an innkeeper, Herr Spressler. He was a brute. Three months later when my family finally came to see how I was getting on I had lost ten pounds and was black-and-blue from beatings. I threw myself on my knees and begged him to take me away. My father had always been stern with me, but I think he might have relented if it hadn't been for my stepmother. You see, I had always wanted to be an engineer, but that cost money. My stepmother needed all the available money for her favourite, Adolf, whom she kept at school. He hid behind her skirts, never doing a day's work or earning a Heller.

'Once, I got into a serious scrape in Vienna. I was threatened with prison for being unable to account for a few crowns I had collected for my master. In desperation I asked for help, begging them to send me the missing crowns. I remember the exact words of the reply I got as though they had been engraved on my soul: "To steal and be caught means you are not even a good thief. In that case my advice is go hang yourself." The letter was in Adolf's handwriting. I can never forget it, and I cannot forgive him even though the letter was dictated by his mother.'

In the book, Alois stated that Adolf used the name of his younger brother Edmund, who died aged two, to evade being drafted for military service and fled to England when the Viennese police discovered the ruse.

The detail in the manuscript was absorbing and I continued to make notes of dates and places in the hope it would tie in with some later inquiry. I was so caught up in the story of Hitler's alleged visit to Liverpool I found myself copying down the entire episode. Was it true? Hitler never mentioned a UK visit to anybody or included it in *Mein Kampf*, but then again, he never referred to the fact that he had a British-born nephew, and he went to great lengths to disown all of his family. Once again, I was asking myself, why should I believe one of the evillest men in history over a very ordinary woman with an extraordinary story to tell?

Before Hitler left for Germany and an unlikely ascent to power, Brigid even claimed she was responsible for his trademark moustache. At the time, she says in the manuscript, Adolf sported a handlebar moustache similar to that of her husband, Alois, and she suggested he should trim off the ends. Years later, when she saw his picture in a newspaper in a familiar pose, she noticed that he had taken her advice. 'But,' she commented, 'Adolf had gone too far.'

The memoir described her brother-in-law's trip to Liverpool, continuing:

Before I go on to describe my brother-in-law's stay, I must interrupt myself with the following remarks. Recently, during an interview in Washington, I was officially questioned about Adolf Hitler, and when I mentioned that he'd been in England the official immediately expressed surprise.

'In what year did this visit take place?' he asked.

'It was in 1912,' I replied. 'Although that's a long time ago, I can give you the exact date he came because it was only a few days after we took the flat in which we remained for several years.'

'This is extremely interesting,' he commented, 'because you are furnishing the answer to a very intriguing question.'

He told me that there had been much speculation by contemporary historians on the subject of a 'lost year' in Hitler's career. The year begins with the second half of 1912 and continues through the first part of 1913. Hitler, himself, in his autobiography, Mein Kampf, states that he left Vienna in May 1912 to go to Munich. In spite of the fact that this was supposed to be an official statement, it was false; all evidence shows that he arrived in Munich a year later than he claims. Conrad Haydn, in his biography of Hitler, Dear Sir, gives the date of Hitler's arrival in

Munich as 1913, as did Rudolf Olden, the famous German anti-Nazi writer whose book, Hitler the Pawn, was published in London in 1936. [The mention of 'Conrad Haydn' and a biography of Hitler supposedly called *Dear Sir* would seem to be a misspelled reference to German-American author Konrad Heiden, who wrote a successful 1944 biography of Hitler titled *Der Führer: Hitler's Rise to Power* (Houghton Mifflin).]

Of course, it's more than understandable why Adolf was so vague about this period. Certainly he would like it to be passed over as quickly as possible. When he wrote Mein Kampf he rearranged the facts of his early life into a more presentable version. To mention his trip to England without giving a reason for it would have been awkward, and the reasons would not have made good publicity for the German prophet. As for feeling grateful for the refuge granted him, it just wasn't in his make-up. My brother-in-law Adolf remained with us from November 1912 until April 1913, and a less interesting or prepossessing house guest I cannot imagine. At first he remained in his room, sleeping or lying on the sofa he used as a bed most of the time. I had an idea that he was ill, his colour was so bad and his eyes looked so peculiar. I felt rather sorry for him in spite of what Alois had told me. When I washed his shirt – he had no luggage with him – the collar was so frayed and worn that it wasn't even worth turning. I persuaded Alois to give him a few things, and as a matter of fact he wasn't at all reluctant to do so. Indeed, I think he would have been more than willing to help Adolf if the latter hadn't been so unappreciative and difficult. Adolf took everything we did for granted and I'm sure would have remained indefinitely if he had the slightest encouragement.

Thinking back, I found him only weak and spineless, but curiously enough I think he preferred my society to that of my husband. After the first few weeks he would often come and sit in my cosy little kitchen playing with my two-year-old baby, while I was preparing our meals. I thought he felt very much at home then. Usually he wouldn't say much, but just sit, from time to time telling me of the different dishes his mother used to make.

Sometimes he would speak of the future. It had been a great disappointment to him that he was not allowed to enter the Kunstakademie, where he had applied several times. 'The reason they gave for refusing me was that I didn't know how to paint, but if I could paint why should I go to the Academy? And that idiot of a professor,' he complained, 'said I had talent for architecture but not painting. I know that was only an excuse. He was prejudiced against me.' 'But why don't you learn a trade, become an apprentice? I don't mean you should become a waiter like Alois, but you might take up something for which your interest in art might be helpful – photography, for example. Or do you really feel you have to be a painter?' 'Oh, I don't know,' he replied uncertainly. 'Up to now I always thought I had the ability to become a good painter. Maybe it's too late, as Alois always tells me,' he sighed. 'Maybe he's right. Of course, if I had another sort of brother, one who wasn't as selfish as Alois, he would give me enough money to live on for a few years while I developed myself.'

This was one mood he displayed to me. Then there was another. In this respect he resembled my husband, but then they were always much alike, like two peas in a pod. Alois had maps of every country and was always studying them. When Adolf was with us, I had to go through the same thing all over again. He would spread them out on tables, or even on the floor, and pore over them for hours, and he would never hesitate to interrupt my housework to explain how Germany was going to take its rightful position in the world. First would come France, then England. Naturally I didn't find this kind of talk very interesting, but whenever I tried to get away, he would begin to shout, although I rarely troubled to contradict him. He would whip himself up into a rage and go on until hoarseness or some interruption stopped him. I put it down partly to the pleasure he took in hearing his own voice – another trick he had in common with my husband – and partly to a desire to domineer me.

As a matter of fact, I didn't pay a great deal of attention to his ravings. I suppose I was beginning to take shouting for granted as a family characteristic – and then, too, Alois's determined friends all talked the same way. I dare say this attitude was indicative of the general feeling of that time.

Only occasionally did I retaliate. Once I couldn't stand Adolf for another minute and burst out: 'You have a fine nerve coming here as you have and saying such things. You will never live to see the day England will be destroyed by Germany. If it ever comes to a fight, it's just as likely that the opposite will happen. Anyway, why do you take such an interest? You and all of us too are Austrians, not Germans.' He stared at me as though I had struck him in the face. For a while he had nothing to say, but his bewilderment soon passed off, to be displaced by what I can only describe as a sly pleasure in the fact that he had made a Britisher lose her temper.

When Alois had time, he took off – to London. Adolf was enchanted by Tower Bridge, and they bribed their way into the engine room to see the immense machinery in motion. Alois had a regular passion for machinery and was pleased to have a companion on his jaunts. He showed Adolf power plants, dynamos, river cranes and the inside of ships. When they came home there would be endless discussions about what they had seen.

They both had an intense interest in anything English and were always going sightseeing. Though I don't mean to say they were storing up information for later use, certainly, at least sub-consciously, they were the forerunners of the tourists who later streamed out of Nazi Germany and brought home the odd bits of information which, patched together, formed a complete pattern.

I think it more than possible that Adolf's English visit gave him the idea. As soon as Adolf knew his way around, he began disappearing by himself, not returning until late in the evening. He said he was looking for a job, but since he knew only a few words of English and never left early in the morning, it was always my opinion that he just wandered about Liverpool or went to stare at the River Mersey, or perhaps he spent his days in the taverns frequented by Germans.

One day he came back quite excited. 'Listen, Alois,' he exclaimed. 'They were playing the Bavarian National Anthem on the river. All of the men took off their hats and stood at attention.'

'That's ridiculous,' commented Alois.

'No, no, there were many people there, and they all showed their respect.' Adolf began to sing, 'Heil unserm Konig! Heil.' The moment Alois heard the tune he laughed. 'You are crazy, Adolf. That's the English National Anthem. The music is the same. Only the words are different.'

There is something else I should like to mention. I believe it was in my house that Adolf first came into contact with astrology. This subject had always interested me. I remember when I was a child, my mother used to talk to me about the planets. She told me that when you are born there are certain planets going over your head. Some are good, some are bad; they influence your whole life. I understood nothing but bothered her to tell me more. Since she didn't know any more, it was years before I had satisfied my curiosity.

Not long before, I had met a Mrs Prentice, who cast horoscopes. My husband despised the idea, but from the moment Adolf first heard about it he kept after me for more details, though never in Alois's presence . . . He asked for Mrs Prentice to do his horoscope again and again. Years later, when my brother-in-law had become famous, there was much comment on his dealing with an astrologist; it was said he never did anything without first ascertaining the astrological aspects. I thought back then to the idle words I had spoken which had served as an introduction to this absorbing interest. One day Mrs Prentice cast a horoscope for Pat. He would go to Germany, she predicted, and would be taught German. I didn't pay very much attention at the time, but it is curious that her predictions came true.

Tiring of Adolf's presence, Alois suggested he should go to America and even went so far as to offer to pay for his steamship ticket. At first, Adolf was enthusiastic, but in a few weeks his interest languished. Adolf argued that he must learn English first, for without it he would be unable to make a living in an English-speaking country.

Alois countered that if thousands and thousands of Germans went there without knowing the language Adolf could too. Adolf agreed to go if Alois would advance him enough money to live on until he could support himself. That was more than Alois could have done, even if he wanted to, so the project fell through. As the visit lengthened, relations between the two brothers became more and more strained. Naturally our family life suffered. Quarters were so cramped it was very difficult for me, and I had my baby to care for.

It is always easy to say, 'Tell him to go', but however

absurd it may sound there was no getting rid of Adolf. He had moved in as a permanent guest.

Time and time again I have tried to think what qualities in the young man I knew then enabled him to make his later career. Actually, the only striking personal attribute that comes to mind is his incredible persistence. He knew we wanted him to leave – my husband even offered to pay for his room in an hotel – yet he managed to stay on.

'First I must learn English,' he had said, but he learnt nothing, although he was always reading – not books, little pamphlets printed in German. These were Adolf's books. I didn't know what was in them, nor exactly where they came from, so I presume he must have got them from the Germans he met around the city.

Alois grew more and more impatient with him, but how could he deal with the situation? As a matter of fact, there wasn't much he could do except be unpleasant, and when he would lose his temper Adolf would repeat, 'You can't expect me to leave until I can make my own way. Surely that's not too much to ask of a brother.'

After months of this Alois had an idea. He would inform our unwanted guest that we were giving up our apartment and moving away from Liverpool. 'But what can I do then?' Adolf demanded.

The accumulated fury raging in Alois for the past months found vent in his retort: 'What can you do? A young man of almost twenty-four years asks that? When I was your age I was managing more than 20 people in the Ritz in Paris, in third place after the director of the hotel, and you ask me what you can do? Well, I don't care. As far as I am concerned you can do as you like. Go and hang yourself, as you told me when I asked for help.' His words ended in an almost hysterical shriek, but being a man of sudden impulses ten minutes later he took out his wallet. This gesture between the two brothers was the equivalent to the signing of a peace treaty.

Alois bought Adolf a ticket to Germany. There was no alternative. During his Liverpool stay Adolf hadn't even picked up enough English to ask directions at the station. He had to go to a country where the people used the language spoken in Austria. He could not return to his own country, for he would have been arrested. Germany seemed the safest asylum because my husband found out by inquiry at the German Consulate in London that there was no danger that Adolf would be extradited from the Kaiser's empire. They informed him that Germany did not extradite political or military refugees from Austria, even if it asked.

Next day the brothers spent selecting the German city in which Adolf should attempt to establish himself. Adolf was unacquainted with Germany, but Alois knew it well, having worked as a waiter in several cities, and advised Adolf to go to Munich because it was in every way – scenery, food, manner of dressing, customs and particularly language – the most like their own Austria.

At this point I pause to ask myself a question. Should I have been more sympathetic to Adolf? Would it have made any difference in thecourse of events, when Adolf was in Liverpool? I was young and thoughtless. Certainly, I didn't concern myself with his future. If I had exerted my influence over him, it is quite possible he might have remained in England. At this time the country was full of Germans. Barbers, hairdressers, carpenters, all varieties of skilled workmen came looking for work. Many of these visitors settled comfortably in England, never to return to the continent. If I had insisted that Adolf learn English, instead of practising my stumbling German on him, he might have shared their obscurity. As I think back to his departure, I see again the pale thin face and haggard eyes of my young brother-in-law, as he hastily kissed me and Alois before he boarded the train. Leaning far out of the window as the train began to pull slowly past the station, he shouted something ending 'zukunft wirst du Erstatten von mir erhalten.'

I looked at my husband in amazement, for I couldn't understand why he suddenly turned red in the face and started forward as if he wanted to run after the moving train. 'What's wrong?' I asked. 'He only said you'd get what he owed you.' 'Yes, that's what he said, but it had a double sense. He meant to threaten me, saying I'd get what was coming to me. But what do I care for the threats of a loafer like him?'

Who would have predicted that this 'loafer' would one day hold my husband's, my own, my son's life – indeed the life of all Europe – in his hands?

Putting down my pen, I tried to read back through my notes, struggling to transcribe the mixed bag of shorthand and scribble that gradually deteriorated as I copied the passages describing Adolf Hitler's alleged Liverpool stay. I called Tim on the mobile phone to let him know I was going to be a while longer at the library.

'Hey Dave, I'm glad you called,' said Tim. 'I just got off the phone with Michael Unger, who said you'd left a message for him about the William Patrick Hitler story. He edited the *Daily Post* in Liverpool and got the Hitler memoirs you're looking at published back in the seventies. Nice guy, actually.'

'He didn't have a copy of his book, did he?' I asked. 'My fingers are killing me copying all this stuff.'

'I don't know. He's over in England and the book has been out of print for years. He said he thought the book was going to do really well and make him a few quid. In the end, all he got out of it was a new fridge.'

'Did he get anywhere in tracking down William Patrick?'

'Not really. He said he tried, but he didn't crack it. He mentioned that guy Toland you've already spoken to but that was about it. Another dead end, I'm afraid. How about the manuscript? Any clues in there?'

'Doesn't seem to be,' I said. 'It's fascinating reading and there's lots of detail, but it's all from before the war. It finishes halfway through a sentence and doesn't say anything about them coming to America. I'm going to stay and make some more notes though. It may come in useful later on.'

'Do you think it's genuine?' asked Tim.

'Yeah, I think so. There's so much detail that either Brigid or someone very close to the family must have written it. And there's a pile of documents with it.'

'Michael Unger said there have been some question marks over it, but he's convinced that the mother wrote it.'

'The thing I don't understand,' I said, 'is that William Patrick was all over the place before the war. It looks like he loved being in the spotlight. He was talking to the *Daily Express* one minute, selling stories to other newspapers, going on lecture tours around America, telling everyone and their mother what it was like living with the name Hitler. And then he literally disappears from the face of the earth.'

'Perhaps he died soon after the war,' said Tim.

'It's possible. That would at least explain why the trail went so damn cold. And yet John Toland says William Patrick was alive and well in the seventies. He could be sitting somewhere now watching *Cheers* reruns on telly. It just doesn't make sense to me that someone so high profile could vanish so thoroughly.'

'There are all sorts of reasons why the last descendant of Hitler would want to lie low. He could have Jewish groups looking for him, Nazis, historians, the press. And no one just wants to shake his hand,' said Tim. 'He may just really, really want to stay away from that name.'

'Well, he's doing a bloody good job,' I said.

CHAPTER FIVE

THE OSS REPORT

10 SEPTEMBER 1943. NEW YORK CITY

Section 32 on the Alien's Personal History and Statement form had proved the major stumbling block when William Patrick Hitler wanted to join the US armed forces and fight against his uncle.

The FBI enquiry, instigated by William Patrick's letter to the president begging to be drafted into the United States Army, had failed to find any good reason why he should not serve his adopted country. But the army hierarchy could not get past section 32 on the form William Patrick completed and handed to his local draft board in Queens, New York, on 21 August 1942.

The section read: 'I have the following living relatives who are in or have been in the armed forces of the countries named:

1. Thomas Dowling. Uncle. England. 1923–1926. Royal Air Force.

2. Adolf Hitler. Uncle. Germany. 1914–18. Corporal.'

William Patrick had written the truth.

Understandably, the military decided it was the wrong answer and blocked his attempts to enlist, prompting William Patrick to tell the *Herald Tribune*: 'My name does make things a bit difficult. The board told me four weeks ago that I had been re-classified as 1-A and would be in the Army in a month. I wanted to get in the Air Force. After all, I do know Germany, and I think I would make a very effective bombardier. I'm going to try and convince the Royal Canadian Air Force of that now that I've been turned down here.'

He said he would change his name if he was accepted into the military in Canada. 'It only costs 50 cents,' he added. 'Hitler is a rather uncomfortable name, you know.'

William Patrick and his mother had left England for the very reason that their surname made life too difficult for them in a country overshadowed by war. After the Japanese attack on Pearl Harbor forced the United States into the conflict it had also become increasingly awkward to be a Hitler in New York.

Although unable to do his bit for America in combat, William Patrick soon discovered there was another way he could help.

The United States Office of Strategic Services (OSS), the forerunner to the Central Intelligence Agency, was established in 1942 under the leadership of General 'Wild Bill' Donovan, and it was his idea to call upon Harvard psychoanalyst Walter Langer to draw up a psychological profile of Adolf Hitler to give Allied leaders a better sense of the man they were up against.

Langer, a former student of Sigmund Freud who accompanied his mentor on his trip into exile in 1938, was given the task of scouring the United States and Canada for anyone who had more than a passing contact with Adolf Hitler and to combine those interviews with any reference material available, plus use his own analytical skills, to come up with a detailed appraisal of the German leader.

With William Patrick still touring the country lecturing about the evils of his uncle, it was not too difficult for Langer to conclude that the disgruntled nephew was a subject worth including on his list. Because of Adolf Hitler's famous reticence about his family background, Langer was seeking more information about the dictator's childhood and his roots in Austria. He contacted William Patrick and arranged for an interview in New York City on 10 September 1943.

Langer tried to keep his interviews as informal as possible and, no doubt, William Patrick believed his co-operation would help prove his loyalty and further his chances both of joining the services and, ultimately, of remaining in the United States, where he was still on a visitor's visa.

However, Hitler's nephew did not make a good impression on Langer. The psychoanalyst was under pressure to finish the report by the end of the summer and William Patrick would have been among his last interviewees. Summing up the meeting, Langer wrote:

> The son of Alois Jr is a young man of thirty-two who has not amounted to much . . . When his uncle became famous he obviously expected that something would be done for his family. He gave up his job in London and went to Germany where he had some contact with Adolf Hitler. The latter, however, was chiefly interested in keeping him under cover and provided him with a minor job . . .

It is my impression that William Patrick was quite ready to blackmail both his father and his uncle but that things did not work out as planned. He returned to England and as a British subject came to this country where he is a professional speaker. He is also engaged in writing a book about his associations and experiences in Hitler Germany.

Irrespective of his personal feelings about William Patrick, Langer had clearly decided he was a reliable source in regard to Hitler's shadowy background. When William Patrick was gone, Langer recorded the interview, parts of which he planned to use in his final report:

The family was not a happy one and his mother left his father several times before he was born. When he was three years old his father deserted his mother and himself and contact was not re-established until 1914.

The immediate cause for the separation was that his father had a passion for beating him when he was a baby and did so several times when the mother went out of the house. When she was at home, she protected him from the father but there were many quarrels in which the father contended that the child had to be disciplined at an early age and had to learn to respect and fear his father. From the time of the desertion until the present day his father has never contributed anything to his support or the support of his mother. In fact, on several occasions, when Adolph gave money which should have been sent to the mother, the father appropriated it to his own ends.

Before the final desertion, there was a separation for a period of time during which the father went to Vienna. Just what year this happened in the boy does not know, but his mother has told him that while he was there he met Adolph who was completely destitute and asked him for money. The father gave him a small amount but told him not to look for anymore and that it was time for him to stand on his own two feet and get a job and go to work – that he could not expect his family to support him forever.

According to what his father told his mother during the years of their married life, and told the boy later while he was in Germany, his relation to Adolph when they were boys was not happy. Alois Sr frequently beat him unmercifully with a hippopotamus whip. He demanded the utmost obedience and expected the boy, Alois, to tow the mark in every respect. Every transgression was another excuse for a whipping.

When asked for specific incidents that the father might have told, he recalled that once when his father was small he had played hooky from school. His father, according to these reports, was very mechanically inclined and liked to build all sorts of things. Alois Sr was in general pleased with these inclinations and tried to foster them. He would in fact promise the boy that when he became older he would send him to an engineering school if his work was good. On the occasion in question, the boy became interested in building a small boat. He became so engrossed in this project that he played hooky from school for three days in order that he might finish it more quickly. When the father learned of this, he became enraged, he whipped the boy and then held him against a tree by the back of the neck until the boy lost consciousness. He then stalked off and left the boy lying at the bottom of the tree until nature would revive him.

Things went from bad to worse when Adolph was born. From the very beginning he became the apple of his mother's eye and would have little to do either with Alois Jr or with Angela, his sister. It is a typical stepmother story in which the son is given all the favors and the stepchildren get the scraps. As Adolph became older, he was still excused from doing any unpleasant chores. He always claimed to be sick and his mother kept him in bed a good part of the time and even carried his meals to him there. He was pampered from early morning until late at night and the stepchildren had to listen to endless stories about how wonderful Adolph was and about what a great painter he would be some day. She even talked the father out of the idea of sending the oldest boy to engineering school; she claimed he was an incorrigible brat and a good-for-nothing and that all education would be wasted on him. The result was that the father put Alois Jr into an apprenticeship as a waiter where he would be away from home and would not cost much money. As a child, Adolph was lazy and disagreeable. He would not do any studying and spent his time wandering around the countryside or sitting down by the river. He was always dreaming or dobbing [sic] and would occasionally get into trouble. When this happened, he would run home and tell his mother that Alois had done it. She in turn would report it to the father who then would whip Alois for Adolph's actions. Alois Jr often said that he had to endure a great many whippings which belonged to Adolph. When asked if he ever heard about the father whipping Adolph, he replied in the affirmative. He said the father used to beat Adolph just as well as Alois but not so frequently. When asked if he had heard of any particular incidents he said he remembered his father telling him one time with considerable glee that when Adolph was about 11 years old, he refused to put up with the maltreatment of his father any longer and resolved to run away from home with two other boys. The plan was to build a raft and float down the river. Preparations were already under way when the father got wind of it and went down to the river, to find the boys engaged in their raft building. He was furious and beat Adolph so violently that when he returned home he was afraid that he had killed him, but Adolph revived.

Things in the Hitler household were not much improved when Adolph's sister Paula arrived. She, too, was spoiled by her mother but not to the same degree as Adolph. As she grew older, Alois Jr developed considerable affection for Paula while Angela developed some affection for Adolph and vice versa. Angela got to the point where she supported Adolph against Alois and Alois supported Paula against Angela. This crossed relationship has continued into adulthood although it is not strong in any direction. It was, however, strong enough at the time of the death of Clara Hitler that Alois persuaded Adolph that since the two girls were destitute it was up to the boys to turn their part of the inheritance over to the girls. According to the report, Adolph immediately said that in that case he would give his share to Angela, which he did, while Alois gave his share to Paula. Paula continued to stay in Linz for some time after her mother's death although he does not know for how long. When asked about other children in the Hitler family, he said that two were born before Adolph. They were called Gustaf and Edmund and they both died in infancy from unknown causes. He is also under the impression from what his father has said that two other children were born to Clara Hitler before Alois Sr married her. They were the children of Alois but were born during the lifetime of his second wife. They, too, died as infants as far as he knows although he admits that he has never been very clear on this subject. [Langer used the incorrect spelling of Clara Hitler, whose first name was spelled Klara, just as he used the variant Adolph for Adolf.]

Alois Jr seems to be a reproduction of his father in many ways. Not only does he go off into rages and want to beat his children, but after leaving his wife he went back to Germany and married another woman without being divorced from the first. The first marriage was performed in the Catholic church and no divorce was possible. In any case he lived with his second wife in Germany and a son named Heinz was born out of this union. When contact was made with the father again, about 1913, or early 1914, he was a very prosperous businessman in Germany and owned a chain of stores dealing in razors and barbers' equipment. This business seems to have gone on the rocks during the World War and the inflation that followed. In any case, the boy's mother sued Alois on the grounds of bigamy in the German courts prior to the War. Before the case came up in court, Alois Jr wrote the mother pleading letters begging her to have mercy on him and that if she did not press the suit he would send her money for their support regularly and threatened to commit suicide if she did press the suit. She agreed not to on condition that he send her money monthly. The case came up in court and, since she did not press the suit, the father was found guilty and given the sentence of one year in prison, which was later suspended. He never kept the promise of sending the money.

They lost contact with Alois Jr during the War and did not re-establish it until the late 1920s when Adolph began to rise in popularity sufficiently to get into the English newspapers. They wrote to Adolph and through him got in touch with Alois again. He again promised to support them but did nothing. In 1930, when Hitler suddenly became famous with over 100 seats in the Reichstag, they thought it was an opportunity of making some money by giving an interview to the Hearst press. Negotiations were under way, but they felt the need of additional information and wrote to Alois asking for further details about Adolph's youth. The reply came in the form of a demand from Adolph to come to Munich immediately for a conference. Tickets for the passage were enclosed. Upon their arrival in Munich, they found Adolph in a perfect rage. He summoned a family counsel at which Adolph, Angela, Alois, William Patrick and his mother were present. The gist of what Adolph said was now that he was gaining some importance the family need not think that they could climb on his back and get a free ride to fame. He claimed that any release to the Hearst newspapers involving his family would destroy his chances for success in view of Alois's record and that negotiations with the Hearst syndicate had to be stopped immediately and the great problem was how this could be done without arousing suspicions. It was finally suggested that William Patrick and his mother return to London and tell the Hearst people that it was a question of mistaken identity and that they had discovered that the Adolph Hitler who was the leader of the Nazi Party was not the uncle they had supposed but an Adolph Hitler who was no kin to theirs whatever. Hitler was pleased with this solution and urged them to get back to London as quickly as possible and disclaim all relationship in the present and the future. He handed Alois $2,000 to cover their expenses while they were in Munich and supplied them with passage home and instructions to give Mrs Hitler what was left over when these expenses had been paid. Alois, according to the story, did everything except pass over what was left of this sum and promised to send it through the mail, which would be much safer, but it never arrived.

[Brigid claimed this was £2,000, but whether dollars or pounds it was a considerable sum in those days. The average salary in Britain was £200 a year so this would have been worth around £250,000 at today's values.]

As Adolph continued to rise to fame and finally came into power, Mrs Hitler chafed more and more under her poverty.

She decided again to try to get some form of support and again approached Adolph in the matter since she was tired of Alois's broken promises and thought Adolph might be willing to pay something to keep her quiet. After some time, Hitler replied and invited William Patrick to Berchtesgaden for a summer vacation. When he arrived there he was greeted by Angela who was keeping house there at that time and roundly upbraided for demanding help from Hitler who, she claimed, was not even his uncle. He did not understand what she meant by all this but soon learned. When Hitler called another conference at which Angela, Alois and himself were present, Hitler was very sweet and told William Patrick that it really broke his heart to tell him this but since he insisted on making demands on Hitler that he could see no way out of it except to tell him the truth. The truth, according to him, was that his father, Alois Jr, was not really the son of Hitler's father but a boy who had been orphaned as an infant and whom Alois Sr had taken into his home and brought up as his own child. He turned to Alois Jr who obligingly confirmed the story. He said, however, that they did not want to be too hard on him and that it would be best for everyone if nothing was said outside the family. He only wanted to make it clear to William Patrick that he had absolutely no claim on him as an uncle and that they were in fact not related at all.

After his return to London, William Patrick and his mother checked on this report through the British Consul General in Vienna who, after some time, said the story was impossible because no adoption papers were on record and the baptismal certificates were clear. From these we learn that Alois Jr was born as an illegitimate child of Alois Sr and his second wife, Fransiska Metselsterger [properly, Franziska Matzelsberger], and that he was later legitimatized by their marriage in 1883. Angela, too, was born of this union. The baptismal certificate of Alois Sr is interesting in so far as his father's name is given as Hitler and not Hiedler, as all the biographers have it. In changing his name from Schicklgruber to Hitler, it would seem that he was taking his father's name and not that of his mother-in-law by his third marriage. William Patrick has also a photostatic copy of Adolph's baptismal certificate showing that he was born in Braunau on April 20, 1889 and not elsewhere on some other date as Otto Strasser's new book will try to show. It also shows that Hitler's Godfather and Godmother are probably not Jewish as Heiden and many others have claimed but a family named Pinx who lived on Loewengasse 28, Vienna III. Furthermore, William Patrick says that his father often talked about his own father's anti-Semitism and it seems that when he was young, he borrowed some money from a Jew in Vienna in order to take some examination in the customs service and that he felt that this person had in some way done him dirt. Just what the details were are not known. In any event, William Patrick leaves it as out of the question that Alois Sr would choose a Jew as a Godfather for any of his children.

Langer clearly found it ironic that Hitler, with all his talk about the Fatherland and the importance of *Deutschland über alles* came from a very Austrian household with a father who held the Germans in contempt. It is yet another clue as to why Hitler should have been so determined to gloss over his family background. As the following excerpt from Langer's report illustrates, Hitler's father considered the Germans to be inferior.

Alois Sr also was very anti-German as was also Alois Jr. He says that his mother used to tell in an amused tone of voice about how she used to jolt him out of his tirades by saying to him, 'Shut up, you dirty German!' This would divert his attention from whatever he was raging about and concentrate his rage on the Germans. He considered it a grave insult to be classed with them and stoutly maintained that he was an Austrian and that that was something entirely different. It was therefore amusing in the family to have Adolph come along and praise Germany to the skies and renounce his Austrian affiliations.

Another interesting sidelight was that Angela had a son named Leo in addition to Geli. After 1930, this son would have nothing whatever to do with Hitler and although he frequently came to Berchtesgaden to visit his mother, he always did so when he knew Hitler would be in Berlin. As soon as he heard that Hitler was coming to Berchtesgaden he would pack up and leave. The reason for his behaviour, according to Angela, was that he held his Uncle Adolph responsible for Geli's death and vowed that he would never speak to him again. After the war broke out, he went to the Balkans and is reported to have been killed there.

William Patrick also met Geli several times and says she was rather attractive in a peasant sort of way; he says she was good-natured and rather pleasant company. When asked if she ever mentioned or talked about her uncle, he said she told him that her life was very hard; that Hitler insisted that she accompany him wherever he went and it was very embarrassing for her, particularly since she knew that Gregor Strasser [early prominent Nazi murdered in Berlin by Hitler's supporters during the Night of the Long Knives, June 1934] was opposed to Hitler's being seen with her and, furthermore, because it prevented her from meeting any other young people. She said that he often insisted that she accompany him on trips to Berlin but no sooner would she arrive there than he packed her in a car and sent her to the airport to be flown to Berchtesgaden where she was to wait until he returned there. According to this report, Angela was always complaining that her life in Berchtesgaden was extremely difficult because Hitler was always complaining about money and would not give her an adequate amount to run the house on or do anything else.

The relationships between Angela and Adolph became very strained when the latter discovered that Angela was conspiring against him. It seems that the farmer who owned the land adjoining Hitler's at Berchtesgaden had died, and that Angela was bringing all kinds of pressure to bear on the wife of this old Party member to sell the land to her. Hitler was outraged when he heard about it and investigation proved that Angela was acting as an agent for Goering who wanted to obtain this land in order to build a house on it. Much as Hitler liked Goering, it seems that he did not like him enough to have him as a next-door neighbor. When Adolph discovered all this, he was beside himself with rage and ordered Angela to pack her belongings and get out of the house as quickly as possible and never come back. It was only through the intervention of others who pointed out the unfavorable publicity that might develop out of such a sudden leaving that he was prevailed upon to allow her to remain in the house a while longer. Goering then got busy and married her off to Prof. Hamitsch of Dresden who was a millionaire and a staunch Party member. Hitler has never had any use for Angela since that time and sees her only rarely and then only to keep down suspicion.

Shortly after he broke up with Angela, he became interested in his sister Paula who was living in Vienna working in an office. Up to this time he had no contact with Paula for a number of years. It seems that when he started out on his political career, Paula thought him crazy and told him that if he kept on he would wind up with his head in a noose. Hitler was offended at this remark and would not speak or write to her for years afterwards. Now he got in touch with her and even had her come on a visit. During the visit he agreed to send her a small monthly allowance on the condition that she stay out of the limelight and particularly out of the newspapers. Also, she was not to mention the fact that she was related to him in any way. William Patrick met Paula during this visit and thought her somewhat stupid, at least, certainly not bright. He says she is the spitting image of Hitler in appearance.

Later, due to the rising sentiment against Hitler in England, William Patrick was unable to get a job. He went to Germany and worked in several jobs before Hitler arranged a job for him at the Opel Auto Co., at a small salary. He would not give him permission to send some of the money to England where his mother was living. Over and over again Hitler warned him about trying to cash in on their relationship and threatened to expose his father if he tried to do so. He said he then acquainted Hitler with the fact that he had documents from the British Consul to the effect that his story about his father was not true and that copies of these documents were deposited with the English government as well as with his mother in London. From that time on, Hitler became more tolerant of him and whenever he began to rage about William Patrick's activities, he had only to mention the documents in order to get Hitler to calm down. He was amazed that even Hitler's closest associates knew nothing about the

Fuehrer, let alone a nephew. At first, they discredited him on the ground that the Fuehrer only had one close relative, namely his sister Angela. Only Schaub and Hoffmann knew of the existence of the brother or anything about the Hitler family. He was under the impression that it was this knowledge that made Hitler fear both of them, because he is absolutely intent on keeping both his present family and his background a deep, dark secret.

At home in New England, Langer worked hard to get the final report written in time and typed the last words just one hour before the Federal Express courier left Boston for Washington on the night before the deadline.

The report contained many of the family secrets Adolf Hitler had been so determined to stifle and, had it been widely circulated to the public, it would certainly have sent the Führer into a rage over the nephew he thought he'd seen the last of. But the study was destined only for the Allied leadership and would not be declassified until long after the war.

At the top of the cover page was the warning: 'CLAS-SIFICATION: SECRET'. Underneath was: 'A PSYCHOLOGICAL ANALYSIS OF ADOLPH HITLER. HIS LIFE AND LEGEND by Walter C. Langer, M.O. Branch, Office of Strategic Studies, Washington D.C.'

The section Langer compiled with William Patrick's help began:

There is a great deal of confusion in studying Hitler's family tree. Much of this is due to the fact that the name has been spelled in various ways: Hitler, Hidler, Hiedler and Huettler.

It seems reasonable to suppose, however, that it is fundamentally the same name spelled in various ways by different members of what was basically an illiterate peasant family. Adolph Hitler himself signed his name Hittler on the first Party membership blanks, and his sister at the present time spells her name Hiedler. Another element of confusion is introduced by the fact that Adolph's mother's mother was also named Hitler, which later became the family name of his father. Some of this confusion is dissipated, however, when we realize that Adolph's parents had a common ancestor (father's grandfather and mother's great-grandfather), an inhabitant of the culturally backward Waldviertel district of Austria. Adolph's father, Alois Hitler, was the illegitimate son of Maria Anna Schicklgruber. It is generally supposed that the father of Alois Hitler was a Johann Georg Hiedler, a miller's assistant. Alois, however, was not legitimized, and bore his mother's name until he was forty years of age when he changed it to Hitler. Just why this was done is not clear, but it is generally said among the villagers that it was necessary in order to obtain a legacy. Where the legacy came from is unknown. One could suppose that Johann Georg Hiedler relented on his deathbed and left an inheritance to his illegitimate son together with his name. However, it is not clear why he did not legitimize the son when he finally married the mother thirty-five years earlier. Why the son chose to take the name Hitler instead of Hiedler, if this is the case, is a mystery which remains unsolved.

Unfortunately, the date of the death of Hiedler has not been established and consequently we are unable to relate these two events in time. A peculiar series of events prior to Hitler's birth leaves plenty of room for speculation. There are some people who seriously doubt that Johann Georg Hiedler was the father of Alois. Thyssen and Koehler, for example, claim that Chancellor Dollfuss had ordered the Austrian police to conduct a thorough investigation into the Hitler family. As a result of this investigation a secret document was prepared which proved that Maria Anna Schicklgruber was living in Vienna at the time she conceived. At that time she was employed as a servant in the home of Baron Rothschild. As soon as the family discovered her pregnancy she was sent back to her home in Spital where Alois was born. If it is true that one of the Rothschilds is the real father of Alois Hitler, it would make Adolph a quarter Jew. According to these sources, Adolph Hitler knew of the existence of this document and the incriminating evidence it contained. In order to obtain it he precipitated events in Austria and initiated the assassination of Dollfuss. According to this story, he failed to obtain the document at that time, since Dollfuss had secreted it and had told Schuschnigg of its whereabouts so that in the event of his death the independence of Austria would remain assured. Several stories of this general character are in circulation.

German steel magnate Fritz Thyssen, mentioned above in Langer's report, was a partner of American tycoon Averell Harriman, himself associated with the Nazis in the early 1920s, and was first introduced to Adolf Hitler in 1923. He later admitted providing Hitler's regime with more than one million marks over a thirteen-year period, mainly from his own private funds. He fell out with Hitler in 1936 and fled to France in 1939. He wrote a book, *I Paid Hitler*, published in 1941, which detailed the financial support he offered to the Nazi Party. The book also included the assertion that Hitler was descended from an illegitimate child of the Rothschild family. Thyssen was one of the first to publicly highlight Hitler's rumoured Jewish family connection. Thyssen was extradited to Germany by the Vichy government in 1941 and survived several concentration camps. After the war he emigrated to Argentina, where he died in 1951.

Hansjürgen Koehler, also mentioned in Langer's report, was a high-level Gestapo officer who wrote about the investigations into Hitler's background carried out by the Austrian Chancellor Dollfuss in his 1940 book *Inside the Gestapo*. In the book, Koehler, who claimed to have worked for the Gestapo for five years and was once part of Hitler's guard at Berchtesgaden, wrote: 'A little servant maid from Upper Austria called Matild Schueckelgruber came to Vienna and became a domestic servant, mostly working for rather rich families. But she was unlucky; having been seduced . . . she went home for her confinement. Her little son, being illegitimate, received his mother's name, Alois Schueckelgruber (in some documents, Schicklgruber) . . . I must repeat that I have no proof of its genuineness . . . the little innocent maid had been a servant at the . . . Rothschild Mansion . . . and Hitler's unknown grandfather must be probably looked for in this magnificent house. But in the margin of the protocol there was a note in the Chancellor's [Dollfuss's] characteristic handwriting: "These data ought to cheer the writers of history who may want to publish sometime in the future the true life story of Hitler. Here is the psychological explanation of Hitler's fanatical hatred of the Jews. Hitler, born in peaceful Upper Austria where there was hardly any anti-Semitism, was filled already in his childhood with a burning hatred of the Jews. Why? This may be the answer . . .'"

Langer provided a detailed analysis of the rumour in his report:

Those who lend credence to this story point out several factors which seem to favor its plausibility:

a) That it is unlikely that the miller's assistant in a small village in this district would have very much to leave in the form of a legacy.

b) That it is strange that Johann Hiedler should not claim the boy until thirty-five years after he had married the mother and the mother had died.

c)That if the legacy were left by Hiedler on the condition that Alois take his name, it would not have been possible for him to change it to Hitler.

d) That the intelligence and behavior of Alois, as well as that of his two sons, is completely out of keeping with that usually found in Austrian peasant families. They point out that their ambitiousness and extraordinary political intuition is much more in harmony with the Rothschild tradition.

e) That Alois Schicklgruber left his home village at an early age to seek his fortune in Vienna where his mother had worked.

f) That it would be peculiar for Alois Hitler, while working as a customs official in Braunau, should choose a Jew named Prinz, of Vienna, to act as Adolph's godfather unless he felt some kinship with the Jews himself.

This is certainly a very intriguing hypothesis and much of Adolph's later behavior could be explained in rather easy terms on this basis. However, it is not absolutely necessary to assume that he had Jewish blood in his veins in order to make a comprehensive picture of his character with its manifold traits and sentiments. From a purely scientific point of view, therefore, it is sounder not to base our reconstruction on such slim evidence but to seek firmer foundations.

Nevertheless, we can leave it as a possibility which requires further verification.

In any event, Maria Ann Schicklgruber died when he was five years of age. When he was thirteen he left the Waldviertel and went to Vienna where he learned to be a cobbler. The next twenty-three years of his life are largely unaccounted for. It seems probable that during this time he joined the army and had perhaps been advanced to the rank of non-commissioned officer. His service in the army may have helped him to enter the Civil Service as Zellamtsoffizial later on.

His married life was stormy. His first wife (born Glasl-Hoerer) was about thirteen years older than himself. She is alleged to have been the daughter of one of his superiors and seems to have been in poor health. In any event, the marriage turned out badly and they finally separated since, as Catholics, a complete divorce was not possible. His first wife died in 1883.

In January 1882, Franziska Matzelsberger gave birth to an illegitimate son who was named Alois. After the death of his first wife on April 6, 1883, Alois Hitler married Franziska Matzelsberger on May 22, 1888 and legitimized his son. On July 28, 1883 his second wife bore him another child, Angela, and a year later, on August 10, 1884, she also died. During the time of his first marriage the couple had taken as a foster-daughter, Klara Pölzl, Alois Hitler's second cousin, once removed. He had reared her up to the time of the separation from his first wife when she went to Vienna as a servant. During the last months of the life of his second wife, Klara Pölzl returned to his home to look after the invalid and the two children. She remained in his home as housekeeper after the death of his second wife and, on January 7, 1885 he married her.

On May 17, 1885 she gave birth to a son who died in infancy. It is alleged by William Patrick Hitler that an illegitimate child was born previously, but we have no other record of this. In any event, at least one child was conceived out of wedlock. Four more children were born of this union. This is certainly a tempestuous married life for a customs officer – three wives, seven or possibly eight children, one divorce, at least one birth and possibly two before marriage, two directly after the wedding, one wife thirteen years older than himself and another twenty-three years younger, one the daughter of a superior, one a waitress, and the third a servant and his foster-daughter. All of this, of course, has never been mentioned by Hitler. In Mein Kampf he gives a very simple picture of conditions in his father's home.

Very little is known about Alois Hitler's character. It seems that he was very proud of his achievements in the Civil Service and yet he retired from this service at the astonishing age of 56, four years after Adolph was born. In very rapid succession the family moved into several different villages and the father tried his hand at farming. It is said, however, that he always wore his customs official's uniform and insisted on being addressed as Herr Oberoffizial Hitler. According to reports, he liked to lord it over his neighbors whom he may have looked down upon as 'mere' peasants. In any event, it seems quite certain that he enjoyed sitting in the tavern and relating his adventures as a customs official and also in discussing political topics.

He died on his way to the tavern in Leonding from a stroke of apoplexy in 1903. He is generally described as a very domineering individual who was a veritable tyrant in his home. William Patrick Hitler says that he has heard from his father, Adolph's elder half-brother, that he used to beat the children unmercifully.

It is also alleged that he was somewhat of a drunkard and that frequently the children would have to bring him home from the taverns. When he reached home a grand scene would take place during which he would beat wife, children and dog rather indiscriminately. This story is generally accepted and yet there is little real evidence in favor of it except what Hitler himself tells us in Mein Kampf.

[Hitler's first biographer] Heiden, who interviewed a number of the villagers in places where the family lived, had nothing of this sort to report. They found the old man rather amusing and claimed that his home life was very happy and quiet except when his wife's sister came to visit with the family. Why this should be a disturbing factor is unknown. Heiden suspects that the legacy was a bone of contention.

There is some doubt about the complexion of Alois Hitler's political sentiments. Hanisch reports: 'Hitler heard from his father only praise of Germany and all the faults of Austria.' According to Heiden, more reliable informants claim that the father, though full of complaints and criticisms of the government he served, was by no means a German nationalist. They say he favored Austria against Germany, and this coincides with William Patrick Hitler's information that his grandfather was definitely anti-German just as his own father was.

[Reinhold Hanisch (1884–1937) was a small-time hustler who met and befriended Hitler in Vienna when the future German leader was at his lowest point, staying in a men's hostel with tramps, drunks and other down-and-outs. Hanisch persuaded Hitler to write to his Aunt Johanna for money, and, with the 50 kronen they received, Hitler bought an overcoat and some painting materials. He used these to paint postcards of Vienna, which Hanisch sold to tourists. He gave an interview to *New Republic* magazine published posthumously in 1939 entitled 'I was Hitler's Buddy'].

Mother Klara Pölzl, as has been said, was the foster-daughter of her husband and twenty-three years his junior. She came from old peasant stock, was hard-working, energetic and conscientious. Whether it was due to her years of domestic service or to her upbringing, her home was always spotlessly clean, everything had its place and not a speck of dust was to be found on the furniture. She was very devoted to her children and, according to William Patrick Hitler, a typical stepmother to her step-children. According to Dr Bloch who treated her, she was a very sweet and affectionate woman whose life centered around her children and particularly Adolph, who was her pet. She spoke very highly of her husband and his character and the happy life they had together. She felt it was a real deprivation for the children to have lost their father while they were still so young.

One could question her background. Her sister is married and has two sons, one of whom is a hunchback and has an impediment in his speech. When we consider that Klara Pölzl may have lost one child before her marriage to Alois Hitler, another son born in 1885 who died in 1887, another son born in 1894 who died in 1900, and a girl who was born in 1886 and died in 1888, one has grounds to question the purity of the blood. There is even cause for greater suspicion when we learn from Dr Bloch that he is certain that there was a daughter, slightly older than Adolph, who was an imbecile. He is absolutely certain of this because he noticed at the time that the family always tried to hide the child and keep her out of the way when he came to attend the mother. It is possible that this is Ida who was born in 1886 and who is alleged to have died in 1888, except that Dr Bloch believes that this girl's name was Klara. He may, however, be mistaken in this particularly since both names end in V and he never had any close contact with her. There is no other record of a Klara anywhere in the records.

The younger sister, Paula, is also said to be a little on the stupid side, perhaps a high-grade moron. This is certainly a poor record, and one is justified in suspecting some constitutional weakness. A syphilitic taint is not beyond the realm of possibility. The mother died following an operation for cancer of the breast on December 21, 1907. All biographers have given the date of her death as December 21, 1906 but Dr Bloch's records show clearly that she died in 1907 and John Gunther's record of the inscription on her tombstone corroborates this. The last six months of her life were spent in extreme pain and during the last week it was necessary to give her injections of morphine daily.

It is often alleged that she was of Czech origin and spoke only a broken German and that consequently Adolph may have been ashamed of her among his playmates. This is almost certainly untrue. Dr Bloch reports that she did not have any trace of an accent of any kind, nor did she show any Czech characteristics. Alois Hitler's first wife was of Czech origin and later writers may have confused her with Adolph's mother.

Siblings: Alois Jr.

Alois Hitler Jr was born January 13, 1882, the illegitimate son of the father's second wife born during the lifetime of the first wife. He is the father of William Patrick Hitler, one of our informants. He seems to have taken very much after his father in some respects. He left the parental home before the death of his father because, according to his son, he could tolerate it no longer. His stepmother, according to the story, made life very difficult for him and continually antagonized her husband against him.

Until his third marriage the father was very fond of his oldest boy and all his ambitions were wrapped up in him. But the stepmother systematically undermined this relationship and finally persuaded the father that Alois Jr was unworthy and that he should save his money for the education of her son, Adolph. She was finally successful and Alois Jr was sent away from home as an apprentice waiter.

Evidently the profession of waiter did not intrigue him, for in 1900 he received a five-months' sentence for thievery and in 1902 he was sentenced to eight months in jail for the same reason.

He then went to London where he obtained a position as a waiter and, in 1909, married Bridget Dowling, an Irish girl.

In 1911 William Patrick Hitler was born and in 1915 his father deserted the family and returned to Germany.

During these four years when his mother and father had separated for a time, his father did go to Vienna. This would agree with Hanfstaengl's conviction that Alois Jr was in Vienna at the same time that Adolph was there.

Harvard graduate Ernst 'Tutzi' Hanfstaengl, the half-American Foreign Press Chief of the Nazi Party, was put under the control of the OSS for his expert help in the propaganda war with Germany.

Langer's report continues:

Alois Jr is not mentioned in Mein Kampf and only a few people in Germany know of his relationship to Hitler.

Angela.

She is an elder half-sister of Adolph. She seems to be the most normal one in the family and from all reports is rather a decent and industrious person. During her childhood she became very fond of Adolph despite the fact that she had the feeling that his mother was spoiling him. She is the only one of the family with whom Adolph has had any contact in later years and the only living relative Hitler ever mentioned. When his mother died in 1907 there was a small inheritance which was to be divided among the children. Since the two girls had no immediate means of earning a livelihood the brothers turned over their share to help the girls along. Adolph turned his share over to Angela while Alois turned his over to a younger sister, Paula. Angela later married an official named Raubal in Linz who died not long afterwards. She then went to Vienna where, after the war, she was manager of the Mensa Academica Judaica. Some of our informants knew her during this time and report that in the student riots Angela defended the Jewish students from attack, and on several occasions beat the Aryan students off the steps of the dining hall with a club. She is a rather large, strong peasant type of person who is well able to take an active part.

After Adolph was discharged from the army at the close of the last war, it is alleged that he went to Vienna and visited Angela with whom he had had no contact for ten years. While he was confined in Landsberg she made the trip from Vienna to visit him. In 1924 she moved to Munich with her daughter, Geli, and kept house for Adolph. Later, she took over the management of Berchtesgaden. In 1936 friction developed between Adolph and Angela and she left Berchtesgaden and moved to Dresden where she married Professor Hamitsch . . . Adolph did not attend her second wedding.

Geli Raubal.

Hitler's relationship with Geli, Angela's daughter, has already been described in the previous section. She died in 1930.

<u>Leo Raubal.</u>

It has been generally assumed that Geli was the only child of Angela. William Patrick Hitler, however, reports that there is also a son named Leo.

<u>Paula Hitler.</u>

Paula Hitler, or Hiedler, is Adolph's real sister and is seven years younger. What happened to her after her mother's death is a mystery until she was discovered living very poorly in an attic in Vienna where she has a position addressing envelopes for an insurance company. She now lives under the name of Frau Wolf (Hitler's nickname is Wolf) . . . Dr Bloch went to visit her in the hope that she might intercede with her brother and obtain permission for him to take some money out of the country when he was exiled. He rapped on her door a number of times but received no answer. Finally, the neighbor on the same landing came to the door and asked who he was and what he wanted. The neighbor explained that Frau Wolf never received anyone and intimated that she was very queer (other writers have also reported this). She promised, however, to deliver any message he might give her. Dr Bloch explained his predicament in detail. The next day when he returned, hoping that he would have an opportunity of speaking to Paula Hitler personally, the neighbor reported that Paula was very glad to hear from him and that she would do everything she could to help him. Nothing more.

During her childhood, according to William Patrick Hitler, she and Adolph did not get on very well together.

There seems to have been considerable friction and jealousy between them, particularly since Alois Jr. was always taking her side. As far as is known, Hitler had no contact with her whatever from the time his mother died until 1933 when he became Chancellor. He has never mentioned her anywhere, as far as can be determined. It is alleged that he now sends her a small allowance each month to alleviate her poverty and keep her out of the limelight. According to William Patrick Hitler, his uncle became more interested in her as the friction with Angela increased. It is said that he has had her visit him at Berchtesgaden and William Patrick met her at the Bayreuth Festival in 1939 where she went by the name of Frau Wolf, but Hitler did not mention to anyone that it was his sister. He said she is a little on the stupid side and not very interesting to talk to since she rarely opens her mouth.

This is Adolph Hitler's family, past and present. It is possible that there is another sister, Ida, an imbecile, who is still living, but if so we have no knowledge of her whereabouts. On the whole, it is nothing to be proud of and Hitler may be wise in keeping it well under cover.

If we let our imaginations carry us back into the early '90s it is not difficult to picture what life was like for Adolph in his earliest years. His father was probably not much company for his mother. Not only was he twenty-three years older but, it seems, he spent most of his spare time in the taverns or gossiping with the neighbors. Furthermore, his mother knew only too well the past history of her husband, who was also her foster-father, and one can imagine that for a twenty-five-year-old woman this was not what might be called a romantic marriage. Moreover, Klara Hitler had lost her first two children, and possibly a third, in the course of three or four years. Then Adolph arrived. Under these circumstances, it is almost inevitable that he became the focal point in her life and that she left no stone unturned to keep him alive. All of the affection that normally would have gone to her husband and to her other children now became lavished on this newly born son.

It is safe to assume that for five years little Adolph was the center of attraction in this home. But then a terrible event happened in Adolph's life – another son was born. No longer was he the center of attraction, no longer was he the king of the roost. The new-comer usurped all this and little Adolph, who was on his way to growing up, was left to shift more or less for himself – at least, so it probably seemed to him. Sharing was something he had not learned up to this time, and it was probably a bitter experience for him as it is for most children who have a sibling born when they are in this age period. In fact, in view of the earlier experiences of his parents it is reasonable to suppose that it was probably more acute in his case than it is with the average boy.

For two years he had to put up with this state of affairs. Then matters went from bad to worse – a baby sister was born. More competition and still less attention for the baby sister and the ailing brother were consuming all of his mother's time while he was being sent off to school and made to take care of himself. Four years later tragedy again visited the Hitler household. When Adolph was eleven years old (in 1900) his baby brother, Edmund, died. Again, we can imagine that Adolph reaped an additional harvest of affection and again became the apple of his mother's eye.

This is certainly an extraordinary series of events which must have left their mark on Adolph's immature personality. What probably went on in his mind during these years we shall consider later on. It is sufficient at the moment to point out the extraordinary sequence of events and the probable effects they had on the members of the family and their relations with each other . . .

CHAPTER SIX

HISTORY COMING ALIVE

12 SEPTEMBER 1995. NEW YORK CITY

Until now, everything I knew about William Patrick came from old newspaper cuttings or in odd paragraphs and footnotes in Hitler biographies. But studying Brigid Hitler's memoir I felt the past had come alive. The tendency of historians to deal in larger-than-life characters and their preordained roles in the grand design often differs from the viewpoint of a journalist who sees events catch up and overwhelm the lives of very ordinary people. Brigid's manuscript, largely ignored in the decades since it was written, at least gave William Patrick's life a context, even if it did not appear to offer any hints to his eventual fate.

Rather than lose heart at another cul-de-sac inquiry, the more I learned about his life the more I needed to know what became of him. The man who had been such a thorn in Adolf Hitler's side surely should not be left on the scrapheap of history.

So, I read on . . .

Soon after Adolf's supposed visit to Liverpool, Brigid's

fragile marriage collapsed. Her husband had dreamed of making his fortune in the burgeoning safety razor industry but had to leave his job in England after an enquiry into missing money. In May 1914, Alois announced he was leaving for Germany, where he hoped to resurrect his career in the razor trade. His then three-year-old son would not see his father again for more than a decade.

The First World War broke out just three months later and it became impossible for Brigid to get in touch with her husband. She heard nothing from him until 1920, when she received a message that he had died in the Ukraine while fighting for Germany.

It was not until 1923 that she learned the truth – Alois was alive and married bigamously to a German, Fledwig Heidemann.

Unknown to his mother, William Patrick, who was now at boarding school, read a newspaper story about the unsuccessful coup d'etat organised by Adolf Hitler in Munich and decided to write to the mayor of the city to ask his uncle for the details of his father's death.

Much to the boy's surprise, an investigation launched by the Munich authorities instigated by the letter discovered that William Patrick's father had remarried and was living with his new wife and their son, Heinz. Either out of pity for the deserted wife and child or, more likely, to cause embarrassment to the upstart Adolf Hitler, the Germans charged Alois with bigamy.

According to the memoir, it was not long before Brigid received the first communication from her husband for nearly ten years. He wrote a letter pleading for her to help get him off the hook. An excerpt, quoted in the book, read:

My solicitor told me that now the only chance to clear me is to have our marriage legally dissolved before the trial of bigamy comes on. It is the only way to save me from the worst, by you doing me this favour. If you deny this to me, then the future will prove to you that you have been doing wrong. It is not only for my benefit, but for yours and Willy's as well. I also want to remind you of one fact. Don't think that I am at present a rich man, for to tell you the truth I am not. But I have got the chance to get rich by the aid of my brother's reputation. This chance will be lost forever if I am found guilty, and if I get sentenced.

You must help me or they'll put me in jail. This bigamy charge is mainly embarrassing, for should the newspapers learn about it they're going to use it against my brother, who, as you must have heard, is the leader of the German political party which has missed reaching the top only by a hair's breadth. Although he is in difficulties now, he has by no means given up. When he is successful, I shall be in a position to compensate you for everything and could recompense you for all the expenses you have had in bringing up our boy and educating him. Up to now I could not share these expenses with you as I have been living in very poor circumstances. Certainly I'll always stand up for my little darling boy, who once was in the sole possession of all my affection. And it is quite as you say. This poor chap, with his lovely, lovely blue eyes and fair hair, of which I still have some in my possession, is a victim of unfortunate circumstances.

Brigid was to relent. Although as a Catholic she would not ask for her marriage to be annulled, she wrote to the court in Hamburg, where the trial was to be held, and asked that her husband should not be punished because he believed his English family had died in an air raid during the war. Alois was spared prison and released with a suspended sentence and the minimum fine of 800 Reichsmarks.

In the grateful letters that followed, Alois began to make plans for William Patrick to visit him in Germany. By now Adolf Hitler was making a name for himself as a political agitator and fast becoming a powerful figure. As his name became more and more prominent, Brigid and William Patrick made the connection that their relationship to him could be beneficial. They left Liverpool, where Brigid had struggled to get by since Alois's disappearance. Setting up home in Hornsey, North London, she took in lodgers to make ends meet.

In a letter to Brigid, Alois made it clear he, too, believed William Patrick's future could prosper with the patronage of his uncle. Referring to his son, Alois wrote:

In England he will always be a young man like millions of others, but in Germany he will be one of the only descendants representative of the man who bears the most prominent name of the present generation of Germany.

It is my intention to put Willy in a Position to enable him to make provision for you in days to come. Willy with his excellent character is well aware of the fact that in our complicated case it is his duty to do so. I, therefore, propose to him to come over here in the course of next summer. In the meantime he must learn as much German as possible, for it is important that he be able to talk at least a bit.

As Adolf Hitler's fame spread, the newspapers in London became increasingly curious about his English sister-in-law and nephew and began calling for comments and asking questions about the Führer's background. At the time, the manuscript says, William Patrick was greatly impressed that his uncle had reached such a high position in the world.

In August 1929, the eighteen-year-old William Patrick was given two weeks' holiday from his job at an engineering firm in Wigmore Street, London, to visit his father in Berlin. I copied four letters carried in full in the memoir describing William Patrick's first experiences with his German relatives.

Dear Mother,

The trip seemed terribly long. I was so anxious to get here, though I must confess after the train crossed the German frontier I wasn't so sure it was a good idea. All I could think of was those stories about the Kaiser they used to tell when we were children.

When I saw the signs 'Berlin Bahnhof Weinbergstrasse' my heart jumped right in my throat. I was going to meet Father. I got out and waited on the platform. I heard someone call me, 'Willy, Willy', and the next minute Father rushed forward and embraced me.

'You didn't know me,' he was laughing, 'but I recognised you right away.'

He grabbed all my luggage and rushed me to a street car, talking every minute. He was in a great hurry to take me home and have me meet his wife and my half-brother. They live on the Luckenwalderstrasse in a third-floor flat. You wouldn't like it – too much furniture and too many pictures. Right on the most prominent spot in the living room is a life-size painting of Uncle Adolf in storm trooper's uniform.

Father introduced me to his wife, whom he calls 'Maimee'. She said I had better call her that too. She was very nice to me and seems very devoted to Father, but it's easy to see that he's the boss of the household. She hardly says a word when he's around. Heinz is eight-years-old and very blond. I can't seem to believe that he and I have the same father. I don't think he looks anything like me, and it's so strange to hear a voice speaking nothing but German, but Father is trying to teach him English. Father always speaks English to me when we're alone. I feel very strange here, particularly with Father, though he acts as if he'd been with me every day of my life. I had no idea it would be so odd to be in a foreign country. I miss you very much.

After we ate a heavy dinner, Father brought out a bottle of wine and poured out a glass for himself and another for me. Then he settled down to talk about you. 'I can't get your mother off my mind. She'll always remain the great love of my life,' he began, but I didn't give him much encouragement. Then he took out his old-fashioned gold watch, opened the back of it and showed me a lock of hair. 'Your mother's,' he said, and quickly put it away again. I didn't like this very much, but I guess you would want to know, so I'm trying to put down exactly what he told me. 'My dear boy,' he said, 'I'm going to tell you our lives run in circles. If we do a good deed or a bad deed it follows up, or we come around and meet it. God has exacted a terrible punishment from me for the way I treated your mother. She is a wonderful woman and no one realises it better than I.' That's what Father said about you and he made a big fuss over me too. Well, goodbye for now, and take good care of yourself while I'm gone.

Your loving son, Pat.

The second letter described William Patrick's first sighting of his uncle.

Dear Mother,

I am writing to you from Nuremberg, where we arrived yesterday. First thing in the morning Father greeted me with 'We're going to Nuremberg.' I didn't mean to be impolite, but I didn't quite understand why he was so excited until Maimee explained. 'Don't you understand? We're going to the National Socialist Party Congress, we're going to see Adolf.' Really, Mother, I think she was more thrilled than Father.

Father, Maimee, Heinz and I were on the train all day. It was frightfully hot. We rode in the third-class compartment, and for dinner we had only sandwiches and coffee Maimee had brought.

I had heard a lot about Nuremberg and looked forward to seeing it almost as much as Uncle Adolf, but actually I saw nothing but flags. They were hanging everywhere, draped over everything. You couldn't even see the houses. It was like a gigantic country fair.

We didn't stay at a hotel. Rooms were at a premium since most of them had been reserved months ahead. We all crowded into a three-roomed flat of a friend of Father's. I heard Uncle Adolf make a speech in the Luitpoldhain, a large park outside the city. There must have been about 30,000 men there, all in S.S. or S.A. uniforms, just like soldiers. I asked Father how that could be, and he said it was because Uncle Adolf was so clever. In the German republican constitution, he said, you can't find one word that forbids men to wear uniforms for a show like this. Father says Uncle Adolf is a genius because he does everything legally, and the Republicans who let him get away with it, Father said, have only themselves to blame because they are so weak and stupid.

Father went to speak with Uncle Adolf, telling us all to stay where we were. We were hoping to get a chance to talk to him too, but Father came back and said it was impossible as Uncle Adolf didn't want to mix his family with business.

The third letter recalled William Patrick's first meeting with 'Uncle Adolf' on his second visit to Germany in 1930.

Dear Mother,

We had just finished dinner last night, and Father was unfolding the evening paper, when the bell rang. Heinz ran to open the door. It was Uncle Adolf, wearing a trench coat with the collar turned up and a homburg hat pulled down in front. Underneath he was wearing an ordinary blue business suit.

He looks much better than in uniform.

Father was very surprised because the newspaper had said there was a big party meeting that night. 'What happened?' he asked Uncle Adolf. 'Why are you alone?' Uncle Adolf was smiling and jokingly said he'd got bored of the meeting and his bodyguards and wanted some of Maimee's good coffee. 'Anyhow,' he added, looking at me with a twinkle in his eye. 'I wanted to meet this Englishman.'

Maimee quickly introduced me, then went out for coffee and whipped cream.

Father was quite excited at the honour of being visited by Uncle Adolf and began to walk up and down the room the way he does. Uncle Adolf sat down on the sofa under the oil painting of himself. When Maimee came back with a large plateful of homemade cake, Uncle Adolf fell to and ate most of it. He seemed to be in a good humour and asked Father if he'd heard his latest speeches. I know Father was familiar with them because he'd been reading them to me out of the papers, translating the words I didn't know, but he listened very attentively while Uncle Adolf told what he'd said.

I had no idea Father could be such a good listener.

Uncle Adolf didn't seem to be disturbed at all by my presence and told us all the news about his sister Angela and her daughter Geli. You remember I told you about meeting them last year.

Geli is the nicest of the whole family, and she can speak English too.

Uncle Adolf complained to Father about his troubles with the industrialists, particularly Herr Thyssen whom he had been visiting. 'I have to keep on good terms with him,' he said. 'After all, the party needs their millions.' He said that the 'few press' is attacking him again, and the others all nodded their heads as they knew what that meant.

Uncle Adolf had been looking at me from time to time as though he were curious about me. Now he turned to me and said, 'And you, you English boy, what is your opinion on the Jewish question? What are they doing about it in England?' I was really embarrassed but tried to tell him as well as I could in my broken German that we didn't have any Jewish question in England, and that we didn't make any distinction about religion. I told him we had many friends whose religion we didn't even know.

'In Germany, it would be different,' he shouted at me. 'Germany is too small for religion and the Party. The Party needs the whole man, not a piece of him. The Party must be everything to him. Even his family must be subordinated.

'That is how we shall build a strong nation. There will be no place for religion in the future. First we must get rid of all the Jews. They are the weakest. And then we must rule out Catholicism. The Catholics are too well-organised. In a few generations no one will know that a Jew called Jesus ever existed, and no German will be ruled by a man in a robe. Germany will be our religion.' And he wound up with, 'Germany is chained, thanks to the Jews and the Catholics.'

'I am a Catholic,' I told him.

'I know,' he said. 'And so am I. But it's true just the same. Catholics drove a dagger into Bismark's [sic] back, and it doesn't matter what country they live in, they all stick together. But Germany must be Germans first. We must make sure of that.' I felt like pointing out that he was an Austrian himself, but thought better of it and contended myself with asking him, 'What about the Protestants?'

I guess he had been a little bit hard on the Catholics then, because he suddenly slapped me on the back and laughed loudly, saying, 'The Protestants are not organised.' Then he asked me jokingly if I went to church every Sunday.

When I said I did, he and Father both laughed. Then Father said, 'I never found going to church paid my rent.'

It was getting late then, so Uncle Adolf had to go.

And the fourth letter is devoted to William Patrick's cousin, Geli, and her bizarre relationship with Hitler.

Dear Mother,

Yesterday Aunt Angela and Geli came for a visit. It's the first time I've seen Geli this year, and I was glad she came, because we always got on well.

You know, Mother, Geli looks more like a child than a girl, though she's actually older than I. You couldn't call her pretty exactly, but she has great natural charm. She's just a nice height, not too short and not too tall. She has deep blue eyes and blond wavy hair. She usually goes without a hat and wears very plain clothes, pleated skirts and white blouses. No jewellery, except a gold swastika given her by Uncle Adolf, whom she calls Uncle Alf. She told me her name is actually Angelica, but Uncle Adolf nicknamed her Geli and gradually everyone has taken it up.

We made a date for today. Geli loves to walk, and offered to show me her favourite haunts in Berlin.

I went to call for her at the Gasthof Ascanischer [properly, Askanischer], the hotel where she and Aunt Angela always stop when they come to Berlin. Usually they live in Munich. The hotel is pretty rundown and shabby. You'd really think they might choose a better one. When I said something about it to Geli she just smiled. 'You don't know Uncle Alf, Willie!' Like all the family, she calls me Willie. 'He wants us to set an example of frugality to the people. He never permits us to spend a penny more than necessary.'

As we strolled through the city, Geli kept returning to the topic of Uncle Adolf. He seems to be very much on her mind. She was very young when she and her mother went to live with Uncle Adolf. Geli's father died in the war, so Uncle Adolf acted father to her and the two other children.

Left: Alois Hitler, father of Alois Jr and his half-brother, Adolf. 'Alois Hitler Sr was an unrepentant womaniser and an arrogant bully who was married three times and always insisted on being addressed with his full title as a middle-ranking Austrian customs official.'
(© *Getty Images*)

Right: Alois Sr's third wife, Klara, née Pölzl; of the four boys and two girls she bore him, only two – Adolf and his sister Paula – survived infancy. Her death from cancer devastated Adolf. (© *Getty Images*)

Left: Alois Hitler Jr at the time of his marriage: '[He] was his father's son, a bigamist and heavy drinker who beat his wife and son and revelled in acting above his social station.'
(© *New York Public Library*)

Right: Brigid Hitler, née Dowling, an Irish girl from Co. Dublin who married Alois Jr in 1910, and by whom she had her only child, William Patrick Hitler. (*© New York Public Library*)

Below: The twenty-five-year-old Adolf Hitler (inset and circled) among the crowd in Munich at Germany's declaration of war, August 1914. Had he visited his half-brother Alois in Liverpool two years earlier? (*© Getty Images*)

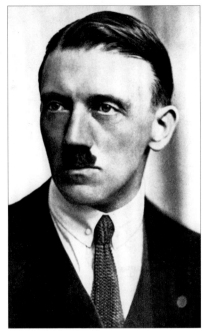

Top left: During the First World War, Adolf Hitler enlisted in the Bavarian Reserve Infantry Regiment 16 and served in France and Flanders, where he was wounded and gassed, and twice decorated for bravery.
(© *Getty Images*)

Top right: Hitler in 1923, the year of the abortive coup in Munich for which he as imprisoned. Ten years later he would become Chancellor of Germany. (© *Getty Images*)

Left: Hitler's niece, Geli Raubal (left) with her mother, Angela. Allegedly Hitler's mistress, Geli died mysteriously in 1931, in what was ruled a suicide, although many believe that Hitler shot her.
(© *Getty Images*)

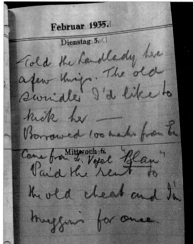

Top left: The front page of the diary kept in 1935 by Hitler's 'loathsome nephew', William Patrick, son of Alois Jr and Brigid Hitler, when he was working in Germany. The diary is in English and written in pencil. (*© David Gardner*)

Top right: A page from the diary, in which William Patrick complains about his landlady and says he'd like to kick her. He seems to have been almost permanently short of money. (*© David Gardner*)

Below: Alois Jr (*arrowed left*), his son William Patrick (*arrowed centre*) and Heinz (*right*), the son from Alois's second, bigamous, marriage, pictured on a canal-boat trip in Germany before the Second World War. (*© New York Public Library*)

Left: Seaman First Class William Patrick Hitler, US Navy, receives his discharge from the service in February 1946. He and his mother had emigrated to the United States in 1939.

(© *Getty Images*)

Right: November 1939: the front page of a prospectus for a lecture tour of America given by William Patrick Hitler. At that date the USA was still more than two years away from joining the war.

(© *Express/Express/Getty Images*)

The Truth About Hitler And His Regime
From One Person Who Knows Them Both Inside Out!

WILLIAM PATRICK **HITLER**

(NEPHEW OF ADOLF HITLER)

Presents His Startling Story
Of The Real Germany
Hidden Behind Nazi Fictions

**WHAT THE
GERMAN
PEOPLE
ARE
THINKING**

Harold R. PEAT, Inc.
Exclusive Agents

Left: Adolf Hitler's former sister-in-law, Brigid, promoting the British War Relief Society in New York in July 1941; there is a photograph of Britain's Prime Minister, Winston Churchill, behind her.

(© *Al Aumuller/ Alamy*)

Above: Brigid says goodbye to her son outside the Astor Hotel, New York, 29 June 1941. The carefully staged publicity shot ostensibly showed William Patrick leaving to join the Royal Canadian Air Force, but in fact he enlisted in the US Navy. (© *Getty Images*)

Right: William Patrick, then aged twenty-eight, and his mother leave St Patrick's Cathedral in New York City, after attending Palm Sunday services, 2 April 1939.

(© *AP Photo/Alamy*)

Above: The house where William Patrick Hitler and his wife Phyllis raised their children. They also ran a blood laboratory from the premises. (© *David Gardner*)

Above: William Patrick at home in later life; he died in July 1987, aged seventy-six. (© *Private collection*)

Left: The stone marking the graves of Brigid Hitler and her son William Patrick. Brigid died in 1969, aged seventy-eight. (© *David Gardner*)

Right: Brian Hitler as he appeared in his high-school yearbook.

(© *David Gardner*)

Left: Louis Hitler, the second of William Patrick's four sons.

(© *David Gardner*)

Left: Alexander Hitler, also a high-school yearbook photo.

(© *David Gardner*)

Right: Howard Hitler performing with his high-school marching band. The only one of Hitler's great-nephews to have married, he died in a car crash in September 1989, leaving a widow but no children.

(© *David Gardner*)

'He was utterly strict,' she told me, 'though more with the others than with me. He was always different with me. I am his special favourite. He would never go to sleep without saying goodnight to me, even when he didn't get home until long after I was in bed. Lots of times he would wake me up in the middle of the night just to say a few words.'

I guess Geli is the only one Uncle Adolf is affectionate with. She told me even when he is in a savage mood, storming about and breaking things, if she begins to cry he pulls himself out of it and comforts her. There were long periods when she scarcely saw him at all. He had no time for anyone when he was fighting for the life of his party.

That was when Geli began to study music seriously. She has a fine natural soprano voice, and her teachers say she could be a success in opera if she would really devote all her time to it.

But Uncle Adolf doesn't want Geli to have a career. He thinks she should learn to be a good housewife first. In fact, I don't think he approves of careers for women at all.

She said only once did he lose his temper with her. That was one night when she was out late after a concert and a boy brought her home. Uncle Adolf was furious and forbade her to go out with boys at all. It was a week before he was nice to her again, and then he began to take her everywhere with him. They would go riding in his car. When he was in Munich, Geli stayed at his Prinzregentstrasse apartment. He even took her on party business to Berlin and Nuremberg. They were inseparable.

I guess if it weren't for Geli's music she probably would allow herself to be completely enslaved by him, for that's what his interest actually amounts to. He wants to take absolute possession of her. He can't bear for her to show the slightest interest in anything or anyone other than himself. Any moment she must be ready to go where he wants, stop whatever she's doing to follow his slightest whim. Sometimes he makes her sit at the movies all day with him, then go back in the evening. Geli gets bored but has to accompany him. She never quarrels with him, but it's only necessary for her to try to get out of going to make him angry. There is never any time for her singing lessons. 'I think he's jealous of my music,' Geli said.

After we talked a while, I found that it wasn't so much the music Uncle Adolf objected to as Geli's teacher, who comes especially from Vienna to give her lessons. He's half-Jewish, and Uncle Adolf doesn't want Geli to have anything to do with him for that reason.

That seems daft to me. As Geli said, 'What difference can his being Jewish really make? He's a fine teacher.' Uncle Adolf is really hipped on the subject. Geli says she can't even talk to him about it.

It's quite a problem for her, because she feels she owes Uncle Adolf a lot for bringing her up and taking care of her mother, and she's sure he's really fond of her, but she doesn't like it that he watches her all of the time and doesn't let her do anything she wants.

I asked her what she wanted to do, and she said, 'go to Vienna and study singing'. She told me sometimes she feels like running away. Anything would be better than being kept down the way she is. She was practically in tears this evening and very upset about the whole thing.

I didn't know what to tell her. She has a very nice voice, but if Uncle Adolf was against her it would be very difficult for her to do anything with it, and of course she has no money except for what he gives her. Anyway, I think it's too bad.

Well, this is much longer than I intended and it's late, so I'll doze.

With love, Pat.

As I read through the manuscript, an episode recounted by Brigid reminded me of two cuttings I had uncovered in the libraries of American publications. One was an article in *Time* magazine, dated 10 April 1939, which was headlined 'Hitler v. Hitler'. The article began: 'With some angry talk, Adolf Hitler last week launched a boat at Wilhelmshaven . . . On the previous day, another Hitler got off another boat in Manhattan, and also delivered some angry talk – against his uncle Adolf. William Patrick Hitler, 23, arriving in the US for an anti-Hitler lecture tour, explained that he hates his uncle because of 1) his policies, 2) his attitude towards his own family.'

It continued: 'William grew up to be a good-looking lad with a slight brogue and not much luck. His worst luck, he said last week, was his name.' But this was the section that caught my eye: 'During the 1934 blood purge, he was arrested but soon released. This year he received hints that he'd better leave Germany. The Fuehrer, says William Hitler, is singularly vulnerable on the question of his family relations.'

It was one thing getting a job in Hitler's Germany; it was quite another going to jail in a country where unexplained deaths and atrocities were frighteningly commonplace. The other newspaper story came from the *New York Daily News* of 31 March 1939, in which William Patrick was reported as saying: 'I was once arrested during the blood purge of 1934 when Capt. Ernst Roehm was killed. I was held for 24 hours. They were arresting almost everybody at that time and perhaps they thought I had some connection with the plot of Capt. Roehm to overthrow Hitler.'

It was this arrest that was described in great detail in the memoir, further convincing me that the manuscript, if not written by Brigid herself, then it was certainly by someone very close to her. In the book, William Patrick describes in detail how he found himself embroiled in the bloody retribution exacted by Hitler on Captain Ernst Roehm, one of his trusted aides, and his followers who were suspected of plotting against Hitler in June 1934.

At the height of Hitler's 'cleansing action', which is thought to have involved up to two hundred assassinations, Brigid said her son was having a drink after a day of work at the Reichsbank in Berlin. The memoir continued:

At ten o'clock that evening, as every evening, Pat was sitting at a sidewalk table, in the Kranzler Cafe, a popular place on the corner of Unter den Linden and

Friedrichstrasse. Berlin's heart was beating with a dulled rhythm, as though drugged with fatigue after the day's sensation. Few people had ventured forth to their usual haunts. New rumours spread through the sparsely populated cafe like the ripples of waves when a stone is dropped. Some came from radio loudspeakers, some were invented.

Every few minutes S.S. patrols passed. One of these, consisting of four men, led by a tall stormtrooper with a scar on his cheek, and a stocky fellow who had obviously had more than a few drinks, entered the cafe. The men officiously went around, demanding to see the papers of all the guests. As each table was cleared, they moved on to the next. Apparently they were looking for someone, rather than making a routine check. But they didn't stop over any of the papers for more than a casual glance until they came to Pat.

Pat had already taken out his wallet containing his working papers, a few letters and his visiting card, which were the only things he had with him. The tall stormtrooper, staring at Pat's National Health card, which he held in his hand, spoke without looking up. 'Your name?'

Since Pat's name was printed on the card in sizable letters it was quite impossible that the stormtrooper could have failed to see it. Nevertheless, Pat told him.

The response came not from him, but from his shorter companion, who bellowed in a voice like a frog, 'The Fuehrer's name is not to be used for stupid jokes.'

'What is your name?' the tall one repeated, emphasising each word as though his patience had been overstrained already.

Pat repeated it. A third was mockingly polite: 'I suppose you claim to be a relative of the Fuehrer.'

When Pat said he was Adolf Hitler's nephew the tall one came closer. 'That's a good joke. Now I'll tell one.' Then in a changed voice he ripped out, 'Get up. You're under arrest.'

Brigid said her son was hustled outside into a waiting Mercedes and driven to the Reichswehr ministry, where he was put under armed guard and questioned. Then the SS men who arrested him pushed him into another car and took him to Lichterfeld, 'a kind of concentration camp' on the outskirts of Berlin.

William Patrick begged his captors to call his uncle to explain it had all been a terrible mistake. 'Please call the Chancellery,' Pat was saying in an authoritative tone.

'Rudolph Hess, or my uncle, will confirm my identity – or his adjutants, Schaub and Bruckner. They know me.'

Although Pat hadn't seen Adolf for some time, he had every confidence that Adolf would help him.

But Hitler's adjutants told the guard, 'Hitler has no nephew,' and William Patrick feared his fate was sealed. But he told his mother he had a flash of inspiration and demanded to be allowed to telephone the British Consulate as he was a British subject. To his surprise, he was allowed to make the call and a diplomat arrived at the prison to help free him.

'I was free,' said Pat. 'But even now I don't know exactly how. The Gestapo is very efficient. I am sure I was on a list. Otherwise, 1 wouldn't have been arrested, particularly in a cafe where I was known to go every evening.'

As unpleasant as the incident sounded, it obviously did not intimidate William Patrick too much as he remained in Germany for another four or so years.

The next chapter in the manuscript dealt with William Patrick's so-called attempts to blackmail his uncle and I was just completing my notes from the book when my phone rang.

'Sorry to drag you out of your history books,' said Tim, 'but I've got a story that is less than forty years old to do. It's actually just the usual two months old but the *Express* wants me to go up to Montreal and take a look at it.'

'Well, have fun. How long will you be gone?'

'Couple of days, I expect. I'm on my way to La Guardia Airport now. Don't forget we're covering for *The Sun* while Neil Syson's away. I think he's back from England next Wednesday.'

'No problem,' I said. 'I'll be back in the office tomorrow. This isn't really going anywhere at the moment. It's fascinating stuff, but I'll put it on the back burner again. I'm beginning to think this story is jinxed. I can't remember ever taking so long to get so little.'

'Don't worry,' said Tim. 'I have every confidence that you'll crack it one day. Just keep practising your goosestep. Oh, and I nearly forgot. The reason I called was because there's apparently been a couple of replies from that ad you put in the Liverpool paper. There are a couple of old boys who say they are either related to William Patrick or knew him. Your brother called from Essex and wants you to call him back. Did you put his number in the paper or something?'

'No, I set up a P.O. Box and he's been checking it for me. I put that ad in the paper months ago. I'd given up on it, to tell you the truth.'

'Okay, well, let me know. I'd better go. This cab driver is driving like a lunatic, and he keeps talking to someone next to him who doesn't exist. It's scaring the life out of me.'

While Tim flew off to Canada to earn us some money, I spent the rest of the day at the library reading through the rest of Brigid's memoirs. Returning home to New Jersey on the 190 bus with a notebook full of passages cribbed from the manuscript, I immediately called my brother, Richard, in Shenfield, Essex, where the time was five hours ahead at just past 11 p.m.

'Rich, sorry to call so late. Tim said you had some stuff on Hitler for me. Is it any good?'

'Could be. There were two letters for you. One looks like a complete whacko. It's pretty hard to understand but some guy says Hitler lived next door to him in Liverpool and they used to go together to watch Everton at Goodison Park. It goes on and on about how he converted Adolf from liking Liverpool when he first came to Britain. So I think we can safely rule that one out. The other one sounds a bit more promising. It's from a Mr Evans who says his mother lived next door to your Mr Hitler and there's a phone number. I'll fax them both to you tonight, if you like.'

'Thanks a lot. You never know, it might lead to something,' I said. 'I'll let you know how it works out.'

Back in the office early the next morning, I worked my way through all the New York papers – the *Post*, the *Daily News*, *Newsday*, *The Times* and the *Wall Street Journal* – to make sure there weren't any stories *The Sun* should know about. When their New York correspondent was out of town on a story or on holiday, the news desk liked to have a reliable fill-in to ensure they didn't miss anything. With the papers read, I called the number left by the mysterious 'Mr Evans'.

The phone rang for a long time before a man with a strong Liverpudlian accent answered.

'I'm sorry to bother you,' I started, 'but I'm trying to contact a Mr Evans.'

'That's me,' he said in a slow, deliberate voice. 'What do you want?'

'You kindly answered my ad in the *Post* asking for information from anyone who knew a gentleman called William Patrick Hitler. My name is David Gardner and I wonder if you could tell me anything about him. I am trying to find Mr Hitler.'

'He's dead,' said Mr Evans.

'William Patrick? Is he dead? Can you tell me when?'

'No, not William Patrick. Hitler. Hitler is dead.'

'Yes, I know. I was actually inquiring about the William Patrick Hitler who grew up in Liverpool. Is he dead?'

'I don't know,' said Mr Evans.

'I understand from your letter that your mother once lived next door to him. Is that right?'

'That's right. She did. It was well known around there that

the Hitlers lived there. There were a lot of stories about the Nazis bombing the Hitler house in Princes Park in the war. Bombed it to bits.'

'Have you stayed in touch with the family at all?'

'No, not really.'

'How about your mother? Did she know the family very well?'

'Not really. She's dead herself, actually. She's been gone twenty years.'

'Did you actually meet William Patrick?'

'Oh yes. He went to the same school as me and we'd play together in the playground. My mother used to say he was a nice, polite boy, but I can't remember much myself.'

'Can I ask you, Mr Evans, why you answered my ad?'

'I thought it might be of some use. You know, we always used to talk about it in the war. It was funny that we used to live next door to the Hitlers in Liverpool.'

'Well, thank you very much for your help, sir. When do you think it was that you last saw William Patrick?'

'Probably about seventy years ago. It may have been seventy-two or seventy-three years. I can't recall exactly.'

'Thanks again. You were a great help, Mr Evans,' I said, putting down the phone.

CHAPTER SEVEN

HITLER'S DIARY

1 JANUARY 1935. BERLIN, GERMANY

A dolf Hitler had been in power nearly two years and he was beginning to turn the screw. One of his chief targets was the Allied Powers who had kept a tight rein on Germany with the Treaty of Versailles drawn up in the aftermath of the First World War, forcing the losing country to disarm and admit its guilt for provoking the conflict. The other target was his own people.

By the end of 1935, Hitler and his Nazi henchmen had announced rearmament despite the treaty, created the Luftwaffe (the German Air Force), the Wehrmacht (the German Army), bought twelve submarines, and stipulated that only 'Aryans' could serve in the armed forces. Even more disturbing was Hitler's announcement at the September 1935 Nazi Party rally in Nuremberg of the 'Reich Citizenship Law and the Law for the Protection of the German Blood and Honour', effectively making Jewish Germans into second-class citizens and banning marriage – and any sexual relations – between Jews and non-Jewish Germans.

While Adolf Hitler was forcing through the laws and the policies that would blight Europe for a nightmare decade, his nephew was scrabbling around in Berlin looking for a job he deemed worthy of a relative of the Führer.

A journal kept by William Patrick during his time in Germany in the 1930s clearly shows how disillusioned he had become with the Third Reich and his inability to get a decent job in the one country where his name was meant to mean something.

On the front page of the old, battered diary that was given to me later as I continued my research are the words 'National Sozalisten' and 'this book belongs to Willy Hitler' written in German, suggesting that, at least for a period, he was a supporter of Hitler's National Socialist Party.

An intimate account of his life in Nazi-run Berlin follows on, describing his trouble getting a job even though his uncle was running the country with an iron hand.

'He was trying to be independent, and his uncle was not doing anything for him,' a family member told me.

On 1 January 1935, 'Willy' was clearly in a thoughtful mood. 'I wonder what is really going to be the end of it all,' he wrote in his diary.

'Received a letter from mother today,' he wrote on 15 January 1935. 'I am utterly desperate. I can see no way out.'

He was equally displeased with his living quarters in Berlin despite his lofty connections. 'Determined to mask this terrible train of difficulties once and for all!!! Moved into new lodgings – a bit of a come down for me but it can't be helped,' he wrote on 2 January.

It clearly didn't go well. 'Told the landlady a few things,' he wrote on 5 February 1935. 'The old swindler I'd like to kick her . . . Paid the rent to the old cheat.'

Although the diary, found with the help of researcher Jennifer Weiss, sheds little light on his relationship with the Führer, other than the fact that he was a supporter, it offers an intriguing snapshot of his life in the German capital at a time of great upheaval.

He wrote about seeking a job with Paramount film studio in Berlin and getting a position at the Opel car company.

After meeting with Paramount movie studio's director for Germany, he wrote on 4 January: 'I am very elated at the prospects which materialise if I am to have any luck at all. Nil desperandum.'

He talked of being offered a position with the Europa Film Company at a salary of 500 marks a month. 'I am in a dilemma now. Shall I go to München for a big salary or remain in Berlin? There are many things to be considered and I don't know what to do for the best,' he wrote on 5 January.

'It will not be my fault if I am still to stay in this awful rut in which I find myself at present,' he wrote the same day, presumably blaming Hitler for his predicament.

'Met Rolf and informed him of my intention to leave Berlin for Munich if I am unable to get a similar position in Berlin,' he wrote on 6 January.

'I did not go in to work today. I am so sick of it all I wish I could lay down and die,' he added three days later.

Blowing off some steam on 18 January, it seems 'Willy' went drinking with a friend who 'challenged me to a duel'. He also wrote that he lost his wallet in the process.

The next day, he wrote that he was offered a new job at the Opel car company with a matching salary. The inference was that Hitler wanted him in a position close by where he could keep an eye on him. He left a meeting with his boss Herr Berlitz 'feeling very grateful to him but nevertheless desperate at my hopeless position. As always it seems that as soon as I have got to leave a town I find that I am supplied with any number of reasons not to.'

'A flimsy hope persists in my mind but the odds are very great. I can foresee quite clear the result of all this hoping. I shall be told it's impossible and so on,' he added ten days later.

But it wasn't all bad. 'Stayed home and went to bed somewhat dazed after the cocktails last night,' he wrote on 25 January. Clearly, despite the lure of the cocktails, it was nearly time to leave.

In truth, 'Willy' was fooling himself if he thought Hitler would offer him a helping hand. The Führer discussed his thoughts about family during his infamous 'table talks' when Martin Bormann, his trusted lieutenant, persuaded him to allow his private conversations to be recorded by shorthand writers as source material for a book he planned to write about the 'Thousand-Year Reich'.

Specifically, he was critical of Napoleon for elevating his relatives after crowning himself as France's Emperor in 1804.

'By looking after his relatives' interests as he did, Napoleon furthermore displayed incredible weakness on the purely human level,' claimed Hitler, according to *Hitler's Table Talk 1941–1944: His Private Conversations*.

When a man occupies such a position, he should eliminate all his family feeling. Napoleon, on the contrary, placed his brothers and sisters in posts of command, and retained them in these posts even after they'd given proofs of their incapability. All that was necessary was to throw out all these patently incompetent relatives.

Instead of that, he wore himself out with sending his brothers and sisters, regularly every month, letters containing reprimands and warnings, urging them to do this and not to do that, thinking he could remedy their incompetence by promising them money, or by threatening not to give them anymore.

Such illogical behaviour can be explained only by the feeling Corsicans have for their families, a feeling in which they resemble the Scots. By thus giving expression to his family feeling, Napoleon introduced a disruptive principle into his life. Nepotism, in fact, is the most formidable protection imaginable: the protection of the ego.

But wherever it has appeared in the life of a State – the monarchies are the best proof – it has resulted in weakening and decay. Reason: it puts an end to the principle of effort. In this respect, Frederick the Great showed himself superior to Napoleon – Frederick who, at the most difficult moments of his life, and when he had to take the hardest decisions, never forgot that things are called upon to endure. In similar cases, Napoleon capitulated. It's therefore obvious that, to bring his life's work to a successful conclusion, Frederick the Great could always rely on sturdier collaborators than Napoleon could. When Napoleon set the interests of his family clique above all, Frederick the Great looked around him for men, and, at need, trained them himself.

Hitler went out of his way to portray himself as a father figure, just as long as the children weren't his own flesh and blood.

'It's in man's nature to act through his descendants,' he said in another conversation. 'Some people think only of their family and house. Others are more far-sighted. For my part, I must say that when I meet children, I think of them as if they were my own. They all belong to me.'

He goes on to suggest that every German family should have four sons, coincidentally the same number and gender that William Patrick and Phyllis raised in America.

'The essential thing for the future is to have lots of children,' said Hitler. 'Everybody should be persuaded that a family's life is assured only when it has upwards of four children – I should even say, four sons. That's a principle that should never be forgotten. When I learn that a family has lost two sons at the front, I intervene immediately.'

Did he have William Patrick in mind when he talked about the 'family black sheep' and discussed the honour system in Japan, his eventual partner in the war?

'Families which exercise considerable political influence have also a corporate family political responsibility,' he said. 'If one member abuses the family influence, it is quite reasonable that the whole should bear the consequences. They are always, after all, at liberty to dissociate themselves from the family black sheep.'

He continued: 'In Japan the principle of corporate family responsibility is so deeply rooted, that every family exercising influence, whether in the Army or in the political field, considers it a duty, as a matter of course, to prevent any member from doing anything contrary to the national interest. If their efforts are not successful and they feel that the national reputation of the family has been smirched by the erring son, then all the male members commit hari-kiri, to clear the family honour.'

In this translation of the table talks, Hitler insisted he had no knowledge of some of his relatives until he became German Chancellor. Again, it is quite possible he is referring to William Patrick, his English nephew.

'For my own part, I know nothing at all about family histories,' said Hitler. 'There were relations of mine, of whose existence I was quite unaware until I became Reich Chancellor. I am a completely non-family man with no sense of the clan spirit; I belong solely to the community of my nation . . . I . . . have to think twice before I can remember my cousins or my aunts; to me the whole thing is uninteresting and futile.'

One of our Party members was most anxious to show me the results of the laborious investigations he had made into the history of his own family. I cut him very short. 'Pfeffer,' I said, 'I am just not interested. All that sort of stuff is a matter of pure chance; some families keep family records, others do not.' Pfeffer was shocked at this lack of appreciation; and there are people who spend three-quarters of their lives in research of this kind. Pfeffer was, however, most insistent in his desire to show me that his wife, at least, was a descendant of Charlemagne. 'That,' I retorted, 'must have been the result of a slip! A faux-pas which can be traced back to Napoleon would be splendid; but of anything else, the less said the better!' Really, you know, it is only the women who transgress who deserve any praise; for many a great and ancient family owes its survival to the tender peccadillo of a woman!'

It soon became abundantly clear to William Patrick in Berlin that if he was going to make any use of his famous name, it would have to be outside Germany.

CHAPTER EIGHT

'HE LOOKS LIKE HITLER, BUT YOU CAN'T BLAME HIM FOR THAT'

29 JULY 1939. HOLLIS, QUEENS, NEW YORK

While I struggled for years to find out what became of William Patrick Hitler, a reporter for the *New Yorker*'s 'Talk of the Town' column found it a whole lot easier in 1939. He just popped in for a chat.

Finding himself rather unpopular with his uncle and somewhat out of step in pre-war England, William Patrick decided to try his luck with his mother in the land of the free and settled into a suburb of New York in Queens where, it seems, he felt quite at home.

Under the title 'Willy Hitler', the *New Yorker* offered an intriguing insight into its subject's life at the time, even if his most illuminating remark about his uncle the Führer was that he liked nothing better than sitting up at night with a book by the British crime writer Edgar Wallace, who was also known, incidentally, for creating *King Kong*.

'William Patrick Hitler, who is not in sympathy with his Uncle Adolf, is living out in Hollis, Queens, working on a book about Germany and marking time until the autumn lecture season,' the article began.

Not having heard a word about him since he was interviewed by the ship-news reporters, we journeyed to Hollis for a chat.

We found him to be a pleasant, relaxed young man, with jaunty clothes and nice manners. He looks like Hitler, but you can't blame him for that.

He is living in a little two-storey furnished house with his mother, Mrs Brigid Elizabeth Downing [*sic*], a jolly, expansive woman who speaks with a brogue.

'Willy told us "that he had been busy writing, seeing movies, and going to night clubs. Willy is as fond of movies as is Adolf, and that's saying a lot. As for the night clubs, Willy is convinced that they provide a chance to meet nice people. He's not yet reconciled to night-club orchestras, however. They play too much, he says, and you don't get a chance to rest."'

Mrs Downing told us that before the World War she used to ask her husband, Alois, why he never wrote to his half-brother Adolf. Alois always replied that Adolf was a good-for-nothing. 'He said Adolf used to just sit by the river watching the straws go by,' she told us. Willy chimed in with some disparaging remarks about his father. 'He'd make a worse dictator than his half-brother,' he said. Alois Hitler deserted his wife and child in England and took a German wife without the formality of getting a divorce. Willy and Mrs Downing don't give a hoot about him now, one way or the other; they're not even interested in the rumor that he's out of favor with his brother.

Apparently, there was a story doing the rounds at the time that Adolf was dead. William Patrick was happy to set the record straight.

'Willy feels obliged to spike the rumors that Hitler is dead,' says the article. It goes on:

'And what would the difference be?' he asked us. 'Things are bad anyway.'

He told us that Hitler is annoyed at the current gossip that makes him out to be a devil with the ladies. Der Führer enjoys carrying a whip. 'It gives him a sense of power,' Willy says. 'His father used to carry one.'

The famous lock of hair on the forehead just happens to fall that way, with no help from Adolf. He really doesn't drink or smoke, his nephew says, but he does enjoy sitting up late with a volume (English translation) of Edgar Wallace.

Willy thinks he got out of Germany just in time, as his uncle had been getting cooler and cooler towards him. He's convinced that Germany is headed for war, and that she's in no shape to stand a prolonged one. You can't get eggs or meat, he says, and there's a good deal of discontent among the upper classes. He's disturbed by the tolerance toward Nazi ideas he found over here, and says he wouldn't be surprised if Hitler saw it as a go-ahead signal.

He and his mother have reacted rather surprisingly to Queens County. 'It's so much like England, they told us.'

William Patrick had gone to the States at the invitation of US publishing tycoon William Randolph Hearst, who was intrigued by all things Hitler before the war. In the case of the Führer's nephew, he was engaged during his lecture tour to detail his unique relationship with his uncle and his fears about the rise of the Third Reich.

But Hearst was one of several newspaper magnates from both sides of the Atlantic who had dalliances with Hitler they would rather have forgotten later as the horrors perpetrated by his regime became clear. In the early 1930s, Hearst had paid Adolf Hitler, Hermann Goering and Alfred Rosenberg – as well as Italian dictator Benito Mussolini – to write articles for his newspapers. He also lobbied through his media empire to keep America out of the conflict as long as possible and remained suspicious of Britain even as American soldiers were dying alongside allied servicemen in the battle zone after Japan's attack on Pearl Harbor on 7 December 1941 brought the United States into the war.

According to the *Washington Post*, Hearst made a deal with Hitler after meeting him in 1934 to show uncensored German newsreels to the American public and praised him for restoring 'character and courage' to Germany. I should add, for reasons of transparency, that the 1st Viscount Rothermere, the 1930s owner of my former employer, the *Daily Mail*, was an ardent supporter of Hitler and the Nazis.

As a newcomer to the United States, William Patrick was happy to embrace the interest shown in him. In England and Germany, he had been shunned. In America, he was feted. For a while, at least, he had found his place in the world.

CHAPTER NINE

'MY NAME IS HESS!'

6 MARCH 1944. SUNNYSIDE, QUEENS, NEW YORK

The classifications specialist did not look up as he waited to tick off William Patrick's name on a list of postings for naval training.

'What's your name?' he asked the tall, brown-haired recruit.

'Hitler,' came the reply.

'Glad to see you, Hitler – my name is Hess!'

So it was that Gale K. Hess, of East Chicago, Indiana, welcomed William P. Hitler, formerly of Liverpool, England, into the United States Navy to fight a Nazi regime that had made their namesakes among the most feared and powerful men on earth. It was the end to a most surreal day for William Patrick, pleased to confound his detractors who suggested he was only boasting of joining up in the military as a publicity stunt to boost his price on the US lecture circuit.

He had arrived at his Local Draft Board 245 at 43-01 46th Street, Sunnyside, Queens to be sworn in as an apprentice seaman and promptly declared he was 'tickled silly to be in the

United States Navy'. After spending four years talking about going to war against the other Hitler's Germany, he was, he insisted, 'raring to go'.

With the cameras rolling as he was sent with fifteen others to the navy recruiting station at 88 Vanderbilt Avenue, Manhattan, to be assigned to a Louisiana boot camp, William Patrick told reporters he had 'more than one score to settle with Uncle Adolf.

'My feelings towards Hitler have never been very cordial. All the time I was in Germany I had to run to Hess or Hitler for anything I wanted. Later, my mother's sister was killed in a blitz on London in 1941. My mother was one of the first to declare war on the Hitlers when she left Alois Hitler, half-brother to Adolf.'

Drawing himself up to his full six-foot-one-inch, he declared: 'I am the only living descendant of the Hitler family bearing that name and I expect shortly to enter the United States Navy. As a member of the armed forces, I hope to take an active part in the liquidation of this man, my uncle, who has unleashed such misery upon the world.'

Still wearing the thin moustache that he would lose as soon as he checked in to boot camp, William Patrick said that in the five years he had spent in the United States he had learned to value the country he volunteered to fight for. 'It's a great testimony to the tolerance of the American people,' he said, 'that I have never heard a discourteous or indiscreet remark about my name.'

The new apprentice seaman had said his uncle once asked him to change his name because he did not want anybody 'waltzing around Europe doing as he pleases with the same name as mine'. But to spite Hitler, he claimed he'd decided to brave on with his unpopular name and never do his uncle the courtesy of changing it. Indeed, William Patrick had profited from his name since his arrival in New York in March 1939, five months before Hitler invaded Poland.

William Patrick had been a one-man Hitler industry from the day he docked in New York to tell Reuters news agency: 'I have just left Germany and Adolf Hitler, my uncle, who I personally have no time for. I believe that Hitler's policy in Europe will not bring any benefit to the human race at all. I hope that the American people in this country will not be kidded by my moustache because, after all, my heart is in the right place and that is the main thing.'

The tone of his rhetoric had changed from his early contact with the British press not so many years earlier when he still gave the impression that he was in thrall to the Third Reich. On 4 January 1938, William Patrick, then twenty-six, told Constance Forbes of the *Daily Express* that he was on a two-month holiday in England.

'It has been a very pleasant experience for me to be back in England after four years in Germany,' he said. 'The constancy, endurance and conventionalism of English customs are refreshing. I suppose I appreciate these things because I was born in England, although it is difficult to persuade my English friends to look upon me as an Englishman.

'Many of them seem to think I am directly answerable for most of the things in Germany which they consider bad. I have a British passport and I should not like to give up my English nationality. I want to settle here eventually, although I want to go back to Germany for a year or two.

'With the mentality of an Englishman I cannot subscribe to everything in National Socialism, but I try to study the Fuehrer in most things. I agree with all the fundamentals. My Uncle Adolf understands this. My uncle is a peaceful man. He thinks war is not worth the candle.'

The following year, the shine appeared to have gone off William Patrick's relationship with his 'peaceful' uncle. In July 1939, *Look* magazine carried a six-page article under William Patrick's byline with the headline 'Why I Hate My Uncle'. One month later, the disgruntled nephew sold a story to French newspaper *Paris Soir* titled 'Mon Oncle Adolf' complaining about England and his ungrateful uncle.

'England was hell for me and I could not remain there any longer. I lost my job, and I couldn't find a new one,' he said, explaining why he decided to look for work in Germany. But his attempts to sponge off his uncle hadn't fared well. 'Why does Germany's great man, who has immense riches at his disposal, allow his family to vegetate in poverty? Although a wave of his hand would suffice to fill the pockets of his nearest relatives, he did not make the slightest gesture,' he told *Paris Soir*.

Brigid was not making any secret of her disdain for her brother-in-law, either. Living in a Britain consumed with talk of war in the late 1930s, she had quickly run into difficulties. When she married Alois, she became an Austrian citizen, and after Austria was annexed by Germany, she subsequently became a German. The unfortunate combination of being both Mrs

Hitler and a German did not go down well in pre-war London and Brigid tried desperately to become a British subject.

She told the *Daily Express* in 1938: 'I want to get back my British nationality. I've seen the Home Office and they want to help me, but unless my marriage can be dissolved, I must remain an alien. Just to think that I, Bridget Dowling that was, am now a German subject since Hitler took Austria.

'As a Catholic, I don't believe in divorce. My husband and I are separated, but that isn't good enough for the Home Office.

'Nowadays it's a bit embarrassing to be Mrs Hitler, but the people who know me don't mind, and the others don't matter. At heart, I'm still Bridget [*sic*] Dowling, but oh! it's my British nationality I want.'

The next time Brigid's name appeared in the newspapers; it was because she had fallen foul of the law. She was summoned along with 800 others by Hornsey Borough Council for non-payment of £9 13s and 10d.

Appearing at Highgate North Police Court on 20 January 1939, Brigid was given six weeks to pay the debt. She said she was 'taking in boarders' at her home at 27 Priory Gardens, Highgate, North London, and explained: 'I was expecting some money from Germany – I can't tell you who was sending it – but it got held up. So, there was nothing for it but to take the devil by his tail up the hill and go to the court.'

Some cheques did arrive later and, according to local gossip, they were signed 'Ribbentrop', who was then Foreign Minister of Germany.

Standing in the drawing room of her home, which showcased half a dozen pictures of William Patrick, then working in a

Berlin brewery, Brigid added: 'You know it seems funny for an obscure little Irish girl like I was to get mixed up in all these international matters.'

A few days later Brigid announced that she had been offered a job as a nightclub hostess in New York and she cabled back saying she was interested. By the end of March, she was setting up home in Manhattan with William Patrick. The speed with which they departed for the United States may not wholly have been a coincidence, for on 2 September the *Daily Express* reported on a bizarre scenario in a London courtroom the previous day. The report read:

Half-way down a list of 15 people summoned for debt, the warrant officer at Highgate Police Court yesterday paused.

News had just been received of Hitler's invasion of Poland and an uneasy tension hung over the court. In a loud voice, the usher called out the next name: 'B.E. Hitler.' It broke the tension like a Max Miller joke. The magistrate smiled. So did the police. An under-cover laugh ran around the public gallery. Even people waiting to answer summonses raised a smile.

The name belonged to Mrs Brigide [sic] Hitler, wife of Hitler's half-brother, Willy Hitler. She was summonsed for not paying a £1 0s. and 10d. electric light bill.

But the summons had not been served. It appeared that Mrs Hitler had not been found at her new address in Lorrimore Gardens, Walworth, S.E.

Later I learned that Mrs Hitler had gone to America

lecturing or touring with a theatrical company. So the summons has been put by. It will be served later.'

Brigid's haste to leave Britain was such that children were stranded at Highgate village hall, waiting in vain for the weekly dancing classes that their teacher, Madame Hitler, had failed to tell them were indefinitely cancelled.

The rumour in the neighbourhood was that the 300 marks a month she had been receiving from the Nazis had finally dried up and Brigid had run out of excuses for her debtors.

Like her son, Brigid had stepped up her public condemnation of 'old Adolf' when she was safe in the United States where, presumably, she did not have to worry about waiting for a cheque bearing the Nazi eagle to bail her out of debt.

A story in the *New York Herald* on 25 June 1941 reported Brigid was 'glad to do her bit to defeat the Nazis'.

The article continued:

Mrs Brigid Elizabeth Hitler, nee Downey [sic], who has been waging a private war against the Hitler family since 1913, joined forces with the Allies yesterday and reported to the British War Relief Society, 730 Fifth Avenue, for her first day's work as a volunteer assistant.

Mrs Hitler is the wife of Alois Hitler, half-brother and second cousin of the German Fuehrer. She left her husband in 1913 because he beat her, and she bears his name today only because the laws of the Roman Catholic Church forbid divorce.

As for Adolf Hitler, 'It's nobody's business what I

think of him,' Mrs Hitler said yesterday. 'Hanging would be too good for him, and electrocution would be too good for him. He should be killed by slow torture, a little bit every day.'

Mrs Hitler explained the relationship between her husband and the Fuehrer as follows: 'Old Adolf, Adolf Hitler's father, married three times. His second wife was Alois's mother, and his third wife was his own first cousin, whose name was also Hitler. Adolf is the son of the third wife. So my husband is his half-brother and his second cousin.' This account differs slightly from other available accounts of Adolf Hitler's parentage, which also differ from each other.

Mrs Hitler told her story to reporters yesterday in a British War Relief Society workroom between bouts with the photographers.

A buxom woman of forty-nine summers, with coal-black hair and smiling eyes, she seemed glad to be doing her bit.

Brigid was equally scathing about her ex-husband, saying: 'I couldn't stand his treatment. He was very cruel – he was Hitler the second. "I'll bend you or I'll break you," he said, and, "Why, you'll break me because I'll never bend," I replied.'

The *Herald* said Brigid had applied to the Pope for an annulment of her marriage to Alois Hitler and for permission to resume her maiden name, which the newspaper gave incorrectly as Brigid Downey. It is possible that Brigid may have known she was following the same path her father-in-law took decades earlier when he appealed to Rome to allow him to wed his maid and niece Klara Pölzl, who was to become Adolf Hitler's mother. Although Alois Hitler Snr's request for special dispensation was initially rejected by the Bishop of Linz in Austria, the Pope granted their appeal and the couple wed on 1 July 1885.

The plea made by Adolf Hitler's parents, dated 27 October 1884, at the Braunau Am Inn, Austria, read:

Those who with most humble devotion have appended their signatures below have decided upon marriage. But according to the enclosed family tree they are prevented by the canonical impediment of collateral affinity in the third degree touching the second. They therefore make the humble request that the Most Reverend Episcopate will graciously secure for them a dispensation on the following grounds: The bridegroom has been a widower since August 10th of this year as can be observed from the enclosed death certificate and he is the father of two minors, a boy of 2 years (Alois) and a girl of 1 year and 2 months (Angela), and they both need the services of a nurse, all the more because he is a customs official away from home all day and often at night, and therefore in no position to supervise the education and upbringing of his children. The bride has been caring for these children ever since their mother's death and they are very fond of her. Thus it may be justifiably assumed that they will be well brought up and the marriage will be a happy one. Moreover, the bride is without means and it is unlikely that she will ever have another opportunity to make a good marriage.

For these reasons the undersigned repeat their humble petition for a gracious procurement of dispensation from the impediment of affinity.

We can only speculate on what would have happened had the dispensation not been granted.

While his mother preferred to gradually ease herself into the background in New York, William Patrick's lecture tour meant he was being paid to court publicity and, for a while at least, it seemed he was revelling in his role as America's resident Adolf Hitler expert. On trips to the West Coast, his agents introduced him to Marlene Dietrich, and he was invited to movie star parties where the famous guests were clamouring for details and gossip about the dreaded Führer.

Emboldened perhaps by his distance from the front line of the conflict and spurred on by his handlers who knew that sensationalism meant bigger purses, William Patrick's lectures painted a more and more lurid picture of his uncle.

A 2 November 1939 article in the *Toronto Star* was typical of reports on his talks at the time. There was also a hint that, like Brigid, he was considering life as a Hitler a little too arduous. The story began:

Patrick William Hitler, here to lecture, plans to change his name. Hitler, wearing a striped dressing gown, opened his bedroom door at the King Edward Hotel. He is six feet two inches tall, has a Ronald Colman moustache.

No, it wasn't Adolf. It was William Patrick Hitler, Adolf's half-nephew, and he is in Toronto to speak at Massey Hall tonight. And while he lectures on Uncle Adolf's maniacal desires to rule the world he is waiting these days for a call from England to join the British army.

William Patrick Hitler is an Englishman by birth and inclination but he has seen quite a bit of Uncle Adolf these last six years in Germany. He is to a Canadian more American in manner, appearance and speech than English. He doesn't look a bit like you'd expect Adolf's nephew to look. He is, as a matter of fact, an easy-going, nice-looking young man of 28, rather enjoying the sensation his name creates.

He is, however, serious about his mission which is to tell the world that the Allies' efforts to control Hitler's imperial desires are well justified, that Hitler and his advisers are sadists, and that 'if for one day there was a free press in Germany the present regime would be swept by the German people into oblivion.' Adolf Hitler's family, he said, is the only family bearing the name in Austria or Germany, and he has applied to the British Consulate to have his own name changed to that of his mother, Dowling, because 'it has become an anathema, not only to everyone else, but to me.'

Hitler, he said, is positively mentally deranged, 'crackers' as he put it, and told stories of orgies that were said to have taken place at Berchtesgaden and at Hitler's chancellery.

Hitler is charged generally by many close to him

of the murder of Angelica Rabid (Raubal), a niece of the Fuehrer and first cousin of William Patrick, said the nephew . . .

Hitler, he said, carried a big bull whip with which he 'stalked' around and which, when he didn't carry it, was borne in state behind him by an aide. He was, he said, a pathological case, talked to individuals, even himself, even in the informality of his half-brother Alois's house 'as though he were addressing an army.'

He agreed with the British White Paper disclosures that there was a great deal of perversion among Hitler's confreres, and said that it was generally known that Hitler's secretary, Schaub, had been convicted of a charge of living on the avails. 'The general outline of what goes on is that they all go up to Berchtesgaden, get drunk and indulge in all sorts of things,' he said.

He himself tasted Hitler's might when he was cast in a prison for 24 hours at the time of the purge that accompanied Captain Ernst Roehm's arrest, and secured release only at the intervention of the British Consul. Roehm was slain.

When he applied to Hitler to help him get a better job in order that he could better support his mother, Uncle Adolf told him, he said: 'I haven't the power. Your mother is young and healthy and she can work and she shall work!'

He left Germany last spring, he said, because Hitler 'called me in and said I had to become a German citizen.' He didn't want to do that and he foresaw war with Germany. 'Besides, if I became a German citizen I would be completely in his power and there might be a little family purge,' he added.

On the same day, the *Toronto Globe and Mail* asked about the British Government's recent White Paper which charged sadistic cruelties in German prison camps. William Patrick said he believed the stories were 'understated rather than exaggerated'.

'Hitler is surrounded by the worst type of men. Sexual perversion is rife among the ranks of his closest friends,' he added.

The article concludes: 'Young Hitler said that he believed the Hitler regime would end in revolution and disaster. 'Germany has been fighting an acute internal war for the past two years, with the people on war rations. Discontent is growing, and I believe that England will be Hitler's master in a year,' he declared.

In January 1942, William Patrick was still touring the country. A promotional article in the *Sunday Star-News* in Wilmington, North Carolina, reported: 'Adolf Hitler may have bludgeoned millions of Germans into acceptance of Nazi doctrines but he did not succeed in intimidating his nephew William Patrick Hitler, who will speak here on January 6 at the Thalian Hall under the auspices of the Community Forum. For six years young Hitler lived in the Third Reich under the direct surveillance of the Fuehrer but the Nazi virus failed to take.' The following month, William Patrick lectured to the Winchester Kiwanis Club in Handley, Virginia, on the by now familiar subject of 'My Uncle Adolph'.

A report in the next day's *Northern Virginia Daily*, said:

Mr Hitler declared that during 1933 he felt at first that there might be some hope that the Utopian state promised the German people would not be impossible and that the Jewish pogroms were a phase of savagery of the storm troopers, and that eventually Adolf Hitler would calm down.

But, he declared, that he realized that his uncle had no designs for anything but personal power and liked to look upon himself as the greatest man in the world. In return for the attempts to make Germany strong and put its industry on a sound basis the German people gave their leader carte blanche. During the question and answer forum following the formal lecture, Mr Hitler said he believed his uncle to be a pathological case; that he considered Hess one of the sanest, most level-headed of the top ranking men around Hitler; that the German people were cut off from the outside world and that it is punishable by death to listen to foreign broadcasts.

As the war continued in earnest, interest in William Patrick's opinions of Germany waned. He made some propaganda broadcasts to Germany and to South America and lectured to dwindling audiences in increasingly smaller towns as America got a first-hand view of Hitler's evil on European battlefields.

After being inducted into the navy, William Patrick was posted to training stations in Upstate New York, south-east Texas and Davisville, Rhode Island, before being co-opted into the Navy Medical Corps. Martin O'Donnell, of Portland, Maine, attended the US Naval Training Station in Samson,

New York, with Apprentice Seaman Hitler and recalled: 'I used to meet him at the company store and we'd talk. He was a very nice man. Had a little moustache. I thought he looked a lot like his uncle.'

Two years later, during which time the papers carried nothing from William Patrick, he was honourably discharged from the navy base at Newport, Rhode Island, with the American Campaign Medal and the Second World War Victory Medal. He told a waiting group of reporters that he hoped to become an American citizen and he planned to change his name and live a quiet, ordinary life.

And that was the last anyone heard from William Patrick Hitler.

CHAPTER TEN

A CHINK OF LIGHT

12 SEPTEMBER 1998. NEWPORT BEACH, CALIFORNIA

I typed the name 'William Patrick Hitler' and clicked my mouse on the same Lexis-Nexis computer search of the world's newspapers for the nth time. I knew the search results by heart. There was a sentence in the 1 March 1994 edition of the *St. Petersburg Times* reporting that '50 years ago today the US Navy announced that William Patrick Hitler, nephew of Adolf Hitler, will report for induction next week'; an article about the Massey Music Hall in the *Toronto Star* on 23 October 1993, which recalled William Patrick Hitler once speaking there to a sell-out audience; a letter in the *Irish Times* on 12 November 1996, confirming the Irish roots of a long-lost relative of Adolf Hitler called William Patrick Hitler; and an interview with novelist Beryl Bainbridge in the 15 April 1979 issue of the *Washington Post* where she talked about her book, *Young Adolf*, a fictitious account of Hitler's supposed visit to Liverpool before he set out to conquer the world.

Even though my family and I had moved from New York to

Newport Beach, California, the previous year, I was still intent on solving the mystery of Adolf Hitler's elusive British nephew. I was still plugging away, following one false lead after another, but this time with an advantage. The internet took moments to make checks that were previously painstakingly slow, and one of the fastest growth areas of the new web culture was in genealogy. Families around the world were floating names over the net in the hope they could fit together lopsided family trees and the new dotcom companies were looking at every available research tool that might attract this hungry new market in information. Whenever I had the chance, I continued to look for the crucial piece of the puzzle I needed to find William Patrick Hitler.

I was intrigued, and heartened, by the fact that a novelist of the stature of Beryl Bainbridge was equally fascinated by Brigid and William Patrick Hitler and had undertaken her own literary investigation into the story. In her subsequent novel and in a play she wrote for the BBC, Bainbridge took the story into the realms of fiction, an option unavailable to me. But it is a curious fact that while her book *Young Adolf* was published in the late 1970s as a novel, and Bainbridge made it clear that it was largely a product of her imagination, many Liverpudlians now accept Hitler's Merseyside adventure as a historical fact.

Reading again the interview Bainbridge gave to the *Washington Post* in 1979 made me all the more determined to find some answers to the mystery.

Asked by the interviewer whether she had ever contemplated non-fiction, Bainbridge said: 'No, I really haven't got the education for that sort of thing. The bit of what I laughingly call research that I did on *Young Adolf* I quite enjoyed. I felt rather educated rushing around looking in libraries.'

She recounted the story as she knew it then, and, even with all my inquiries, I did not know a lot more. The Liverpool writer, on a promotional trip to the United States, said: 'The facts are that Adolf Hitler's half-brother owned a restaurant in Liverpool as early as 1910. He married an Irish Liverpool girl called Bridget Dowling. They had a son called William Patrick Hitler. That's fact. He's here now, in the States. In 1941, through some amazing ridiculousness; Britain's war effort, she worked for the Red Cross in Washington. William Patrick went lecturing at American universities on "My Uncle Adolf". Obviously, they thought they could cash in on their relationship with Hitler, so they went first to Germany, but they were a terrible embarrassment to Uncle Adolf. By this time, they'd already caused trouble at home in Britain by claiming their relationship to Der Fuehrer, so they weren't really welcome anywhere. And so they came here. In 1941, Bridget wrote her memoirs and the first four pages say that in 1912 she and Alois went to meet Alois's sister Angela, arriving from Linz, and off the train instead came Adolf.

'I read the memoirs pretty thoroughly, because I'm doing a two-part play for the BBC based on the memoirs. The part of them that seems the most real is the part about Adolf coming to Liverpool. It's the most understated, whether it's true or not. There's no proof that he came, but there's no proof that he didn't.'

She went on to explain her take on Adolf which, again, I found interesting. 'I've got a disposition to see normality in oddity,' she explained. 'Certainly, had Adolf been around now, and applied to a college of art in England, he'd have been in like that. So you had a persecuted lad who lost his mother to cancer; and his whole thing was that he'd been done out of art school. He felt very frustrated as an artist. In that sense, one can see why he was so odd.

'Actually, he was no more anti-Semitic than any other German, because anti-Semitism was absolutely taught in the schools and the universities. And he wasn't particularly interested in politics, but the war gave him a family unit for the first time – the army – although he didn't mix very well. He won the Iron Cross, and that gave him a sense of security. Then the war ended, and he was nobody again. He just wandered in out of the cold, into a meeting in Munich, and somebody thought, "By God! That boy can speak," and dragged him in, and he was away! And it was as random as that.

'You read all the time about famous people who groomed themselves from the age of 15, but Adolf never did that. Never! He went in every other direction you could think of.'

I still spoke regularly to my old partner, Tim, entertaining him with the latest dead-end Hitler inquiry, but now he was back in England. We had decided to part after four successful and hugely enjoyable years together. Towards the end of our time in New York we had both considered a move back to Britain, but while Tim and Wendy eventually settled back in London, Michelle and I decided, after enduring a bone-chilling weekend at an East Anglian country house hotel around the Christmas of 1996, that we would move to California.

And in January 1997 our family of five was settled into an old beach cottage on the peninsula at Newport Beach, California, a short hop to Los Angeles and a long way from the frosty fens of England's East Coast.

In the months after that, I had concentrated on establishing myself as a Los Angeles correspondent for a number of British newspapers where I still had old friends and contacts.

Short of time to devote to the Hitler story, I sent a cheque for £300 to a West London company specialising in finding family records. They were to research in Ireland to try and trace the roots of a Bridget Elizabeth Dowling, the maiden name of William Patrick's mother, using the spelling with a 't' of her Christian name as set out in her memoir in the New York library.

In the meantime, when I was not covering stories on the West Coast, in Mexico or South America, I decided to discover more about William Patrick's life before the Second World War in the hope of establishing just why he had escaped from public view.

One of the most important themes running through those of Hitler's biographies which mentioned William Patrick was his role as his uncle's protagonist. He had supposedly dared to try and blackmail Adolf Hitler in two ways: initially by threatening to expose the sleazy antics of his own father, Alois, and the prosecution for bigamy after deserting Brigid; and secondly by hinting he would leak family stories to the press concerning the possibility that Alois Sr – the father of Adolf and Alois – was fathered by a prominent Austrian Jew.

I returned to Brigid's memoir. While it contained nothing about her family's supposed Jewish connection, she launched into great detail about Hitler's furious response when he learned she and William Patrick had talked to a curious press about him.

Brigid and her son gave unimportant family facts about Adolf's background to the London *Evening Standard* and the London *Evening News* after Alois wrote from Germany suggesting they should set the record straight on their infamous relative while at the same time telling them: 'Don't give it away for nothing.'

Shortly after the articles were published, William Patrick received a telegram from Germany, which read: 'Father dying, stop. Come Berlin at once, stop. Aunt Angela.'

According to the memoir, the message was just a ruse by Alois and Angela Hitler to ensure William Patrick hurried to Berlin to face his uncle's wrath. They were met at the Hotel Kurfürstenhof on the Linkstrasse by Rudolf Hess who ushered the three family members in to see Adolf Hitler standing with his back to them, dressed in a business suit and staring out of the window.

The subsequent scene, as it was told to Brigid by her son, was recounted in detail in the manuscript:

Adolf turned around and glared at the three of them, and then began to walk nervously up and down the room. This must have gone on for several minutes before he pulled up sharply and shouted: 'To me, exactly to me, this has to happen.'

But instead of explaining, he started off again raging up and down, mumbling to himself, to the blank walls, to the air, to anything except his relatives. 'I am surrounded by idiots. Yes, you, you are idiots. You're tearing down everything I have built up with my own two hands.'

Adolf's hair was tumbling over his forehead, but this

time he didn't bother to fling it back. His arms flailed the air in wild violence. He turned to Alois. 'You criminal. You succeeded in smashing everything.'

'But Adolf . . .' Angela tried to reason with him. But he didn't pay any attention.

'What did you tell the newspapers?' he rasped at Pat. 'Who gave you permission to appoint yourself an authority on my private affairs?'

This was so unexpected Pat didn't know what to say, but Alois immediately tried to defend him, by saying he knew nothing, they hadn't told him.

'Then tell him now,' Adolf roared, turning his back on Pat. Alois explained that two days before the New York office of the Hearst papers had called up the Braunhaus in Munich and demanded to speak to Adolf Hitler personally. They wanted to know if he had a nephew in London who was an authority on the Hitler family.

Adolf furiously interrupted: 'They put personal questions to me, to me.'

Pat still couldn't grasp why Adolf was so angry. After all, Alois had asked us to correct a false impression created by the English journalists. Pat thought he was doing Adolf a favour. Why didn't Alois explain?

But Adolf had only begun. 'My personal affairs are being discussed. Anyone can say who I am, where I was born, what my family does for a living. They mustn't learn about this stupid bigamy. I can't have it. No one must drag my private affairs through the newspapers. I never have said one word they can use, and now this happens.'

'I don't understand anything,' Pat said to his father. 'I didn't tell anything except the truth, as you—'

'The truth!' yelled Adolf, nearly beside himself. 'The truth! I'm being attacked from every side. I have to stand before them without the slightest stain, the slightest blemish. The shadow of a suspicion would be enough to ruin me.' His voice faltered.

'Can't you understand that? Or are you too stupid? I am surrounded by fools. My own family is destroying me.'

His voice trailed off almost into nothing as he allowed himself to sink into a chair, his hands lifting to hide his face. 'I have been so careful. I am only a step from attaining the top. I might even become Chancellor. And now there is a "nephew" to tell them all the miserable little details they want to know. They'll hound me.'

At this moment the door opened to admit an SA officer carrying a briefcase. Adolf looked round and thundered at him with a violence Pat wouldn't have believed possible. 'How dare you come in here? I left orders not to be disturbed. Get out, out!'

The astonished intruder gone, Adolf again dropped into the chair. Grasping the edge of the desk, he began to sob. His eyes brimmed with tears and he cried out choking: 'Idiots, idiots! You will destroy everything. You will ruin me, you.' As though tortured beyond human capacity to endure, he rose painfully and gasped hoarsely: 'I'll kill myself. I'll put a gun to my head.' And he lurched out of the room through another doorway.

Stunned by what had happened, bewildered by the situation, Pat turned to Angela. 'But what harm did I do by telling the truth?'

'What was the title of the article,' she asked.

'My Uncle Adolf!'

'It's not true,' Angela cut in, looking sharply at Alois. 'Even if your father said so in his letters, you'd better understand once and for all that it's not true. Your father isn't related to Adolf so naturally you aren't either. Your father had a different father and a different mother. He just lived in our family as an adopted child. By rights, he is no Hitler at all and has no justification for using the name.'

'Is that true, father?' Pat asked Alois.

'Yes, that is so.'

A few minutes later Adolf returned. He was in complete control of himself, and came directly to Pat. 'I know none of this is your fault, but you must help me put things to rights.' Angela took advantage of this new mood to plead: 'You are right, Adolf. After all the boy is innocent. He didn't understand he was doing anything wrong when he told the newspaper reporters he was related to you. Now that he sees things clearly, I am sure he will be willing to return and put things right by telling the newspapers he was misinformed, and that he was mistaken in claiming relationship with you.'

'Yes,' agreed Adolf. 'That's the only way to proceed.' He offered Pat his hand and spoke in a very sincere, serious tone.

'Will you go back to London and make amends for this, even though it wasn't really your fault but your father's? He should have told you the truth long ago.'

Adolf sat down on top of his desk and they all looked at Pat.

'When you get back to England, I presume the reporters will get in touch with you. All you have to do is tell them you made a mistake.'

Brigid's manuscript corresponds with an American magazine article written by William Patrick himself. In the 4 July 1939 issue of *Look*, he wrote: 'I published some articles on my uncle when I returned to England and was forthwith summoned back to Berlin and taken with my father and aunt to Hitler's hotel. He was furious. Pacing up and down, wild-eyed and tearful, he made me promise to retract my articles and threatened to kill himself if anything else were written on his private life.'

Brigid claimed Hitler gave £2,000 to his half-brother to give to William Patrick as an incentive to do his bidding. But rather than follow his uncle's directions, and deny his ancestry, William Patrick set about trying to prove that he was, in fact, related to the new German Chancellor.

In the *Look* story, he explained: 'When he saw Hitler's repudiation of me, my father also turned on me and sent me back to England. I realised then that if Hitler should decide to denounce me as an imposter, my father would certainly side with him, and that what I needed was unassailable proof that I was Adolf Hitler's nephew. Since I could not get work in England without changing the name which I had in no way disgraced and was therefore determined to keep, I spent the following year rounding up the proof.'

William Patrick contacted Dr Frederick Kaltenegger, the British Embassy's lawyer in Vienna, who tracked down birth certificates for both Alois and Adolf Hitler that clearly showed they shared the same father. William Patrick also traced marriage and baptismal records, which he copied, and kept the originals at a London bank.

Perhaps William Patrick was foolhardy, but he returned to Germany in 1933 armed with his family documents and determined to benefit from his uncle's elevation. If his name was so detrimental to him in London, he reasoned, it ought to have the opposite effect in Germany.

This time, having been informed of William Patrick's extracurricular family history homework, Hitler was in a cordial and more accommodating mood, offering his nephew 500 marks to set himself up in Berlin and promising him a job. Rudolf Hess was reportedly instructed to again help the young Hitler find work, but things did not work out as William Patrick had hoped.

In the manuscript, Brigid reported her son was increasingly disillusioned with his poor pay and lack of attention from his uncle. 'I was led to expect I could make a decent wage, not just barely exist. If I couldn't do any more than pay for my own food the whole project was a failure,' William Patrick told his mother.

In *Look*, accompanied by a copy of a summons from his uncle issued by Hitler's adjutant, Wilhelm Bruckner, he wrote: 'I found work in a Berlin bank and for a time all went well with me – but not with my mother, who was in England. For months on end afterwards all my requests for permission to send her money were flatly refused. Finally, in October 1934, I received the above summons from Hitler, signed by Bruckner, his personal adjutant. My uncle was in an ugly mood when he received me. He said my mother was an able-bodied woman, that I could send no money out of the Reich, to her or to anybody else. Then with a curt 'Heil' he turned on his heel, swept out of the room.'

The memoir quotes William Patrick saying Hitler had a secret personal bank account in the very English name of Birkenshaw and joint accounts with several aides, in spite of his claims to be the only statesman in the world without a bank account. It seems, however, that the nephew's persistent pleas must have touched a nerve.

After being continually rebuffed in his attempts to try and contact Hitler to get either his bank salary increased or help to find another better-paying job, William Patrick decided to return to England and try his luck away from the ominous shadow of his uncle.

'Pat determined to conclude the whole affair and, with this object in mind, wrote a letter to Adolf, in which he not only said he was returning to England but poured out all the bitterness he had stored up for months,' recorded Brigid's memoir. It continued: 'He would try to find work in England, and if he couldn't get it because of his name he would make a public declaration that he had nothing to do with Adolf Hitler and wanted nothing to do with him.'

More than sixty-six years after William Patrick wrote that

'blackmail letter', it was discovered by chance among some correspondence belonging to Hitler's sister, Angela. The letter, now in the Archiv zur Zeitgeschichte des Obersalzbergs, once again serves as independent corroboration to the memoir's historical accuracy – and underlines the foolhardy courage of the impetuous nephew who dared to challenge Hitler.

Dated 29 November 1934, the letter was in German and addressed to Julius Schaub, Hitler's general factotum. It read:

> It has been made clear to me that I will not be able to leave the Reichs-Kredit bank without giving eight weeks' notice. I wanted to leave Germany shortly before Christmas and I am asking you if you can make that possible.
>
> But in any case, it would be as impossible for me to live in England under the Hitler name as it would be for the Fuehrer to live there. In actual fact, I would really like to start in the same way as my uncle did. I really want to make it absolutely clear that I have the intention to distance myself from the political influence that has affected my life and that of my mother's for many years. In order to clear that up I am intending to make a statement to the English press to this effect so that my situation in England can be more secure.
>
> Because of this I must accept that there will be a conflict between myself and my uncle. This is unavoidable because this is the life I have chosen.
>
> Because I want to spend Christmas with my mother it is impossible for me to fulfil the conditions of my business contract. As I have no intention of returning to the Reich,

I would ask you once again to bring this matter to an agreeable conclusion.

Yours truly,

W. Hitler

There were immediate repercussions after William Patrick's letter was received. Hitler's adjutant, Bruckner, appeared at the bank the next day to escort William Patrick to the Chancellery.

Bruckner railed at him as soon as he climbed into Hitler's private car, saying: 'What arrogance, after all the Führer has done for you, to write such a letter . . . Have you no shame that you dared blackmail against the Führer? There will be no question of your leaving the country until we know what you propose to tell the English press.'

According to the memoir, William Patrick was shown in to see his uncle.

'You wrote me a letter,' Adolf began, 'not a very courteous letter, you must admit.'

I grant it wasn't very courteous,' Pat interrupted, 'but after all, when I came to Germany I was promised I'd be able to make a living, and send something extra to my mother.

'Otherwise I would never have come. I know I could get a better job if you would consent. It seems quite clear now that I made a mistake. I can take a hint. I think it would be best if I return to England.'

Obviously annoyed, Adolf began to speak, his tone conciliatory, 'You have a job and you can maintain yourself on your earnings,' he told Pat. 'What more can you expect? I didn't become Chancellor for the benefit of my family. You must understand that a Chancellor is in a peculiar situation. I can't have people saying I show favouritism to my family. No one is going to climb on my back.'

The meeting ended with Hitler warning his upstart nephew that he was getting regular reports on him and had been informed that William Patrick was falling into bad company. He added: 'By the way, about your trip to England, I feel quite sure, when you think it over, you'll change your mind. I don't believe it would be desirable for you to go just now.'

When William Patrick returned to his job at the bank, he discovered his wage had been doubled on the orders of the Führer and accompanying the manuscript at the New York Public Library is a copy of a German money order for 100 marks stamped by the adjutant of the Reichsführer, described by Brigid as her son's 'first and last present from the Fuehrer'.

This first blackmail episode involving William Patrick is detailed in a number of Hitler biographies. Ron Rosenbaum, in *Explaining Hitler*, published in 1998, found the comparison between the uncle and the nephew particularly telling.

He wrote of William Patrick's 'eerie ability to echo his Uncle Adolf's characteristic fusion of cravenness and boastfulness' when he depicts himself 'as the kind of fellow who could stroll into Hitler's Reichchancellery and make the raging Fuehrer of the German people quail into quiet submission'.

Rosenbaum continued: 'One really has to laugh at this

picture for its peculiarly Hitlerian self-aggrandizement: the preening little blackmailer supposing he's got the world-conquering Fuehrer wrapped around his finger. If there's something Adolfian in William Patrick, there's also something William Patrickian in Adolf; that combination of low cunning and grandiose imagination. The glimpse William Patrick Hitler gives us into the thought-world of the blackmailer – his own and that of his uncle – brings us closer to the Munich Hitler. This is the Hitler his disreputable Brown House cronies knew [Nazi Party HQ in Munich, destroyed by Allied bombing in 1943].'

The Brigid Hitler memoir curiously made no mention of the other alleged blackmail plot said to involve the two 'troublesome relatives' from Liverpool – the suggestion that Adolf Hitler had Jewish blood – even though it has since proved central to historians when attempting to explain Hitler's twisted psyche.

It was two weeks later when, just as I had begun to research the Jewish grandfather story, my fax machine rumbled out a message from the genealogy firm reporting on its efforts in Ireland.

They had found two Bridget Dowlings, one the daughter of William Dowling and Elizabeth Reynolds, from Dublin, which seemed correct because Brigid's marriage certificate gave her father's name as William. But then the birth date came up as 3 July 1901, which would have made her ten when she had William Patrick. The other Bridget Dowling was born on 6 January 1890, the daughter of William Dowling, a policeman, and Esther Cullan, which seemed more likely. The fax finished: 'Would you like us to continue with our inquiries? If so, please contact us concerning an additional payment.' I took a deep breath, picked up the phone and promised to send another £300.

The next day I was telephoned by the genealogy company saying there had been a mistake and that the first Bridget Dowling, the daughter of Elizabeth Reynolds, was actually born on 3 July 1891, not 1901. So I had two possible dates of birth for William Patrick's mother.

A week later, I received another fax, this from a contact saying he had found the man I was looking for. My momentary elation soon deflated as I realised the William Patrick Dowling he had traced was the one in Connecticut we had investigated several years earlier. I called the investigator to tell him not to waste any more time on that and he insisted he had another 'fascinating' breakthrough in the case. Patrick Dowling was alive and well and living in Malaysia.

It was not altogether unfeasible that William Patrick might have ended up in the Far East. He had served in the navy, and he may well have been in that part of the world fighting the Japanese. It would certainly have offered him an escape from the burden of his name. I typed 'Patrick Hitler' into the search engine once again on the off chance that it would trigger a newspaper cutting from Malaysia and, to my surprise, three stories from the *New Straits Times* popped right up.

It transpired that the coach of a football team called Sarawak, an Englishman called Alan Vest, was considering using a number of younger players to 'beef up' his defence, among them a talented goalkeeper, Patrick Hitler. The cutting was from March 1998, when the Patrick Hitler I was looking for would have been eighty-seven. I called my contact and told him to keep looking.

It was a quiet afternoon and I spent most of it on the phone to Washington, trying to get some details about William Patrick's naval career. Passed around from department to department, I was getting nowhere. There did not appear to be any record of a William Patrick Hitler and one government employee even mentioned a 1972 fire at an archive storage facility in St Louis that could have destroyed the file. I kept asking questions anyway and kept being put on hold while another bureaucrat was found to tell me he or she was not in the right department. While waiting I noticed an addition to a genealogy web page I had been trawling for missing Hitlers. The social security death records database boasted millions of names of people who had died in the US together with their social security numbers and the area code of the town in which they had died.

I put William Patrick's name in, with all its variations, to no avail. There were ten Hitlers who all died between 1887 and 1947, but none of them appeared related in any way to the British nephew. Then I typed in Brigid's name and one record was highlighted on the screen. It gave her date of birth as 3 July 1891, which fitted with the age mentioned in the memoir for when she married Alois. It also fitted with the corrected date of birth for one of the Bridget Dowlings from Dublin unearthed by the London genealogy company. The date of death was given as November 1969. Most importantly, a New York area code was included for her home at the time of her death.

After three and a half years of dead ends, I could see a chink of light. At last, I felt my meandering investigation was heading in the right direction. But, with the Malaysian Hitler still fresh in my mind, I was not going to hold my breath.

CHAPTER ELEVEN

WAS HITLER PART JEWISH?

16 OCTOBER 1946. NUREMBERG, GERMANY

It was on this day that Hans Frank, the 'Butcher of Poland', was hanged with eight others from the Nazi hierarchy. Despite his conversion to Catholicism and his statement that 'a thousand years will pass and the guilt of Germany will not be erased', there was little doubt hanging would be his fate.

He died a horrible death, dangling and writhing on the rope for almost twenty minutes before his body was cut down – but one of the stories he told in his memoir continues to divide historians seeking the origins of Hitler's evil to this day.

It concerned a top-secret investigation Frank was ordered to carry out in 1930 after Hitler received a 'disgusting blackmail threat' from his 'loathsome relative'.

This reference to William Patrick was made after he had supposedly written to Adolf Hitler pointing out 'very odd circumstances in our family history', namely the possibility that Hitler's grandfather may have been an Austrian Jew named Frankenberger.

In the two-page account written from his death row cell, Frank wrote: 'One day, it must have been towards the end of 1930, I was called to the residence of Hitler at Prinzregentenplatz. He told me, with a letter lying before him, of a "disgusting blackmail plot" in connection with one of his most loathsome relatives, with respect to his own ancestry.'

Frank said the relation in question was 'a son of Hitler's half-brother Alois who was gently hinting that in view of certain allegations in the press it might be better if certain family matters weren't shouted from the roof tops. The press reports in question suggested that Hitler had Jewish blood in his veins and hence was hardly qualified to be an anti-Semite. But they were phrased in such general terms that nothing could be done about it. In the heat of the political struggle the whole thing died down. All the same, this threat of blackmail by a relative was a somewhat tricky business. At Hitler's request, I made some confidential inquiries.'

Frank did not give details of his research, saying only that he had 'all kind of sources' including letters between Hitler's grandmother and a Jewish family that he obtained from a Hitler relative living in Austria. But he wrote: 'intensive investigation elicited the following information: Hitler's father was the illegitimate son of a woman by the name of Schicklgruber from Leonding, near Linz, who worked as a cook in a Graz household . . . But the most extraordinary part of the story is this: when the cook Schicklgruber (Adolf Hitler's grandmother) gave birth to her child, she was in service with a Jewish family called Frankenberger. And on behalf of his son, then about 19 years old, Frankenberger paid a maintenance allowance to Schicklgruber from the time of the child's birth until his 14th year. For a number of years, too, the Frankenbergers and Hitler's grandmother wrote to each other, the general tenor of the correspondence betraying on both sides the tacit acknowledgment that Schicklgruber's illegitimate child had been engendered under circumstances which made the Frankenbergers responsible for its maintenance ... Hence the possibility cannot be dismissed that Hitler's father was half-Jewish as a result of the extramarital relationship between the Schicklgruber woman and the Jew from Graz. This would mean that Hitler was one-quarter Jewish.'

According to Frank, when he reported back to his boss, Hitler said he knew about the child allowance payments and boasted his family tricked the Jewish Frankenbergers into believing the child was theirs so they could make money out of them.

'Adolf Hitler said he knew that his father wasn't the product of sexual intercourse between the Schicklgruber woman and the Graz Jew,' wrote Frank. 'He knew it from what his father and his grandmother told him. He knew that his father sprang from a premarital relation between his grandmother and the man whom she later married. But they were both poor and the maintenance money that the Jew paid over a number of years was an extremely desirable supplement to the poverty-stricken household. He was well able to pay, and for that reason it had been stated that he was the father. The Jew paid without going to court probably because he could not face the publicity that a legal settlement might have entailed.'

The story would certainly explain Hitler's wariness in dealing with William Patrick, and Frank had no obvious reason to misrepresent his leader or to invent the story. But his memoir is littered with other inaccuracies and even his own son, Niklas, who was seven when his father was hanged, maintained he was an inveterate liar. He recalled the last time he saw his father: 'When we were allowed to see him one final time in Nuremberg before his execution, I knew he was going to be hanged. He told me, "Well, Nikki, soon we'll all be together again for Christmas." If only he'd said, "Dear Nikki, I'll be executed because I did terrible things. Don't lead the kind of life I led." But I left this last meeting seething mad. I'm against the death penalty, but I believe my father's execution was totally justified.'

In his biography, *Hitler 1889–1936*, British historian Ian Kershaw summarily dismissed Frank's claims. 'Hitler's grandfather, whoever he was, was not a Jew from Graz,' he wrote. Kershaw said there was no Jewish family called Frankenberger living in Graz during the 1830s, adding that no Jews at all were allowed to live in that part of Austria until the 1860s. He also questioned Frank's account of Hitler being told by his grandmother that there was no truth to the story as his grandmother had been dead for over forty years when Hitler was born. As to whether Hitler received a blackmail letter from William Patrick, Kershaw wrote: 'If such was the case, then Patrick – who repeatedly made nuisance of himself by scrounging from his famous uncle – was lucky to survive the next few years, which he spent for the most part in Germany, and to be able to leave the country for good in 1938. His revelations when they came in a Paris journal in August 1939, contained nothing about the Graz story. Nor did a number of different Gestapo inquiries into Hitler's family background in the 1930s and 1940s contain any reference to the alleged Graz background.'

Another Hitler expert, Bradley F. Smith, came to a similar conclusion in his book, *Adolf Hitler, His Family, Childhood and Youth*. He wrote: 'It assumed importance for Frank, who was seeking a way to escape from his feelings of guilt, and it has, of course, been seized upon by anti-Nazis as the final irony in Hitler's career. It may even provide some small comfort to his surviving victims. Unfortunately, it also appears most unlikely and, without substantiating evidence, must be considered inadmissible to the Hitlerian canon.'

Smith maintained there was little prospect of the mystery of Hitler's grandfather ever being solved. Frank's memoir got wider attention only when it was published by his family under the title *Im Angesicht des Galgens* (In the Face of the Gallows) in 1953. By then the only other person involved who could throw fresh light on the story was William Patrick Hitler – and he was never heard from again after he was released into obscurity by the US Navy in 1946.

What of the other Hitlers? Ironically, it was Adolf's determination to distance himself from his family that saved them from serious recrimination as the Second World War drew to a close. With the exception of Brigid and William Patrick, all of the other close family members had remained in Germany and Austria but none had been given positions of any importance in the Third Reich.

It was not just the Jewish grandfather rumour that had dogged Hitler. There was also widespread gossip that some of his relatives were deranged. In January 1944, Gestapo chief Heinrich Himmler sent Martin Bormann a top-secret report containing unsubstantiated claims that their boss had relatives who were 'half-stupid and insane'. In the light of the Nazi's harsh treatment of the mentally ill, it was proposed that the allegations, whether true or not, should be kept strictly under wraps to avoid any embarrassment.

In a 3 December 1942 OSS memo on the subject of 'Biographical Sketches of Hitler and Himmler', Roosevelt's anthropology expert Henry Field writes that, 'a glance at Hitler's family tree reveals the fact of almost incestuous breeding'.

It goes on to quote Brigid Hitler as a key source, saying: 'Hitler's mother Klara Pölzl according to Mrs Brigid Hitler (mother of Patrick Hitler) had Czech blood, besides being a blood relation of her husband, Alois Schicklgruber, subsequently legitimized to Hitler.'

Field continues: 'Hitler's father was twenty-three years older than his wife and was fifty-two years old when Adolf Hitler was born in 1889. All evidence obtainable points to the fact that this marriage was unhappy. The one fact which seems to emerge from the cloud covering this marriage is that Hitler's father was a sadist. This fact was learned by Dr Sedgwick from Mrs Brigid Hitler, the ex-wife of Alois Hitler II, half-brother of Adolf Hitler.

'She called on Dr Sedgwick on August 10, 1937, at his London home and told him that her ex-husband Alois had described his own father as of a very violent temper, in the habit of beating his dog until the dog wet the carpet. He also beat his children and upon occasion in a bad temper would go so far as to beat his wife Klara.

'The pattern thus becomes clear. On one side was the hated father and on the other the suppressed mother, who quite possibly enjoyed this treatment, and young Adolf, at this period just reaching the age of puberty, and constitutionally opposed to his father. The result of this domestic situation on Hitler was a mixture of Narcissus and Oedipus complexes.'

Field again refers to Brigid, writing: 'Brigid Hitler is the wife of Alois Hitler II, who is seven years older than his half-brother Adolf. Separated from her husband, she is now in the United States with her son, Patrick Hitler, the author of a book, *I Hate My Uncle*.

'Mrs Brigid Hitler was born in Dublin during 1894. Her husband, when last reported, was keeping a restaurant in Berlin. He was allowed to return to Berlin in 1937 where he opened a restaurant on the Kurfuerstendamm near the Kaiser Wilhelm's Gedächtnis-Kirche, which is frequented by SA and SS men. The name Hitler does not appear in connection with this restaurant, but it is well-known that the proprietor is a half-brother of Hitler, whom he has seen in the Chancellery.

'During his youth Alois Hitler II had several convictions for theft and subsequently went to Dublin where he was a waiter and met and married Brigid when she was seventeen in 1911. Two years later he was expelled from England on a charge of being a souteneur. In *Mein Kampf* Hitler of course never mentions his half-brother, Alois II, who is the skeleton in the Hitler family cupboard.'

'Souteneur' is a French-derived term meaning a pimp, which has not been publicly mentioned elsewhere but might explain why Alois's marriage to Brigid ended so abruptly with his departure from Britain. It's certainly not a matter of pride and for many families Alois would be considered a 'skeleton' in the cupboard. But it pales into insignificance when your half-brother is Adolf Hitler.

Field writes that Alois and Adolf spent time together in Vienna before the First World War. 'During this so-called "Vienna-period" Mrs Brigid Hitler states that Adolf Hitler saw a great deal of his criminal half-brother Alois II, who was bumming around Vienna. In Dr Sedgwick's opinion, it is unlikely that Hitler indulged in any homosexual relationship at this time but rather represented, as he does today, the type of egocentric and masturbic Narcissus with the craving for the unfindable woman and occasional hysterical outbursts of a sado-masochistic nature.'

Field writes that Hitler was once asked why he didn't marry. He answered: 'Marriage is not for me and never will be. My only bride is my Motherland.'

He writes that Hitler often walked around with a whip, gesticulating with it in the company of women. 'All this wielding of the whip seems to be connected with a hidden desire on the part of Hitler for some state of erection which would overcome his fundamental sexual inferiority complex,' he adds. 'The truth is that Hitler is in all probability still in the stage of puberty, and still in the essential meaning of the word a virgin.'

Alois opened a restaurant in Berlin in 1937 and managed to keep it open for the duration of the war. A story in the 18 September 1937 edition of the *Daily Telegraph* highlighted the difference between the Hitler brothers. It read: 'Herr Alois Hitler, the Fuehrer's innkeeper half-brother, who has opened a new restaurant in Berlin, speaks good English. He spent eight years in England before the war studying hotel keeping.

'As he confided to me one evening in his original inn in the poorer quarter of Berlin, "Why shouldn't I speak good English, seeing how often I fell in love with English girls during that time?"

'Herr Alois Hitler plays the concertina, wears a moustache cast from the authentic family mould, and has a sense of humour.

'He is several years older than the Fuehrer. He does not, however, trade on his connection with his half-brother, who, in fact, does not keep in touch with him.

'I remember hearing an American tourist remark loudly to him, "Say, let me get this straight. You say you are the brother of the Fuehrer and Reichschancellor?"

'Herr Alois replied with quiet dignity: "In this inn I am the proprietor – nothing else."'

Although Adolf Hitler made no secret of his annoyance with his brother trading in the fashionable West End of Berlin, the restaurant became a favourite with Nazi leaders. At the end of the war, he tried to sneak through the occupation forces by changing his name to Eberle but was arrested in the Hamburg area for being in possession of false identity papers. He was held by the 21st Army Group of the British Army in July 1945 and questioned for a couple of weeks before being released. He supposedly told his captors: 'Adolf seemed ashamed of having a brother who owned a wine shop.' A statement issued at the time by the British military government authorities said it was clear Alois had led 'a perfectly blameless existence, being absolutely scared stiff of being associated in any way with the former Fuehrer's activities'.

Later that year he applied for permission to change his name to Hiller, claiming: 'The name Hitler has sometimes been a source of embarrassment to me. In Berlin, I had a restaurant with the name "Alois" in big neon letters, and the name Hitler in small letters. People used to wait for hours, hoping that the Fuehrer would come, but he never came. I have never seen my brother since we were boys together in Linz.'

Although it is true Hitler never gave his brother any power and ensured he was side-lined, Alois was certainly in contact with Adolf. During the war, there was a strong suggestion that he even pretended to be his brother at times. Alois was said to have donned Adolf's uniform and walked out onto the porch at Berchtesgaden to take the salute of the crowds gathered below. With his lookalike moustache, the older brother apparently gave a very creditable impression of the Fuehrer.

By November 1953, when presumably enough years had passed to make Alois a little bolder, he was prepared to be recognised as a Hitler. Running a Munich beer hall under the name of Hans Hiller, he protested over a documentary about his brother, *Five Minutes Past Twelve*, which carried intimate scenes from the private life of Hitler's mistress, Eva Braun. Ironically, Alois complained the programme brought 'discredit' on the family name.

Two years later, Alois had almost returned to his old adoration of his half-brother. He led an obscure ultra-nationalist political organisation called the National Democrat Party and was selling postcard-sized photos of Hitler to foreign tourists from his latest bar, in Hamburg. A German magazine reported an alleged sighting of Alois in 1968, but family members say he died twelve years earlier in 1956.

Alois's son, Heinz, from his second, bigamous marriage

fought on the Russian front in the Second World War and was captured by Soviet soldiers. He died in captivity.

Paula, Adolf's full sister, died in 1960, aged sixty-four. According to her memoir, Brigid had stayed with her in Vienna for several days in the 1930s and William Patrick stayed in close contact with the spinster when he was in Germany. With Alois, she was the chief source of family stories passed on to William Patrick and his mother. A devout Catholic, she resented her brother's attacks on the church and maintained her independence, insisting on remaining in Austria in spite of Hitler's repeated demands for her to live at his alpine retreat at Berchtesgaden.

Paula was interrogated on 12 July 1945 by an army intelligence agent from the 101st Airborne Division and released. Her classified statement does not mention Brigid or William Patrick, but it nevertheless makes fascinating reading and gives a real sense of Hitler's treatment of even his closest relations:

I was born at the estate of my father in Hartfeld, Austria, in 1896. My father was 60 years old at the time of my birth. He died when I was 16. 1 know nothing about my father's family.

My brother and I spent little of our time together, as he was seven years older. He attended the Realschule in Styria and spent only his vacations at home. The death of my mother left a deep impression on Adolf and myself. We were both very much attached to her. Our mother died in 1907 and Adolf never returned home after that.

Since I was much younger than my brother, he never considered me a playmate. He played a leading role among his early companions. His favourite game was cops and robbers, and that sort of thing. He had a lot of companions. I could not say what took place in their games, as I was never present.

Adolf as a child always got home too late. He got a spanking every night for not coming home on time.

After my brother finished school he went to Vienna. He wanted to go to the Academy and become a painter, but nothing came of it. My mother was very sick at the time. She was very attached to Adolf and wanted him to stay home. That's why he stayed. He left the house after her death in 1907. 1 never saw him from 1908 until 1921. 1 have no idea what he did at this time. I did not know if he was even alive. He first visited me in 1921. 1 told him that it would have been much easier for me if I had had a brother. He said, 'I had nothing myself. How could I have helped you? I did not let you know about myself because 1 couldn't have helped you.' Since my father was an official we received a pension of 50 kronen. This should have been divided between Adolf and myself. I could have done nothing with 25 kronen. My guardian knew that Adolf supported himself in Vienna as a labourer. Adolf was interviewed and he renounced his half in my favour. Since I attended the Higher Girls' School the money came in handy. I wrote him a letter in 1910 or 1911, but he never answered.

I never had any particular artistic interests. I could draw rather well and learned easily. My brother was very good in some subjects, and very weak in others. He was the weakest in mathematics and, as far as I can remember, in physics, also. His failures in mathematics worried my mother. He loved music. He preferred Wagner even then. Wagner was always his favourite.

My brother came to Vienna in 1921 for the express purpose of seeing me. I did not recognise him at first when he walked into the house. I was so surprised that I could only stare at him. It was as if a brother had fallen from heaven. I was already used to being alone in this world. He was very charming at the time. What made the biggest impression on me was the fact that he went shopping with me. Every woman loves to shop.

I did not see him regularly. About a year later he visited me again. We went to our parents' grave near Linz. He wanted to go there. Then we separated, he going on to Munich, and I to Linz. I visited him in Munich in 1923. This was before November 9th. He still looked the same to me. His political activities had not changed him. The next time I saw him was in the Dirsch Strasse in Munich. The only person that I met among his political friends was Schwarz, treasurer of the Party. The next time I saw him was on the Nuremberg Party Day. This was the first time that he invited me to a Party Day. I received my tickets like any other person.

(At this point the interrogator said, 'We found some of your brother's letters to you. They are very short. A lady who worked with him once said he had absolutely no family sense.') There is something to that. I think he inherited that from our father. He did not care for our relatives either. Only the relatives on our mother's side were close to us. The Schmieds and the Koppensteins are our dear relatives, especially a cousin Schmied who married a Koppenstein. I knew no-one of my father's family. My sister Angela and I often said, 'Father must have some relatives, but we don't even know them.' I myself have a family sense. I like my relatives from the Waldviertel, the Schmieds and the Koppensteins. I usually wrote my brother a birthday letter, and then he wrote a short note, and sent a package. This would contain Spanish ham, flour, sugar, or something like that that had been given to him for his birthday.

I did not see my half-sister Mrs Angela Hamitzsch very often. She lived in Dresden. She had her husband and children and was happily married. I spent the last few days before the arrival of the Americans with her, as she was also in the Berchtesgadener Hof [a Nazi-run hotel in Berchtesgaden].

During the Party Day in Nuremberg my brother received me in his hotel, the Deutscher Hof. He wrote me very rarely, as he was 'writing lazy'. He wrote only a few words, and only once a year.

From 1929 on I saw him once a year until 1941. We met once in Munich, once in Berlin, and once in Vienna. I met him in Vienna after 1938. His rapid rise in the world worried me. I must honestly confess I would have preferred it if he had followed his original ambition and become an architect. (The interrogator interrupted to say that this was the most classical statement that she would ever say.) It would have saved the world a lot of worries.

My brother did not live on a special diet in his youth. Our mother would never have permitted that. He never cared much about meat. I suppose that he later became a vegetarian because of a stomach complaint.

The first time that my brother suggested my changing my name was at the Olympic Games in Garmisch. He wanted me to live under the name of Wolff, and maintain the strictest incognito. That was sufficient for me. From then on I kept this name. I added the Mrs as I thought that less conspicuous. I was ordered to remain incognito also when I was moved from my home in Austria to the Berchtesgadener Hof.

I lost my job in a Viennese insurance company in 1930 when it became known who my brother was. From that time until the Anschluss he gave me a monthly pension of 500 marks a month. In 1940 I went to Berlin to see my brother. I was never under the observation of the Sicherheitsdienst. I could always move about freely. The criminal police once came to check on all the guests when I lived in a hotel in Munich during Mussolini's visit. Even they did not know who 'Frau Wolff' was.

I am a Catholic, and the church is my biggest outside interest. My brother was also Catholic, and I don't believe he ever left the church. I don't know for sure.

For the last few years I was employed as a typist in a hospital. My brother knew about it. He fully agreed that I should employ myself. I had to give it up later as it was too much for my health.

My coming to Berchtesgaden was very strange. I was

in my house in Lower Austria between Vienna and Linz. I wanted to remain at home. It is very important that someone keeps their vegetable garden in order, and see that everything thrives.

One morning in the middle of April of this year a passenger car stood before the door. A driver entered the house and told me he had the task of bringing me to the Obersalzberg. We were supposed to leave in two hours. I was amazed, since I had made no preparations. I said that under no circumstances could I leave in two hours. Then he agreed to drive away the next morning. I don't know who the driver was. I think the car was a Mercedes. There was also a second driver in the car.

(The interrogator, who believes that the trip was arranged by Martin Bormann and that Miss Hitler was in grave danger of being killed, then asked, 'That was done by Martin Bormann?')

I don't know about that. I knew Bormann only slightly. When we were half way to Berchtesgaden the one driver said to me that they hadn't reckoned on me coming along. I said, 'Why didn't you tell me that before? Then I wouldn't have come along.' The driver was not armed and I've forgotten how he looked.

I saw Eva Braun only once. That was in 1934 in Nuremberg. My brother never discussed the subject with me. I have never visited my brother's place on the Obersalzberg, either with him or now that the Americans are here. I was never invited. When I arrived at the Dietrich Eckert Hatte, where Farbe of the Berchtesgadener Hof put me, no-one knew who I was. I took my meals in my room, and didn't talk to the people. I knew no-one there. At present we are learning English. I still have to go over my vocabulary for today. I studied English at school but have unfortunately forgotten most of it.

The personal fate of my brother affected me very much. He was still my brother, no matter what happened. His end brought unspeakable sorrow to me, as his sister. (At this point Miss Hitler burst into tears, and the interrogation was ended.)

Hitler's older half-sister, Angela, who shared the same mother as Alois Jr, was the closest to him and worked for years as his housekeeper, died in 1949.

It was Angela's tragic daughter, Angelica, who featured in another sinister mystery in Hitler's past that was never solved. Once again, William Patrick played a pivotal role.

On his lecture tours around the United States in the early years of the war, William Patrick's revelations about Hitler's alleged murder of his niece and mistress Geli Raubal were a central theme of his talks. Geli had been found dead on 14 September 1931, aged twenty-three, at the Munich flat she shared with Hitler, with his revolver on the floor and an unfinished letter on the table. The death was said to have had a shattering effect on Hitler. But William Patrick suggested his uncle played a much more sinister role in Geli's death than had been previously believed.

After one speech in Canada in 1939, the *Toronto Globe and Mail* reported:

Most dastardly crime charged to the German Chancellor, said his nephew, was the murder of Angelica Raubal, niece of the Fuehrer and first cousin of William Patrick.

'This young girl was a great favourite of Hitler. He had a most unnatural affection for her. She was found dead, shot through the heart in his house. Hitler's army revolver was found in the room. After she was discovered dead, Hitler ran sobbing out of his house and almost collapsed into the arms of Goering, who arranged all the burial details for the girl. They have a way of arranging these affairs in Nazi Germany.'

It was Geli whom William Patrick met on one of his first trips to see his father in Germany. Brigid Hitler's memoir offers a version of Geli's death that she claimed was told to her son by Alois's second wife, Hedwig.

The woman William Patrick knew as 'Maimee' said Hitler became infuriated when Geli told him she was pregnant by her Jewish music teacher, and tried to attack her with a riding whip before being stopped by his sister, Angela. Later that night, Hitler and Geli were supposedly heard in a shouting match in her room at his Prinzregentenstrasse apartment.

Angela left for Hitler's mountain retreat but Geli remained, and the housekeeper returned to the apartment the following morning to find the place in uproar and called Angela, telling her to rush back because of an emergency involving her daughter. Brigid's memoir continued:

As soon as Angela realised what had happened, she rushed towards Geli's room, but was not allowed to enter. Beating on the door with her fists, she demanded to see her daughter, but was kept outside, although Geli lived for some hours more.

Only Adolf and Dr Brandt remained with the dying girl. Suddenly the door opened. Adolf stood in the doorway, eyes bloodshot, face waxy pale, hair hanging in a matted tangle.

Seeing his sister, he abruptly retreated towards Hermann Goering, who stood a short distance away, and collapsing against the latter's shoulders began to weep hysterically, saying, 'She's dead, she's dead.'

Angela, who had automatically started towards her daughter's room, when she saw Adolf come out stood before him as though powerless to take another step. 'She's dead,' Adolf cried, 'and I am her murderer.'

At these words Goering intervened. 'You're upset, Adolf. You mustn't say a thing like that. Frau Raubal might misunderstand. Tell her the truth, that Geli committed suicide.'

He turned to Angela: 'My Fuehrer was not even here.'

Goering's emphasis on the fact that Adolf was not present when Geli was shot became the keynote of Adolf's alibi. He wasn't there when it happened. According to the account Angela publicly gave of the fatal evening, Adolf left for Munich and then Geli committed suicide.

'I don't know what happened that night,' Pat said to me in a troubled voice, 'and I didn't have time to find out, but from what Maimee told me I don't see how it could have been a suicide.'

Later in the manuscript, Brigid reports a conversation she had with her sister-in-law, Paula Hitler, who supposedly claimed outright that her brother killed Geli. Paula told Brigid the pregnancy story was invented by the Nazi hierarchy as an explanation for Geli's suicide. Paula is quoted in the memoir as saying: 'He was in love with her, his own niece. When I learned about it I begged Angela to send Geli to me in Vienna. According to Angela the gun went off by accident while the two of them were struggling. It was in Adolf's hand.'

Of the pregnancy story, Brigid's memoir claimed Paula said: 'Not a word of truth in it. That fiction was circulated by Goering to establish a possible motive for suicide. Angela had always protected Adolf and found excuses for him. And it's difficult to find excuses for a man who brandishes a revolver during a discussion with a member of his own family, in his own home. Ach! What a fool she is, Angela. Adolf twists her right round his little finger, the way he did my mother. No matter what he does, she stands up for him and turns everything to make it look right. It was a scandal that he should be running around with Geli, but Angela let it go on. Then when he killed her, she passed it off as suicide.'

Questioning the accuracy of Brigid's memoir, some historians argue that Angela was not present at Hitler's apartment the night before Geli's death and say Brigid names Hitler's housekeeper as Josephine Bauer, when, in fact, he had two housekeepers at the time named Maria Reichert and Anna Winter.

But independent confirmation was offered by Hanfstaengl, the Harvard graduate who was a close pre-war confidant of Hitler and one-time foreign press chief for the Nazi Party. In his book, *Hitler – The Missing Years*, Hanfstaengl wrote that while living in exile in London in the autumn of 1937 he 'was visited by Mrs Brigid Hitler. She maintains that the immediate family knew well that the cause of Geli's suicide was the fact that she was pregnant by a young Jewish art teacher in Linz, whom she had met in 1928 and wanted to marry at the time of her death.'

Hanfstaengl viewed the Geli scandal as a major stepping stone in Hitler's gradual transformation into a cold-blooded monster. 'I am sure that the death of Geli Raubal marked a turning point in the development of Hitler's character. This relationship, whatever form it took in their intimacy, had provided him for the first time in his life with a release to his nervous energy which, only too soon, was to find its final expression in ruthlessness and savagery. His long connection with Eva Braun never produced the mooncalf interludes he had enjoyed with Geli and which might in due course, perhaps, have made a normal man out of him. With her death the way was clear for his final development into a demon, with his sex life deteriorating again into a sort of bisexual Narcissus-like vanity, with Eva Braun little more than a vague domestic adjunct.'

There is no mention anywhere that Hanfstaengl was involved with William Patrick when he was working for the OSS, but it is quite possible he could have had some hand in the Brigid memoir mystery.

I have no firm evidence for my theory, but it strikes me as possible that William Patrick could have worked with the FBI and perhaps even Hanfstaengl in preparing the memoir, but then the project was shelved because the propaganda war was essentially over by that late stage in the conflict.

There is no doubt that William Patrick provided a wealth of information to a supposed writing collaborator who may possibly have been linked to the FBI. The FBI would certainly have had access to that information.

A memo to J. Edgar Hoover, dated 2 July 1942, underlined Hanfstaengl's wartime role in the US. It read: 'The Board of Psychological Warfare, a joint committee of the State, War and Navy Departments, has recently effected the release from internment in Canada of an individual who is known in this country as Ernest Sedgwick, who was formerly a high ranking and influential member of the Nazi regime. It should be stated at this point that . . . this individual is undoubtedly Putzi Hanfstaengl, former Nazi Party official, who has been interned in Canada.'

Hanfstaengl, the memo continued, 'will be used on varied assignments such as analysing propaganda, preparing biographies of Nazi leaders and "such other assignments as the Board of Psychological Warfare may think up for him".' A second FBI memo explains: 'When Hanfstaengl arrives in the United States he will be used primarily by Colonel Donovan's organisation and to this end Irvin is being placed on Donovan's payroll to handle Hanfstaengl and to work with him. Hanfstaengl will apparently be used primarily in matters relating to propaganda material to be distributed through Colonel Donovan's organisation in Germany.'

As more details emerged in the aftermath of the war, historians sought out William Patrick to see if he could add any more substance to his second-hand story. He could not be found.

CHAPTER TWELVE

MEETING THE FAMILY

15 SEPTEMBER 1998. LONG ISLAND, NEW YORK

The faint lilt of German folk music floated through the open window of the dark-wood alpine bungalow shrouded in trees and shrubs as I walked down the short path to the front door. The property straddled two small roads on a forested private estate nestling into one of the bays tucked behind slithers of land protecting the New York coastline from the full impact of the Atlantic Ocean. Neither close enough to New York City to be overrun by urban sprawl nor fashionable enough to compete with the wealthy weekend getaways in the Hamptons, it was a community where neighbours still talked to one another, where the Stars and Stripes hung from many homes, and where at that time life went on untouched by dramas beyond American shores. This was the town William Patrick Hitler had chosen to escape his past.

I had driven past the bungalow twice already, once to check the address and then to compose myself before knocking on the door and asking the elderly woman inside the question she must have been dreading for nearly fifty years: 'Is your real name Mrs Hitler?'

Many people think journalists are inured to feelings of anxiety about approaching strangers for details of their private lives. But it is not easy to turn up unannounced on the doorstep of a stranger and ask them the most personal of questions, sometimes about the loss of a loved one or about an incident that could cause them embarrassment and perhaps even harm. Some, understandably, will be upset by the intrusion and turn you away. Others gladly invite you in, appreciating the chance to talk. There was no way of telling how this woman I had travelled so far to meet would react to the knowledge that the fictitious barrier she had hidden behind all these years was about to be destroyed. I was hoping her overriding reaction would be one of great relief, but I suspected her emotions would be far more complicated and, possibly, hostile. The response I feared most was a blank denial, which would place me in the invidious position of having to prove not only that she was, indeed, Mrs Hitler, but also that she was intentionally misleading me.

There was no doorbell and I knocked with my knuckles on the frame hoping that anyone inside would be able to hear. I rapped again, harder this time, filled with a nervous sense of the knowledge that I had spent countless hours making inquiries and flown across the USA to get to this point and possible rejection.

My premise was simple. History had treated William Patrick and his mother badly. They had been written off as sleazy opportunists and blackmailers, largely on the word of Hitler himself and his murderous functionary Hans Frank. Here was a chance to finally state William Patrick and Brigid's version of events and to correct the biased impressions that had damned their memories so unfairly.

I knew William Patrick would not be answering the door. I had just been to visit his grave, a twenty-minute drive away, at the closest Roman Catholic cemetery. Now I was standing outside his old home, hoping to speak to his widow.

The story of Hitler's lost nephew had been stalled for so long but once one fact dropped into place, everything else quickly followed. Armed with Brigid's hometown and the date of her death from the social security deaths database, I had called the local library for the town in New York from my office in Newport Beach. A helpful librarian offered to search through the archives of the local newspaper kept on microfiche in the reference section to see if it carried an obituary for Brigid in the days after she passed away.

He called me back an hour or so later to say he had found the obituary and would be happy to read it slowly over the phone if I wanted to take it down. He said Brigid was seventy-eight when she died. She was born in Ireland and had lived in the Long Island town for eighteen years. The funeral home, the Catholic church and the cemetery were all named. But one short sentence made my heart stop. It read: 'She is survived by a son, Patrick.'

My wife had thought there was an earthquake when she heard the crashing coming from my upstairs office. She ran upstairs to be greeted with my excited yelps: 'Yes, yes, yes!'

'What on earth's happened?' she asked as I continued banging my fist on the desk.

'I think I've cracked it,' I said. 'I think I know what happened to the Hitlers. Well, I know where they went, at least.'

I telephoned the cemetery to check Brigid was interred there and was given the location of her grave – section 10, range BB, plot 215. Then the cemetery clerical assistant said something else that took me aback. 'There is a second name listed for that plot. Do you want that, too?'

'Yes, please,' I said.

'The other name is Patrick, and it looks like he was her son. He died on July 14, 1987 and was buried on July 17. He was seventy-six when he died in hospital.'

'Do you have a next of kin?'

'Yes, the widow's name is Phyllis.' She gave me Phyllis's address and asked: 'Are you a member of the family?'

'No, I'm not, but I'm trying to contact them.'

'Okay, well good luck. That's all the information I have here. You'd be best to try the widow for any further information.'

'I will, thanks,' I said.

Mathematics was never my strong point, and I scribbled the figures down on a scrap of paper. The year 1987 minus 76 years = 1911. It was the year of William Patrick's birth. It had to be him.

I did not have a telephone number for the widow, but if I had one I would still have gone and knocked on the door without an appointment. The simple truth is that you learn early as a journalist that it is harder for people to say no in person. A phone call can be brushed off quickly and the journalist's personality does not always get the chance to make any impact. It is much easier to put down the phone than to close a door in someone's face. Besides, with a story as sensitive as this, I reasoned that a phone call coming out of the blue from a total stranger would only worry the woman, who was bound to be elderly, even more than a personal inquiry. At least she would be able to see me.

Later that morning I called Tim in North London, where he now lived, to tell him the news.

'You old dog,' he said. 'You managed to find him at last. Excellent! You certainly get top marks for persistence. I didn't know you were still working on it.'

'I never stopped really. I just kept going back to it when I had a spare moment.'

'Are you going to go over and knock on the door?'

'Yeah, that's the plan. It's why I called, actually. Can you get across to New York in the next few days? I figure we started this together, so it's only right we should work on it together now.'

'I would love to, I really would. But you know that TV series I wrote about women killers? It's been picked up by ITV and I'm working on it as executive producer. They're putting quite a bit of money into it and I can't exactly just clear off right now. Damn, a couple of weeks ago it would have been perfect. It'd be great to get back to New York and see everybody.'

'Don't worry. I'll let you know how it works out.'

'When did you get the name?'

'Earlier today.'

'When are you heading over?'

'I'll probably go tomorrow morning if I can get a flight. I just hope the family talks to me.'

'Even if they don't, it's still a great story. People have been trying to find out what happened to this guy since the war. It'll make a great read. Are you going to use a photographer?'

'No, I think I'll go by myself if you can't make it. The less people who know the real name the better.'

'Okay, well good luck. Let me know how it goes.'

Arriving at Newark Airport in New Jersey the following afternoon, I hired a car and drove across Manhattan and through the Midtown Tunnel to get on the busy Long Island Expressway to take me through Brooklyn and Queens and out to rural Long Island, where I found a small hotel. I decided to find the cemetery where William Patrick and Brigid were buried first thing the next morning. Everything pointed to the fact that this was their last resting place, but I needed to see the headstone myself to feel certain. Only then did I want to turn up at William Patrick's widow's door and request an interview.

It was raining when I drove through New York, and I had a very real sense of being caught up in history. I had felt this before on some of the more meaningful stories I had worked on around the world. Most of the time as a journalist you are reporting on events that have happened; they may have happened years, weeks or just moments before but they are usually in the past tense. You know what you are looking for, be it a central figure, a key witness, or some vital evidence to back up and confirm what you may already know or suspect. Just occasionally you find yourself in the middle of a story rather than on the outside looking in. Your actions are changing history, even in the smallest ways, and your choices can affect people's lives. It can be disconcerting when you nevertheless must continue to look on the unfolding story as an observer.

Having searched in vain for a half-decent hotel, I contented myself with a motor inn that was convenient, if a little basic,

situated in between the cemetery and the address I was given for
Phyllis Hitler. In the telephone book in my room, I found one other
listing with the same surname as Phyllis but with the first initial A.
A computer check using my laptop provided an address to go
with that name, together with details of a landscaping business
filed as an incorporated business and linked to Phyllis's address.

I was waiting at the wrought-iron gate of the Catholic
cemetery in a neighbouring town when it opened at 10 a.m. the
next morning to see for myself the headstone that would prove I
was on the right track. A downpour from earlier that morning had
blown itself out, but as I walked through the graves crisscrossing
the meticulously tended lawn the heaviness in the air promised
another storm. I came to the plot number I had scrawled in my
notebook. If I needed any confirmation, this was it. Underneath
Brigid's name and the dates of her birth and death was the name
'William Patrick' and with it was his date of birth – 12 March
1911 – the same date on the birth certificate from London I had
in my pocket, and the date of his death in 1987. Needless to say,
the name 'Hitler' was nowhere to be found.

Driving back towards the hotel I decided there was little point
in delaying; I should go and see Phyllis Hitler as soon as possible
and see if she was prepared to talk to me about her husband.
While disappointed that he was dead, I remembered reading in
John Toland's Hitler biography that William Patrick had a son
called Adolf. Could this be the telephone listing with the initial
A that I had noticed the night before? There were so many
questions from my years of research.

I knocked again and this time I heard the music stop and
someone shuffle towards the door.

'Hello, can I help you?' The voice came from behind the closed door, with a distinct German accent.

'I'm sorry to call on you out of the blue like this,' I answered, 'but there's something I would like to talk to you about concerning your husband, William Patrick. I'm from England,' I added, thinking, for some odd reason, that might make a difference.

The door half-opened, but the tall, elegantly dressed woman remained behind the screen door. 'He passed away some time ago,' she said, still composed. Even through the grey mesh I could tell the reason for my visit was already dawning on her. She must have envisioned this very conversation countless times over the years.

'But he was your husband, was he not?' I asked, needing to be sure.

'Yes, but why? What do you want?' she asked.

I took a deep breath and explained: 'My name is David Gardner, and I'm a British journalist. I'm sure you know that a great many people have spent years trying to find your husband because of his relationship to Adolf Hitler . . .' I paused, half-expecting her to ask me what the hell I was talking about, but she said nothing, politely waiting for me to finish.

'I know that both your husband and his mother have passed on, but I would very much like to talk to you about them.'

'I'm sorry you have wasted your journey,' she said. 'But please leave it alone, will you? Let sleeping dogs lie.'

'The last thing I want to cause is any upset, but this is a matter of history. So much has been written about your husband and he never had the chance to put his side. Could you possibly help me set the record straight?' I persevered.

But she was adamant: 'Perhaps we will talk about it when my boys are older. We were married for a long time and my husband never wanted anyone to know who he was. Now my sons don't want anything to do with it. It was all too long ago. There has been enough trouble with this name.'

'I understand your worries, honestly I do. But I would be happy to keep your adopted name a secret and not mention where you are living. That way no one would be able to find you,' I said.

'There are always people out there,' she said, seemingly close to tears. 'We had to move once before when someone found out who we are. We don't want to keep moving and moving. It is so upsetting. I will have to talk to my boys.'

'My story will be published in England, so it's unlikely anyone will ever be able to trace you to here,' I added, hoping to reassure her.

'I have family in England,' she answered, quickly. 'A lot of my family is from England, and he was English, you know. He grew up in England and I am from overseas.'

'I heard your accent,' I said. 'Are you from Germany?'

She just smiled and said again that she was sorry I had made a wasted journey.

Desperate to keep her talking, I asked: 'There were a couple of things I'd really like to know. For instance, how did you come across your assumed name? What made you choose that name?'

'Oh, I don't know where the name came from. It was all a long time ago. It doesn't matter now. It's in the past.'

'The other thing that has intrigued me is that there is a memoir written by William Patrick's mother in the New York

Public Library. Is there anything that you can tell me about that? Do you know whether William Patrick or Brigid wrote it?

'That book. Oh, it was all made up.'

'Could you tell me anything about how it came about or who wrote it?'

'I'm sorry, but I don't want to say anything. This makes me very nervous. Just forget it, will you? Forget all about it.'

'I honestly don't know if I can do that,' I said. 'Could I leave you my name and phone number and perhaps you could talk with your family about how they feel about talking to me? I would treat any interview with complete confidentiality, I assure you. I'll just have to get my card from the car.'

'Okay,' she said. 'You can leave your number in the mailbox. But I can tell you now, we will not be speaking about this.'

The door closed and I walked slowly back to my car, unsure whether to be pleased that my story had, at least, been confirmed, or dejected because so many more questions remained.

As I sat in the passenger seat with the door open, searching in my bag for some note paper and an envelope to write a letter explaining my intentions and giving my home and hotel phone numbers, Phyllis came out of the house and beckoned me over.

'I just want to ask you one question,' she said. 'How did you find us?'

Glad of the chance to resume our conversation, I recounted in detail how I had traced her mother-in-law via her death record and the obituary in the local newspaper. I also showed her a property record I bought through an internet service, KnowX, offering tax details about her home.

'I'm afraid there's a lot more information out there about people than there used to be. I went to visit the grave before I came to see you,' I added.

'I'm sorry I can't help you,' she said. 'Did you fly all the way from England for this?'

'I'm actually based in California. I came from there,' I said. 'I really don't want to cause you any problems.'

'I know,' she said, 'but we will have to move now. There's nothing else for it.'

'But I won't tell anyone your name or address.'

'I know, I know, but we don't have a choice. Look, have a good trip back to California. I don't think you will be hearing from us again.'

'Well, thank you anyway. I'm sorry to have troubled you,' I said, watching her walk back into the cabin-style house. There did not appear to be anyone else at home, but I noticed a gardening truck in the driveway, with rakes and lawnmowers piled in the back. On the side was the adopted family name with a phone number offering landscaping services.

It was only when I drove away from the house that I realised the implication of what Phyllis had told me: that the Hitler line did not die out with William Patrick Hitler in 1987. It lived on through his sons.

Although she called them her 'boys' it was clear the new generation of Hitlers were almost certainly grown up and could have been raising families of their own. It was incredible to think that the dreaded Adolf Hitler's great-nephews grew up as all-American kids in this rural safe haven protected from the terrible consequences of their birthright. It hardly seemed possible that William Patrick and Phyllis would risk that anonymity by naming their first-born son Adolf.

I decided my best bet to find out more about the sons was, once again, the local public library, where I asked to see a pile of copies of old high-school yearbooks. Combing through countless yearbooks for the adopted surname, I finally came across a photograph of Alexander, the eldest son of William Patrick, as a clean-cut eighteen-year-old from the Long Island high school's Class of 1967.

Two years later, his brother Louis graduated in the Class of 1969 and there was a Howard with the same surname in the 1975 yearbook. The beaming face of William Patrick's youngest son, Brian, did not appear until the 1983 yearbook.

While many of their fellow students belonged to a plethora of clubs and societies, the sons apparently kept a lower profile, with their names appearing under their stock class pictures. Once again, I could not help noticing that the eldest son, Alex, had a middle name beginning with A.

I walked across town to the office of births, deaths and marriages to look at birth certificates for the sons, only to be told that in New York State, unlike in Britain or many other US states, birth records were only available to immediate family.

Working on another hunch to put a name to that suspicious middle initial, I drove to the local city hall to inquire at the voters' registration department. There was no record for Howard, although I learned that the other sons were registered Republicans, for what that was worth, and their names were listed with middle initials. Brian's middle initial was W, so there was a good chance it was William; Louis was followed by initial P, probably for Patrick.

Could the A after Alex possibly stand for his grandfather, Alois? Or was it, as historian John Toland suggested, an A for Adolf?

Evening was drawing in as I drove back to my hotel, certain now I had a story, but unsure exactly how to proceed. I knew that the spectre of the *Hitler Diaries* would be foremost in the mind of any magazine or newspaper editor considering publishing such an unlikely revelation.

The *Hitler Diaries* saga started out as one of the greatest scoops of the post-war years: the apparent discovery of sixty bulky leather-bound volumes written in Adolf Hitler's own hand. In April 1983, West Germany's largest weekly news magazine, *Stern*, trumpeted its publication of excerpts from the diaries having paid an obscure military relics collector from Stuttgart, Konrad Kujau, up to £1 million for the rights. But within weeks, the diaries were being hailed in a very different light – as the fraud of the century.

It turned out that Kujau's painstaking forgery was so skilfully penned that he managed to fool both the *Stern* magazine hierarchy and Hugh Trevor-Roper, the eminent Cambridge historian and Hitler expert, whose declaration of authenticity prompted the *Sunday Times* and *Paris Match* to buy reprint rights from *Stern*. Then the bubble burst when German government officials who tested the diaries' paper, ink and bindings revealed them to be 'grotesque, superficial' fakes.

Both Kujau and Gerd Heidemann, the top *Stern* reporter who brought the story to the magazine, ended up in jail and all the publications involved faced scathing public condemnation of their methods. For good reason, editors were likely to be extremely sceptical of another major Hitler scoop.

I had the bones of the story together with a confirmation from William Patrick's widow, but while I knew an extraordinary amount about his life before the Second World War, I still had very few details about William Patrick's second life, his anonymous years in America.

With the story finally beginning to come together, I also had to wrestle with an ethical dilemma. How did my professional desire to publish a story I had been working on so long and so diligently fit in with the ardent requests for privacy from a family that had tried so hard to distance itself from the past? I decided there and then that I would not reveal the new name adopted by the Hitlers. Nor would I give any clues to the town where they lived. It was a commitment I carried through to the writing of this book and to the publication of this updated version. In the intervening years, historians and journalists researching the story used the clues in my book to deduce both the family's assumed name and the town where they lived, and they can now be found with a simple Google search, but I shall not include them here.

On the way back to the hotel, I was passing close to the street address given in Brigid's newspaper obituary as her last residence and decided as a long shot to knock on the doors of some of the neighbours in the hope that someone might remember her.

Like many residential streets in the area, it branched off an ugly main highway littered with fast food restaurants, car showrooms and gravel yards filled with heavy machinery. Then it became a pleasant side street of detached houses with mowed lawns and pretty gardens. The white clapboard cottage I was looking for was about halfway down and seriously in need of painting. I knocked on the door of Brigid's old house and those of several neighbours asking if anyone remembered an old Irish woman named Brigid who died in 1969. I did not need to explain why I was looking for her because nobody remembered her.

It had been a long day and I was about to give up when I decided to knock on one more door. It was a habit I had never shaken off from my time at the *Daily Mail*, which proudly maintained a demanding reputation of always asking its reporters to make one more check, knock on one more door or stay one more hour on the scene of a story than any of its competitors.

The couple living in the house had just arrived home from work in Manhattan when I called and asked if they remembered Brigid living in the street. They said, yes, she lived at number 67 and her son lived next door with his family.

'Do you remember the name of the son?' I asked.

'It was Pat,' said the woman, who was aged in her early thirties. 'I used to play with his son, Brian. They lived next door to my parents.'

She stopped and looked at her husband, who asked: 'Can we ask why you want to know all this?'

I told them I was a British journalist making inquiries about Brigid and tried at first to dance around the reason for my interest. But as it became increasingly evident that the woman, at least, knew the family well, I decided to tell them the truth.

'That is so amazing,' said the woman. 'I didn't have a clue, but, you know, it does make sense to me. I would never have thought in my wildest dreams that they were related to Hitler, but it does fit with some of the things they used to do that seemed a little strange at the time.'

They invited me into their kitchen, made me a drink and christened me Austin Powers – not, I hope, because I had bad teeth, but because I was a Brit snooping around like a spy. They agreed to talk to me on the condition I would not use their names.

It seemed that while in the navy, William Patrick had worked in the medical corps and developed an interest in medicine. He later trained as a phlebotomist, or blood technician, and set up a laboratory in a room attached to his house. Initially, he was sent blood samples from hospitals for microscope analysis and, according to the neighbours, later put up a 'Medical Lab' sign outside the large, four-bedroomed house. Patients, mainly elderly, would visit to have their blood work done.

Patrick and Phyllis had moved from the street around 1978, nine years after Brigid's death, but two of the sons ran a landscaping business and regularly mowed lawns and tended gardens in the area, said the former neighbour, who said she lost touch with the youngest son, Brian, after he moved away. There had also been a fourth son, Howard, she added, but he died in a car crash.

She mentioned that the family never made any secret of its fascination with Germany. They drove a VW Beetle, played German music in the house and the parents would often slip into speaking German, particularly when they did not want friends to understand what they were saying.

'They would talk about the war all the time,' said the neighbour. 'They used to tell me that Hitler was a great man. Brian's mother would say that Hitler was a great man, but he went wrong along the way. He had some problems that made him go the wrong way.

'We'd be playing, and I might kind of say that Hitler was really evil. Brian would say that Hitler wasn't so bad. It was a very strange thing for an eleven-year-old to come up with unless he had someone saying it in the house.'

She added: 'Brian had a toy ship called the *Bismarck*. I would have some American ship I'd call the *Enterprise* because I was into *Star Trek*. But he would always try and win for Germany. Brian had all sorts of war toys. They had these great English toy soldiers with bright-red jackets, and they had toy guns. The boys were very rough with each other and would drag one another down the street.

'They visited England. They did a big trip to Europe, and we got a postcard from England. They brought me back a little black, yellow and white German flag. They had a little German kid stay with them once. I remember he couldn't speak any English.

'Pat was a very kind man. He was tall and slightly balding, and he was always laughing and cracking jokes. I knew Pat was in the war. He used to talk about having shrapnel in his leg.

'Phyllis was said to be intensely proud of her German roots, even though she wasn't able to return to her native country until decades after the war. For years, she would subscribe to German fashion magazines. She was heavy duty German,' said the neighbour.

'She was always a little bit mysterious. If she didn't want us to hear something she would start talking in German. Pat could obviously speak it too because he knew what she was saying.

'I think Phyllis had lived on a farm in Germany. She was very beautiful, a handsome woman. She was always dressed very stylishly. She reminded me of Ingrid Bergman.'

She added: 'Blood patients would go right to the house. Phyllis would answer the phone and give patients tea while they waited. My dad said that Pat worked at one time for the state hospital before setting up at home. We had to be quiet and go out to play when people were in the waiting room.

'The sons are really close to their mother. She was always very domineering. Everyone said that was why the boys never married.

'Alex left home first. My father and I used to joke that Alex was in the CIA because no one would ever say what his job was. You would ask him, and they'd go all strange. Alex had dark hair and a moustache.

'Louis worked in Macy's department store before he started the landscaping business with Brian. Brian was very sweet and innocent. He was the baby of the family. I think his mother wanted him to do more with his life. She wanted him to be an accountant or something. But he was happy just being close to his family.

'They had a beach house, which I think Pat's mother owned. I remember going out there. There were bunks and it was right by the water. Pat was very upset when his mother died. Brian said it was the first time he had seen his dad cry. I remember his mother as being very sweet and nice.'

Although Brigid and Phyllis were not said to be particularly close, the Irish grandmother lived next door in her white-painted cottage until her death, aged seventy-eight.

When her husband died eighteen years later, it was Phyllis who was left alone to shoulder the burden of the Hitler legacy that came complete with her marriage vows all those years ago.

CHAPTER THIRTEEN

BLOOD MONEY

30 APRIL 1945. FÜHRERBUNKER, BERLIN

The woman with the harsh blonde hair, her darks roots spreading from the left-of-centre parting, shrugged off her heavy coat to reveal a blue silk summer dress. The sounds of shellfire and rough Russian voices could be heard from just outside the Führerbunker near the Reich Chancellery in the centre of Berlin and, although the heaters inside were turned on full, Eva Braun couldn't help shivering.

'Take my fur coat as a memory,' she told Gertrud 'Traudl' Junge, one of her husband's secretaries. 'I always like well-dressed women.'

With a flourish, she took her husband's arm, and they went back to their rooms for the last time. 'It is finished,' she said over her shoulder. 'Goodbye.'

Earlier, according to eyewitness accounts from interrogations carried out by MI5 agents after the war, Adolf Hitler had gone from room to room, thanking his staff. He had just learned of Mussolini and his mistress Claretta Petacci's execution at the hands of Italian partisans and was determined that he and Braun should not suffer the same fate. Hitler's SS bodyguards had destroyed all his personal papers and his doctors used poison capsules to kill his Alsatian dog, Blondi, and Braun's spaniel. The Red Army was closing in and his time was up.

On the afternoon of 30 April, Hitler shot himself, while Braun – the loyal mistress he had married in that same bunker just twenty-four hours earlier – took one of the same poison pills that so effectively killed her pet.

The MI5 papers also revealed that Hitler drew up a will shortly before his wedding. Quite apart from the stolen artworks and treasures the Nazis had plundered from across Europe over the previous six years, the Führer was a very rich man in his own right. He had been raking in almost a million pounds a year from sales of his ideological 1925 autobiography, *Mein Kampf* ('My Struggle') in the 1930s, largely because he made it mandatory for every German couple getting wed to be given a free copy that was bought from him by the state. Every soldier fighting at the front also received the anti-Semitic diatribe. It had sold an estimated 12 million copies by the end of the Second World War.

Conveniently, Hitler sidestepped some enormous tax bills after becoming Chancellor by declaring himself exempt and was said to have stashed away a fortune in excess of £100 million. Even now, all these years later, it is unclear what happened to it all.

In the small hours of 29 April, Hitler dictated his will and a final personal testament – yet another tirade against the Jewish people – to Junge, his secretary. The will, translated here into English, read:

As I did not consider that I could take responsibility, during the years of struggle, of contracting a marriage, I have now decided, before the closing of my earthly career, to take as my wife that girl who, after many years of faithful friendship, entered, of her own free will, the practically besieged town in order to share her destiny with me. At her own desire she goes as my wife with me into death. It will compensate us for what we both lost through my work in the service of my people.

What I possess belongs – in so far as it has any value – to the Party. Should this no longer exist, to the State; should the State also be destroyed, no further decision of mine is necessary.

My pictures, in the collections which I have bought in the course of years, have never been collected for private purposes, but only for the extension of a gallery in my home town of Linz on Donau.

It is my most sincere wish that this bequest may be duly executed.

I nominate as my Executor my most faithful Party comrade,

Martin Bormann.

He is given full legal authority to make all decisions. He is permitted to take out everything that has a sentimental value or is necessary for the maintenance of a modest simple life, for my brothers and sisters, also above all for the mother of my wife and my faithful co-workers who are well known to him, principally my old Secretaries Frau Winter etc. who have for many years aided me by their work.

I myself and my wife – in order to escape the disgrace of deposition or capitulation – choose death. It is our wish to be burnt immediately on the spot where I have carried out the greatest part of my daily work in the course of a twelve years' service to my people.

Hitler's first beneficiary, the Nazi Party, didn't last much longer than he did, and the state of Bavaria ended up seizing his property, as his home was registered as his mountaintop retreat in Berchtesgaden. Bavaria also claimed ownership of the copyright to *Mein Kampf*, ensuring the book wasn't republished. However, German law protects a copyright for only seventy years after the author's death and so it effectively became public property after 2016, and several new versions have been published since.

Did he hide away millions in offshore bank accounts? Just as he liked to project the impression that he had no care for his own family, only the 'Fatherland', Hitler also promoted the idea that he wasn't interested in money or material things. He travelled without cash and lived relatively modestly. Yet this was a man who copyrighted his own image, which meant that every stamp sold with his face on it earned him a royalty payment. Just because he didn't spend money didn't mean he didn't covet it.

Dr Cris Whetton, author of the book *Hitler's Fortune*, put the dictator's wealth at his zenith at 1.1 billion Reichsmarks, which would be more than £4 billion today.

'He felt paying taxes was beneath him,' Dr Whetton said in a Channel 5 documentary, *The Hunt For Hitler's Missing Millions*. 'The tax authorities always wanted to know what happened to the collections and admission fees for the meetings he spoke at, and he would say, "I don't know. It doesn't come to me. It goes to the National Socialist Party."

'By the time we get to 1944 he's definitely in the billions of Reichsmarks . . . which wouldn't have been far off billions of euros today. He loved money,' continued Dr Whetton. 'He just wasn't prepared to do much work for it.'

According to the documentary, American intelligence discovered in 1944 that Hitler had a secret bank account for his foreign royalties containing today's equivalent of £250 million. Documents from the US National Archives show that a bank account was opened at the Union Bank of Switzerland in Bern for Hitler by Max Amann, the Nazi media chief and publisher of *Mein Kampf*.

A 1944 intelligence report by the Office of Strategic Services, titled 'Objectionable Activities by Switzerland on Behalf of the Nazis', said that '. . . it is quite possible that Hitler's foreign exchange revenues from his book and foreign exchange revenues of the Nazi Party abroad are held at this Swiss bank in Ammann's [sic] name.'

The discovery was part of an attempt by World Jewish Council researchers to trace money and treasures plundered by the Nazis during the Second World War, reportedly including bullion worth at least $5.5 billion. The Allies put a value on Hitler's confiscated estate at only around £40,000 immediately after the war.

Hitler did make a vague concession to his family by including his 'brothers and sisters' in the 1945 will and some experts have suggested that his surviving descendants should challenge the interpretation of the hastily drawn-up document.

The possibility of a family claim to any inheritance left by Hitler is one that has consistently been raised over the years. Historian Dr Werner Maser represented a group of relatives – Austrian cousins related to Hitler's half-sister Angela, his former housekeeper – who considered a possible bid for royalties from sales of *Mein Kampf.*

Leading that group was Leo Raubal, the son of Hitler's half-sister, Angela, who had been the Führer's favourite nephew and was such a dead ringer for his uncle that he occasionally worked as Hitler's double in Berlin. He was captured by the Russians at the Battle of Stalingrad in 1943 and was eventually released in the mid-1950s and allowed to return to Germany.

The family attempt to challenge the will imploded after Raubal – who died from a heart attack in 1979 – insisted he should keep 50 per cent of any royalties they might recoup, according to Maser.

The only family member who tried was his sister, Paula, then living under the surname of Wolff, whose claim was dismissed by a Munich court that ruled the Hitler will as void because of 'formal legal deficiencies'.

Officials from Bavaria's Finance Ministry told historian Timothy Ryback that all assets of the higher-ranking Nazis were confiscated under a binding order in 1948.

'There is absolutely no legal basis on which the Hitler heirs could lay claim to the royalties,' said a former overseer to the *Mein Kampf* copyright.

Paula, Hitler's only full-blood sibling, died in 1960 and is the one relative to be buried with a headstone bearing the surname she shared with her brother.

The American Hitlers understood there was a chance they could have been the legal heirs to Hitler's estate, but they wanted none of it. William Patrick and Phyllis dismissed any potential claim, calling it 'blood money'.

At one stage, the brothers also considered writing their own book telling their father's extraordinary story, using photographs he had kept from the time that were still stored in the family albums. In the end, they decided that no amount of money was worth the trouble it would bring.

The only other surviving members of the direct family line – although they are not Hitlers – are the descendants of Angela, Adolf's elder half-sister.

Angela had three children through her first marriage to Leo Raubal Sr (1879–1910) – Leo Jr (1906–1977), Geli (1908–1931) and Elfriede (1910–1993). As you have read, Geli supposedly killed herself, but Leo Jr and Elfriede married and had a child each, both boys.

Those boys, Peter Raubal, a retired engineer born in 1931, and Heiner Hochegger, about whom little is known other than that he was born in 1945, are both reportedly living in or near Linz, Austria, although one or both may have passed away. According to reports, neither had any children.

I have no information that they decided not to start families because of any concerns over their DNA. But if the reports from Austria are correct, the fact that the five men with the closest bloodlines to Adolf Hitler do not have heirs does mean that the gene pool will die with them.

There is the story, of course, that Hitler never died in the Berlin bunker and that his suicide was a ruse to cover up his escape to South America, Japan, or even the South Pole. As with every historical event that is shrouded in secrecy, his death has fed countless conspiracy theories. The Soviets gave them a head start with Stalin initially insisting the Allies were told Hitler could have flown out of Germany at the eleventh hour as the Red Army troops closed in. The Cold War was fought through any number of small, pointless victories and keeping the Americans, in particular, ignorant to Hitler's final hours was just such a petty battleground. The Americans would be forced to launch a pointless, time-wasting intelligence operation to find out where Hitler went. So began a factory farm of theories giving birth to books and documentaries following a spurious trail of Hitler and Braun to Paraguay or Argentina. It would be all the less likely if it wasn't true that the monstrous Josef Mengele successfully eluded capture by fleeing to first Argentina and then Paraguay and Brazil before suffering a stroke while swimming off the coast. If one of the most wanted Nazis – the Auschwitz 'Angel of Death' – could escape, the argument went, why not Hitler?

While the Russians finally confirmed Hitler's death in the bunker, they continued to bedevil attempts at independent corroboration of the facts, first reburying the bodies and then destroying them and refusing to release the witnesses to Hitler's final hours for a decade.

Other than the witness statements, the only solid proof lies in part of a skull and a jawbone said to be all that was left of Hitler's body. In 2009, Nicholas F. Bellantoni, an archaeologist at the University of Connecticut, claimed the skull fragment with a bullet hole was from a forty-year-old woman and not from Eva Braun, throwing new doubts on the bunker suicide theory.

But in a 2018 book, *La Mort d'Hitler*, two investigative writers, Jean-Christophe Brisard, from France, and the Russian-American Lana Parshina, wrote that they were able to confirm the jawbone stored in a cigarillo box in the Russian archives was not a 'historical forgery'. They enlisted the help of a French scientist, Philippe Charlier, who analysed the jawbone and Hitler's teeth (no sign of meat colouration confirming his vegetarianism, but evidence of poor care, which explains the rumours about his bad breath). His findings left the journalists sufficiently confident, according to *Slate* magazine, to declare: 'We can state that Hitler died in Berlin on April the 30th, 1945. Not in Brazil at 95, nor in Japan, nor in the Argentinian Andes. The proof is scientific, not ideological. Coldly scientific.'

'The teeth are authentic, there is no possible doubt. Our study proves that Hitler died in 1945,' Charlier wrote in the *European Journal of Internal Medicine*.

There will continue to be conspiracy theories concerning Hitler's death. The circumstances and the idea that the twentieth century's most enduring bogeyman could somehow have evaded justice is too tempting a storyline, especially when one of the superpowers has been so happy to fuel the idea that Hitler spent his twilight years sunning himself on a Copacabana beach.

It underlines why Hitler's true descendants are so worried about what might happen if they shrug off the cloak of secrecy that has shrouded their entire lives. Hitler took his own life nearly eighty years ago, robbing the families of the many millions whose deaths he caused of any hope of justice and leaving his innocent heirs to a life lived in his shadow.

CHAPTER FOURTEEN
THE BROTHERS' PACT
18 SEPTEMBER 1998. LONG ISLAND, NEW YORK

It must have been a shock when the girlfriend of one of William Patrick's sons announced she was considering starting a family. Nothing was ever written in stone, but there was a firm understanding among the latest generation that the Hitler bloodline should end with them. None of the three brothers were married and they had decided there would be no children. They did not want sons and daughters to suffer the same fears and problems they had encountered. But now they faced a dilemma: no one outside the immediate family knew the truth about their name. How could they tell the girlfriend that if she was to have a baby, the child's true name would be Hitler?

The situation was even more complicated by the fact that the girl was Jewish and was committed to having children. In the end, according to a source close to the family, it was decided that she had to be told and the relationship crumbled shortly afterwards.

A similar dilemma was faced by the family when one brother

became involved in a serious relationship with a Puerto Rican girl. That relationship also came to a premature end when she was told she would effectively be the next Mrs Hitler if she married her boyfriend.

While the perils of publicly acknowledging a direct lineage to Adolf Hitler were clear, the price of keeping it a secret were also heavy. After hiding their true identity their whole lives, any alternative would add an extra dimension of fear, not only from people trying to exact some warped retribution for the acts of Adolf Hitler, but also from any changes in the way other people perceived them in their everyday lives in small-town America – the only place the sons had ever known.

I was told the last of the Hitlers were prepared to sacrifice some of their happiness to ensure they did not leave heirs to face the same fate.

For three days, I spoke to people in Long Island who had been close to William Patrick; people who knew him not as the Führer's nephew but as a devoted family man who doted on his wife and sons. While asking not to be identified, they helped answer many of the questions left when William Patrick vanished from sight fifty years before.

He was last heard from as William Patrick Hitler in February 1946, when he was discharged from the navy at Fargo Barracks in Boston, Massachusetts. He said he was heading back to New York to meet Brigid and was hoping to become a US citizen 'very soon'.

Any records of William Patrick's naval service seem to have disappeared, but I was told: 'He saw action in the navy and caught some shrapnel in the leg. He paid his dues.'

An internal FBI memo sent on 25 January 1946, less than a month before he was discharged, reported that 'Hitler is presently at Newport, Rhode Island and is due to be released.'

It continued: 'The office of Naval Intelligence in Boston, Massachusetts is conducting an investigation with reference to subject's application of naturalization and has requested copies of FBI reports in this matter.'

Perhaps while waiting for his citizenship to be approved, he went back to school at the City College in New York and graduated with a Batchelor of Social Science before enrolling at the City College's School of Business and Civic Education, now known as Baruch College, in an MBA programme, studying economics, law, accounting and Spanish. According to college records, he left after four terms without completing his degree.

In October 1946, he applied for a social security card under the name of William Hiller and the following year he married his wartime girlfriend Phyllis. The attractive young German girl was twelve years younger than William Patrick, who was a close friend of her brother when he lived in Germany in the 1930s. The couple met briefly in Germany, when they were introduced by Phyllis's brother, and William Patrick continued writing to the family when he returned to Britain and then moved on to the United States.

With war looming back in Europe, the brother asked William Patrick to look after Phyllis if he could send her to New York. They became fast friends and although there was a suggestion among their friends that the wedding was initially a way for Phyllis to remain in America, there is no doubt it grew into a strong and stable union.

With a wife to support and children on the way, William Patrick took a job in a urologist's office in uptown Manhattan and then worked as an administrator in the urology department of a major Manhattan hospital, thought to be Bellevue. Later he worked at a state hospital on Long Island.

He also changed his name, so it was unrecognisable from Hitler or Hiller or even from his mother's maiden name of Dowling. I have pledged not to divulge the family's adopted name but, intriguingly, the double-barrelled alias derived from an English author admired by William Patrick and whose racist texts helped mould Hitler's Nazi doctrines.

William Patrick, Phyllis and Brigid moved out of the city to Queens, a busy suburb of New York, and, later, to the quiet town further out on Long Island where there were fewer prying eyes and where no one knew their real identity. William Patrick wanted to start a family and allow his children to grow up in America without the burden of the family name – and he vowed never to speak about his hated uncle in public again.

One of the factors contributing to his decision to fade deliberately into the background was a threat made by Himmler who was said to have ordered Nazi sympathisers in the United States to 'go to no limit' to stop William Patrick from speaking out against his uncle.

Although the sinister threat was supposedly made at the beginning of the war, William Patrick feared that Hitler fanatics could still target him and his family.

Using his medical training in the navy and his experience in various hospital departments, William Patrick set himself up in business analysing blood samples and worked long hours while Phyllis looked after the house and their growing family.

In 1949, they had their first child, Alex, followed two years later by Louis. The third boy, Howard, came in 1957 and Brian was born in 1965.

If he was strong and somewhat set in his ways, William Patrick was also eloquent, intelligent and very cosmopolitan. 'Pat was not intimidated by anyone,' said one person who knew him well. 'If you chose to accept him that was fine and if you didn't accept him, then you could go to hell. Let's face it, this was a man who stared down Adolf Hitler.'

He was also a loving father to his sons. 'He was a very caring person. I wish you could have known him,' said the friend. 'He took very strong care to protect his family. His sons and his wife were everything to him.'

The couple were sociable, but they remained close-knit, eschewing clubs and community groups. Phyllis's best friend was another German woman who lived across the street.

Getting on in years, Brigid never remarried, but her brother, Thomas, moved to the same town. In her twilight years she walked with a cane, but she remained in control, still determined to protect her only son. Described as 'a very rigid person' she clung steadfastly to her Catholic faith throughout her life. Even after her death her family kept up the subterfuge. Not wanting 'Hitler' on the death certificate, the family are said to have replaced it with 'Hiller'.

In time, the money I invested in making inquiries in Ireland to track down Brigid's roots paid off. It transpired she was born in the Dublin suburb of Tallaght in the year, as I now knew for sure, of 1891. The house where the former convent girl grew up still stands today.

It seems she may have first met Alois Hitler at a staff dance at the Royal Hibernian Hotel on Dawson Street in Dublin, not at the horse show as she claimed in her memoirs. 'He fairly won my heart with his sugary talk and his foreign ways,' Brigid told the *Daily Express* in a pre-war interview I discovered only after establishing her original hometown. She continued: 'My father – rest his soul – was a real Irishman. He would not hear tell of a wedding to a foreigner. Alois and I used to meet every afternoon in the museum and make plans to elope. Four months later, when Alois had saved enough money, we went to England on the night boat and came to London. I wrote to my mother and said I would not return until we got permission to marry. She talked my father around and he gave his consent.'

After marrying Alois in London, Brigid said she 'took him straight back to Dublin to meet the family, and then we went to Liverpool. He got a job in a restaurant as a waiter and then became an agent for a razor firm. Willie, our only child, was born in March 1911.

'My husband used to talk about his family. He told me of his younger brother, Adolf, who was a dreamy sort of lad and was studying architecture when we were married.'

Brigid's father, William Dowling, was a farm labourer from Kilnamanagh and her mother was Bridget Reynolds, from Ballymount. Her grandparents were Martin and Elizabeth Dowling from Cookstown, and John and Bridget Reynolds, from Ballymount and, earlier, from Kilnamanagh. In her youth, Brigid spent some time living in the town of Clondalkin. Her brother, Thomas, served in the Royal Air Force in the 1920s.

When Brigid was born, her mother was illiterate and marked herself down as 'X' on the birth certificate.

According to Tallaght journalist Donal Bergin, Brigid's marriage to Alois was kept secret in the close-knit Catholic community where she grew up. 'That was hidden,' he quoted a source. 'The next generation weren't told much about it.'

One cottage in which the family lived was leased to Brigid's father by a man called Andrew Cullen Tynan, father of the poet Katharine Tynan. In the opening page of Brigid's memoirs, she describes the day she first met Alois and recalls that 'father was discussing horses with Mr Tynan, a neighbour'. Surely this was yet another clue that the memoirs could not be 'all made up', as Brigid's daughter-in-law had claimed.

But if Hitler was a taboo subject in front of strangers, at home with the family there were lots of stories to tell. William Patrick described taking tea with Hitler, and how everything his uncle surrounded himself with was the very best – the best-looking women, the most elegant furniture and the most ostentatious surroundings. But he told them: 'Hitler got lost in the grandeur of it all. He became a madman.' This message obviously impressed the boys because they talked this way themselves. Their father would sometimes show them photographs of himself with politicians and Hollywood movie stars, mementos from his days on the lecture circuit.

William Patrick spoke also of his bold decision to stand up to his uncle, his refusal to relinquish his British citizenship in return for a grander role in the then all-conquering Third

Reich. He talked of being invited to Hitler's private hideaway at Berchtesgaden where he was told to pick his side. If he wanted to stay and 'partake in the glory of Germany' he should become a German. Hitler's deputy, Rudolf Hess, had apparently told him earlier that he would be doing 'a service to our Führer' if he changed nationality. 'You must surely realise,' Hess said, 'that it's a little embarrassing for the Führer to have English relatives.'

Considering his previous ambition and past requests to his uncle to help him find better-paid jobs in Germany, it was a curiously brave decision. But William Patrick said he had seen enough of Hitler's grand design by then to know he wanted nothing to do with it. The snub meant that to stay in Germany any longer would be suicidal, and he was warned to leave quickly while he still could, stealing over the border with Holland in a friend's car. 'He could have been very high in Hitler's regime. That was the offer Hitler made. But he said no – he knew it was the wrong thing to do – and he told Hitler right to his face. He had no choice but to leave pretty quick after that,' said a family friend. 'Pat had the option to stay, but he chose not to because he didn't like what he had seen.'

Forsaking Germany was particularly hard for Phyllis, who maintained strong ties to her homeland and sorely missed her old life, but she kept in touch with relatives and made several trips back to Europe to visit with her children.

She was said to have been so worried her own family would be torn apart by the Vietnam War that she had all of her sons ordained as Lutheran ministers so they could not be drafted into combat.

Their identity had been discovered once before and they had

left home in the middle of the night to settle in a new town, so desperate were they to preserve their secret life.

'They literally picked up and left under cover of darkness on the night they were tracked down. They felt they could be in harm's way, and they got out of there. They ran,' said a source with intimate knowledge of the family. 'This wasn't a journalist or writer – it was someone who they believed posed a threat to them.'

William Patrick's death in November 1987 took everyone in the family by surprise. He developed a fever and was treated for a bronchial infection. He died days later, aged seventy-six, at a local hospital. Phyllis and her sons considered burying him without a headstone, allowing him in death the anonymity he so prized in life. But in the end, they felt they could not leave a loving father without a memorial. He was buried with Brigid in the three-person plot, which had a space left for his wife.

While the eldest son, Alex, worked counselling Vietnam veterans, the other boys ran their landscaping business from their mother's home. All show a remarkable resemblance to their father – and their great-uncle.

Less than two years after her husband's sudden death, Phyllis and her family suffered another terrible blow. Driving between jobs as a New York-based investigator for the Inland Revenue Service, the third son, Howard, was killed in a head-on collision with a car full of teenagers which veered across the double yellow lane and smashed into him.

While his brothers always kept a lower profile, Howard cut a more dramatic dash, both in school and in life. He was the only son to look for a wider role for himself away from the security of the small town the rest of his family treasured as a safe haven. He was the only brother to work in Manhattan. And he was the only one to get married.

A photograph of Howard in a white suit strutting at the head of his school band as drum major attests to the fact that he inherited his father's showman side.

An old school friend, who also played in the marching band, remembers Howard as a 'jokester. He was an all-American kind of boy. He didn't show any sign of his English and German descent. He certainly never talked about being related to Adolf Hitler. Son of a gun! I would never have associated him with any kind of Nazi. He was either very close-lipped about it or maybe he just didn't know.'

Another friend went to elementary and high school with Howard, played at the family home and, when they grew up, jointly owned a house at an East Coast ski resort. But he never had the faintest idea about Howard's secret heritage.

'Howard was one of the tallest kids in the school and he used to kind of walk with a bounce. He would take a bit of joking about that, but he was very popular, and he was good at his studies. His mother was heavy duty German with a very thick accent. She was always the one who would take him to parties and functions and stuff. His father had a blood lab at their house and spent a lot of time working. He seemed to be a very large man and he was very diligent and cordial. Both of his parents were very nice and kind. But Howard wouldn't really say very much about what was going on at the house.

'It was a pretty tight-knit sort of family. I remember Alex, the oldest brother, and Brian, who he was very close to. I don't remember Louis very well. Brian was really a dead ringer for Howard. We listened to rock music together, played football; he was always involved in something. Nothing was ever said about his real name being Hitler. I guess that was something that was supposed to be kept a secret. It's a really interesting concept. A lot of people in this area served in World War Two and a lot of people didn't come back. It is not something that you would want to let out – that you are a relative of Adolf Hitler.

'He was intelligent, kind and outgoing and he took his life and whatever business he was involved in very seriously. I can't believe that Howard was in some way related to Adolf Hitler.'

After leaving school, Howard worked for a while at a truck rental company, but, in his dreams, perhaps fuelled by tales of his father's pre-war exploits, he had always wanted to work for the FBI or some similar government agency. In the end, he settled on the investigation branch of the Internal Revenue Service and had been working as an agent for two years when he was killed travelling in heavy rain between two fraud inquiries. Howard, then aged thirty-two, died instantly. He had been married for less than four years to a loving young wife whose parents, like his, came from Europe. Friends say that of all the brothers, Howard was the one most likely to have defied the blood pact of the Hitler sons. 'But fate intervened,' said one friend. 'I think Howard and his wife would have loved to have kids. It was definitely something they were thinking about. I guess it just wasn't to be.'

Friends and relatives packed the church for Howard's funeral. Everyone whose lives he had touched wanted to pay their last respects. Howard's name is remembered on memorials in Washington, D.C. and Georgia commemorating the lives of agents killed on duty.

For Phyllis, the loss of one of her beloved sons, particularly so soon after William Patrick's death, was almost unbearable.

Although there are some distant relations living equally quiet lives in Austria, the three American sons are the only descendants of the paternal line of the family. They are, truly, the last of the Hitlers.

I could not help thinking, as I pulled my notes together in my hotel room on the night before I left New York, that the post-war years of the Hitler family could have been ripped from the scrapbooks of any family in America. They had lived quiet, hard-working lives to protect the people they loved. All they had asked in return was to be left alone.

Before flying back to California, I made one further polite approach to the family, who were all now very aware that a British journalist had finally managed to track them down. I was told, equally politely, that I was wasting my time.

CHAPTER FIFTEEN

HITLER'S FAKE SON

25 MARCH 1918. SEBONCOURT, FRANCE

It comes as little surprise to most people that the legitimate last living descendants of the paternal Hitler line would go to great lengths to hide their identities from the world. As you are discovering in this book, their ancestry has placed a terrible burden on their lives.

After the Second World War, the Russians levelled the Chancellery buildings in Berlin and the Americans destroyed Hitler's Berchtesgaden home in Bavaria as part of a demolition campaign to wipe out every trace of Hitler and Nazism to prevent them from becoming far-right shrines to the Third Reich. The American Hitlers have spent all their lives dreading a knock on the door from fanatics who still consider their despotic great-uncle a god.

So, it is all the stranger to wonder at the motivation of men who would court publicity with their claims that they were related to Hitler. If there was any lingering doubt over your parentage, surely the last person you would want to be connected to is the most reviled man in history?

Perhaps the warped personalities of these men offer some clues. Taken to visit Dachau, the first concentration camp set up by the SS, where at least 28,000 people perished between 1940 and 1945, Frenchman Jean-Marie Loret, who claimed to be Hitler's illegitimate son, crossed his arms, looked around him and said, 'If my father did this, then he must have had his reasons.' He also reportedly once gave the Nazi salute to Japan's National Assembly.

Another man claiming to be related by blood to the German dictator, Romano-Lukas Hitler, was reportedly convicted of sexual misconduct in 2019.

Loret's claims received the most publicity, despite being dismissed by leading Hitler historians, and the French railway worker went to his grave in 1985 insisting he was the Führer's long-lost illegitimate son. He maintained that his mother, Charlotte Lobjoie, confessed on her death bed in 1948 that the young Hitler got her pregnant when he was serving in France during the First World War. They supposedly met in 1914 when Hitler was a corporal in the German Army on leave in Lille and Lobjoie was a sixteen-year-old. Their drunken affair that, according to Loret, stretched over several years and different regions of France, resulted in his birth in Seboncourt, France on 25 March 1918. The father was recorded on Jean-Marie's birth certificate as an 'unknown German soldier'.

Loret was brought up by his grandparents and was later adopted, which explains his surname, but he claimed to be ignorant of his father's identity until his mother's bombshell revelation. Loret's son, Philippe, insisted his father's claims are true, telling the *Daily Mail* in 2012: 'I believe I am Hitler's grandson. Of course, I am. The evidence is there. If people don't believe it, that's their problem.

'My father told me. My mother is still alive and also believes it. He is part of my family, that's why I have him on the wall. Hitler is my family. It's not my fault that I ended up as his grandson or that all the things happened during the war. What he did has nothing to do with me. He will always be family for me.

'When I was first told, all I was interested in was girls, and so I didn't think about it too much. I knew who Hitler was – I studied him at school – but I did not tell any of my school friends. My private life had nothing to do with them. By the time my father told us about Hitler being his father, he was proud of being Hitler's son. He had trouble accepting it at first. He didn't like this fact, but gradually he came to terms with it.

'My father told me the relationship lasted for only a few months. Hitler came under gas attack and went back to Germany to recover. He came back again for a few months and left again for Germany, and she never saw him again.'

The family wasn't afraid to go into detail. 'My father said Hitler was a good lover and was gentle with my grandmother,' said Philippe Loret. 'But apparently, he was a jealous person and did not like other men giving her the eye. As far as I know he never had any sexual perversions – I don't want to make him more than the monster he is.'

Loret went to considerable lengths to back up his story, employing scientists to find he had the same blood type as Hitler and similar handwriting. His children also took DNA tests to much fanfare, but the results were never made public. Unlike the American Hitlers, who had steadfastly refused to go public with their story, Loret wrote a book, calling it *Your Father's Name Was Hitler.*

Genetic tests carried out by Belgian researchers, journalist Jean-Paul Mulders and customs official Marc Vermeeren, also appeared to exclude Loret from the Hitler family.

The Belgians followed Alexander, the eldest Long Island brother, around for a week and eventually fished a napkin he'd used in a chicken fast food restaurant out of a rubbish bin. They then matched it with what Mulders described as 'DNA of Hitler that we keep in a sealed, armoured chest'.

Although hardly scientific, the results confirmed the brothers' lineage and the researchers claimed to have unearthed thirty-nine distant relatives of Hitler in Lower Austria, but there was no match for the unfortunate Loret.

Historians such as Sir Ian Kershaw and Anton Joachimsthaler, who both wrote seminal biographies of Hitler, gave little credibility to Loret's claims either. The only thing the Frenchman had in common with the dictator, it appears, was his boorishness.

Romano-Lukas Hitler's story is, if anything, even more bizarre. This lonely man, who lives in Goerlitz in east Germany and works as a boat helmsman, claims to be the great-grandson of Hitler's father's younger brother, an ancestor who was previously unknown and experts suggest did not exist. *Bild* newspaper in Germany said the bachelor was unable to prove his lineage although he uses the name Hitler.

He was happy to discuss his alleged connection on screen for the 2014 documentary *Meet the Hitlers.*

'People always ask me why I haven't wanted to change my name, and I ask back, "Why haven't you wanted to change your name?"' he said. 'I'm not proud about why I'm so unique. For me it's normal how things are. It's part of me and that's that. I can't change it. I have no apartment. I have no money. My parents dropped me off at an orphanage in Bratislava. My parents wanted to go to Austria and told me they would pick me up after one or two months. They never came back for me. I still love my parents. Every child wants to have and see his parents. I didn't have them.'

Hitler, who has a lion tattooed on his head, insisted his ancestry was impressed on him by his family. 'My parents always told me that because of my uncle, I couldn't play with other children or go to kindergarten, etc. I knew from my parents that it was because of my uncle. I didn't understand who Adolf was. That's why I learned at an early age to keep my distance from people.

'Yes, I am the only and last relative of Adolf Hitler on earth. After Adolf there is me, and then after me we are done with the family. Absolutely nobody else is left. I feel like the nephew of Adolf. That's a matter of faith. I only have Adolf as my family. No one else can have it. I'm the only one in this world. For me, Adolf is the only person I have.'

He said he had always dreamed of starting a family and naming his own son Adolf.

In 2019, he faced some less welcome publicity when he was reportedly convicted of kissing a thirteen-year-old girl on the neck and cheek after her father complained to the authorities. According to the *Daily Mirror*, the judge rejected his claim that the kiss was an innocent greeting.

He was adamant that he, and not the three American brothers, was the very last of the Hitlers. Told about their background as the Führer's great-nephews, he said only: 'I don't think so. I don't believe that.'

There has been one other claim that Hitler fathered a child, but, once again, the evidence was flimsy. It involved his bizarre friendship with Unity Mitford, a member of the notorious aristocratic family with a penchant for Nazism.

The 1930s socialite became what would be known today as a stalker, going to Hitler's favourite restaurant, Osteria Bavaria, every day for ten months until he finally invited her to join his table. The fourth daughter of Lord Redesdale, she was fervently anti-Semitic and an outspoken advocate of fascism in 1930s England.

She went from being Hitler's groupie to a member of his inner circle and was on the balcony with him in Vienna when he announced the Anschluss in 1938. An intelligence report described her as being 'more Nazi than the Nazis'.

There's no evidence of the relationship going any further than hero worship on her part, but they were certainly close for four years and only parted ways after Germany invaded Poland in 1939 and Hitler cooled towards her. Mitford didn't take it well, shooting herself in the head in her Munich flat in an unsuccessful attempt at suicide. To be fair, she had vowed to commit suicide if the two countries she loved went to war against one another. But while her follow-through was commendable, her aim was not. The bullet lodged in her brain, leaving her with substantial brain damage and she eventually died in 1948 after being cared for the rest of her life by her mother, Lady Redesdale.

It would have stayed at that but for a story in the *New Statesman* in 2007 suggesting that Unity may have returned to England with a little more than her tail between her legs. According to author Martin Bright, he had been told by a source that Mitford had a baby at an Oxfordshire maternity home during the war. Asked who the father might have been, Bright says he was told: 'Well, she always said it was Hitler's.'

The baby boy was given up for adoption, the source was informed, but Bright was suspicious about the story, as were Hitler's biographers, who have given it short shrift.

Bright quotes the diaries of MI5's wartime number two Guy Liddell, who wasn't persuaded that Mitford had even tried to kill herself. He wrote: 'Unity Mitford had been in close and intimate contact with the Führer and his supporters for several years and was an ardent and open supporter of the Nazi regime. She had remained behind after the outbreak of war and her action came perilously close to high treason. Her parents had been associated with the Anglo-German Fellowship and other kindred movements and had obviously supported her in her ideas about Hitler.

'We had no evidence at all in support of the press allegations that she was in a serious state of health, and it might well be that she was being brought in on a stretcher in order to avoid publicity and unpleasantness to her family.'

Liddell's suspicions were unfounded as Mitford eventually died from her injuries, but the suggestion that she may have been pregnant lingered on, despite her family's fierce denials. One clue may have been that a woman whose sister worked at the maternity home – Hill View Cottage in the village of Wigginton,

Oxfordshire – told Bright that Mitford wasn't there to have a baby, but to recover from a mental breakdown.

There wasn't any evidential proof as the British authorities hadn't even bothered to interview Mitford even though she had made no secret of her closeness and adoration of the German leader. No doubt that had she come from less salubrious beginnings, she would have been asked to explain just how close that relationship became.

Unity was one of six Mitford sisters who grew up to varying levels of notoriety. They were kept out of school because their parents, Lord and Lady Redesdale, feared they would get thick ankles through playing hockey and Unity's older sister, Diana, had an open dalliance with Oswald Mosley, leader of the British Union of Fascists, whom she later married at the German home of Joseph Goebbels, with Hitler as the VIP guest. After being arrested and interned, along with Mosley, she was asked if she agreed with Hitler's abhorrent policies targeting Jews. 'Up to a point,' she said. 'I am not fond of Jews.'

So, Unity had the motive and the breeding to bear Hitler's offspring. There's a very good chance that she wished it could have been so. But, as with Jean-Marie Loret, there are just too many holes in the story to give the idea of a Hitler wandering anonymously around the Cotswolds any credibility.

It is why so much fascination remains around the true-life story of the only remaining Hitlers.

CHAPTER SIXTEEN

LET SLEEPING DOGS LIE

24 APRIL 2001. LONG ISLAND, NEW YORK

Not surprisingly, after thirty years he was greyer and stockier than he looked in his high-school yearbook photo from 1967, but Alex Hitler still had the family resemblance that might make people stop and look twice – if only they were aware of his real name.

I began to introduce myself, but it was not necessary. 'I remember you,' he said, standing at the front door of his house, less than ten miles from where his mother lived. 'And I know why you are here.'

I had returned once before since first contacting the family more than two and a half years earlier and was relieved to find my inquiries had not driven Phyllis from her home nor worried her sons enough for them to seek a new start with a different name in another town. That time Alex had met me at the door of his mother's house. He was extremely polite, even friendly, but was equally certain that the family still had no intention of discussing the past. The time was not right for his mother or the rest of the family to let their secret slip. A bouquet of flowers I sent to the house the next day was returned to the store.

This time, because I did not want to worry his mother anymore, I called at Alex's small bachelor home in a busier Long Island suburb. With me were British film-makers David Howard and Madoc Roberts, who were interested in making a documentary about the life of William Patrick Hitler. I had been talking with David about the project for more than a year and he and Madoc had managed to unearth some fascinating old newsreel tape of William Patrick and his mother, both in England and America. David had also gone back to Brigid's pre-war address in Highgate and found an elderly woman who remembered the Irish Mrs Hitler and remained in contact with the family for some years after they moved to the United States. She even remembered receiving a photograph of Brigid with her first grandson in the post from America. Curiously, the name of the baby scribbled on the back of the photo was 'Alf' – the same pet name Geli Raubal had used for her uncle, Adolf Hitler. It was yet another indication that Alex Hitler's middle name might be Adolf as John Toland had claimed.

Further inquiries in Liverpool revealed a wide circle of local people who knew the story of Adolf Hitler's visit to the city without, sadly, being able to present any firm proof. The story had been passed on down the generations to be accepted into the historical lore of Liverpool, whether it was true or not.

Clearly, to make a documentary or, indeed, to write a book about William Patrick, it would help a great deal to have the co-operation and assistance of his surviving family. 'We want to ensure that it's as accurate as possible,' I told Alex, who was dressed in an old T-shirt and jeans.

'I realise this is fast becoming an annual visit,' I continued. 'But there is this huge gulf out there between the material written painting your father and grandmother in a poor light and the reality that they spent most of their lives determinedly remaining out of the spotlight and raising a loving family. This is an unfair perspective that, with your help, we would like to correct. I honestly think it's important to show a balanced portrait of your father.'

Alex had not long been home from work and answered with a tired acceptance. 'Have fun,' he said. 'Make your programme about my father, or whatever you intend to do. I know that in England there's still a lot of interest in Hitler, and it's on the television and in books and newspapers more often than it is here.

'Just make sure you say good things about my father because he was a good guy. He came to the United States, he served in the US Navy, he had four kids, and he had a pretty good life. It's rubbish that people have called him a black sheep. Nothing could be more wrong.

'For everyone else this is probably very interesting. But for us it's a pain in the ass. It's like, why do we have to be burdened with this? We have always said that we're not going to get anything out of this but aggravation.

'I have read some of the letters my father wrote to my grandmother and all I can say is that it was all a very unhappy experience. He loved living in England, but then he was living in Germany and everything. That was why he came to the United

States – because he wanted to disappear. It was past history and unfortunately it was negative past history.'

Just in case people were still in doubt, Alex wanted to spell it out: 'My father was definitely anti-Nazi and anti-Hitler. I guess that's because they did such terrible things in Germany when he was there. He decided he was going to the US to become an American and that was it.

'If he wanted to make his experiences known, he was the one to do it. They were his experiences. I was after him all the time to write a book. He said, "If I write a book, the moment I die you will go out and release it." I said, "Oh no, I wouldn't."

'We wanted him to write the book just because he knew everything, and I didn't really know anything. I have spent my whole life in the United States. I don't know anything about what went on over there. I have been to Germany a couple of times. It's a nice place, but it's still a foreign country to me, that's all.

'I was asking my father to write his book for a couple of years but towards the end of his life his memory got a little bad and he said to me, "It looks like it's not going to happen." So, it never happened. It was as simple as that. Why is everyone so fascinated with him? Is it because he was English?'

'It's interesting that a Hitler grew up in England and lived in America,' I said. 'What is so fascinating is that he did such a good job in vanishing from the face of the earth that no one ever knew what happened to him. And I know I keep on saying it, but because he never came out to tell his side of the story, he hasn't been remembered very kindly by history. That's why I think it would help so much if you decided to help tell his real story.'

Alex smiled, but he was not moved to change his mind.

'This came up with my father in the early eighties and he just told me, "I am not saying anything." My grandmother felt the same. Her idea was that we should all let sleeping dogs lie and we have said that all along.

'You can bet your bottom dollar we are not going to be associated with anything. It's something you are going to have to write. I may be able to take a look at it but before I do that I will have to speak to my family. I'm glad you came and talked to me because my mother has not been feeling very well.

'I think that if the name didn't have such a bad connotation, we would probably do it. I spoke to one of my closest friends and he said, "What's the big deal? You should say something. They will make a big drama about it for fifteen minutes and then it will all be over."'

'He may have a point,' I said. 'Part of the fascination is in the mystery and the fact your family hasn't said anything about this whole thing since your dad left the navy. Once the story has been told, you may be able to get on with your lives without having to worry about journalists like me turning up at your door.'

'Yes, but I think it would simply start a chain of events where somebody will say, "Look, they did say something. Let's go and try and speak to them, too." We all finally got together and decided that we are just going to say that we are not going to talk about it. In another fifteen or twenty years, who knows? It's one of those things that isn't going to do anything for me. Every time I talk to you a little bit more comes out, but what good does it do for me? A couple of million dollars might be nice, but otherwise, it's not worthwhile. We don't see why we should take the risk of saying anything.'

While a source who had been close to William Patrick believed 'a lot' of the manuscript purporting to be Brigid's memoirs is true and, indeed, many stories from William Patrick's own wartime lectures and the articles he wrote for *Look* and *Paris Soir* seem to verify and confirm episodes from the book, the family still insist it's a fake.

Phyllis told me the memoir is 'all made up' and Alex agreed. 'We read it,' he said, 'and it was the funniest thing I ever saw in my life.'

'But if it wasn't written by your grandmother or your father, then who did write it? I asked. 'There's so much detail in it that nobody else could have known.'

'It's not something we are interested in pursuing,' said Alex. 'Maybe a publisher wrote it anonymously. It may have been a way of him making some money. But the information was false.'

All of a sudden, Alex registered that he had talked for longer than he had intended, and he suggested I return the following day when he got home from work. By then, he said, he would have asked the opinion of his mother and brothers as to whether he should agree to review our material about his father.

Before we left, I asked Alex outright if his middle name was Adolf. He just smiled at me and closed the door.

When I returned at the agreed time there was no sign of Alex. But there was a note addressed to me pinned to the door. It said any further inquiries should be made through the family lawyer and included a local number. There would be no co-operation.

CHAPTER SEVENTEEN

TRAGEDY OF THE MARRIED HITLER

14 SEPTEMBER 1989. LONG ISLAND, NEW YORK

For one of the last living descendants of the most hated man in history it was perhaps a strange choice of occupation. IRS agents, after all, are not usually regarded with great fondness.

But like his father before him, Howard Hitler was determined to do all he could to serve his country, and by all accounts the Long Island native was a popular and hard-working employee as well as a loving husband.

So, when he was killed in a car crash on 14 September 1989, as the first Internal Revenue agent ever to die in the line of duty, the shock to his family and the community he grew up in was all the more heart-breaking.

The church was filled to overflowing. His sudden death at the age of thirty-two left his wife, his mother and his three brothers devastated.

With one exception, none of Howard's closest friends had any idea that he was born a Hitler. The born-and-bred New

Yorker was buried at a Long Island cemetery under the same assumed name that his parents had chosen to cover up the truth about their blood ties.

Howard Hitler was interred just a few rows away from the final resting place of both his English-born father and his Irish mother.

Unlike his three brothers, Howard was outgoing and sociable, the life and soul of any party. He was also the only sibling who refused to be constrained by the burden of his name and would not be a party to the pact the other siblings agreed to end the family line at their generation. Not only did he get married, but he also wanted to have children before his life was tragically cut so short.

Some of his friends agreed to speak to me to offer a unique insight into the life of a man who grew up with the ultimate family secret.

'I want the world to know what a wonderful human being Howie was,' said his best friend, Joe Sirhan. 'He was one of the nicest guys you could ever wish to meet, and I'll carry him around with me forever.'

Despite the extraordinary secret behind their name, there was nothing particularly out of the ordinary about the Hitlers' upbringing. Howard was the third of the four brothers. All four went to the same high school, but Howard stood out as the most outgoing, playing in the school band and always with a big circle of friends.

Kathy Masem-Zguris, who still runs a music shop in their hometown, was Howard's high-school prom date and they played in the school band together. 'I didn't have a clue that

Hitler was his real name. I don't know how well that would have gone over. I still can't really believe it,' she said, adding: 'He was an absolute gentleman and always great fun.'

'We were all the best of pals and band geeks, so we had a great time. My brother was a year ahead of us and we were out the other night and I said, "You'll never guess who Howard was related to. You remember him from band?" He said yes and I told him, "Adolf Hitler!" He was just dumbfounded at that point, totally dumbfounded. That name is associated with torture and killing. I could understand them not wanting to have it.'

Howard's marriage to girlfriend Marie came like a bolt out of the blue to the rest of the close-knit family, who were used to keeping outsiders out.

He confided his Hitler secret to just one person, his best friend, Joe Sirhan, who also knew him from their band days together.

'It was a few days after his father died and it was in his backyard. He had to tell me a few times before it really sunk in because I'd known him that long and he was my best friend,' said Joe. 'His mum was pretty upset once she found out that he told me. There was that instant family blockage that no outsiders should know this terrible story.

'It was a cloudy day and Howard said, "I have a little story to tell you. Well, my father is the nephew of Adolf Hitler." I said, "Come on!" He said, "No, it's true." He then took me through the lineage and how they changed their name. It was for anonymity. That's a big burden to bear and, because we were so close, I didn't say anything to anybody about this for twenty-five years.

'The whole secrecy thing fell into place; why they were so guarded. They kept to themselves. There are some whackos in the world and they're afraid of that. That was always the big deal, they were afraid of someone coming and evening up the score with any kind of Hitler. Howard did say that was why they kept it secret because there were a lot of strange people out there. They had nothing to do with their great-uncle, but they've been handcuffed to him. The whole family is handcuffed to each other over this.

'There would be strange cars outside their house. It was pretty much a little fortress.'

Joe still misses his friend. 'Howard did so much for me. He was a big, big galoot and a fun guy,' he said. 'He kept a good secret, but I'm positive it damaged them all. When I look back now it was a very dysfunctional family. All the brothers lived with them in a minute house. It was a postage stamp.

'They invited me everywhere. Every Friday night they went to a restaurant called the Good Steer. That was a tradition for the whole family. Howard's favourite colour was black. He always dressed in black. He had a black Camaro car like the "Knight Rider". He was heavily into *Star Trek* and *Star Wars*.

'Willy was great,' he added, referring to William Patrick. 'He treated me like a son. He loved to laugh. He was at my wedding when I got married in 1979 and Howard was an usher. Willie's voice was a dead ringer for the actor Michael Caine. That was exactly what Willy sounded like. He was very heavily into astrology. He could read your charts. He loved that. Astrology was his passion.'

Joe said the family was hit hard by William Patrick's sudden death from heart failure in 1987 at the age of seventy-six.

'William died very quickly but there was a problem,' he explained. 'They didn't know what to do with the tombstone. They were afraid if they put the Hitler name, which is what it should have been, it would become a neo-Nazi shrine and they didn't want that. They felt he might want to be buried under his real name to set things straight for a final time, but in the end, they decided against it.

'Howard's marriage was pretty much of a shock to the family,' said Joe. 'His mother didn't see it coming and I didn't see it coming. They just went ahead and went to a justice of the peace.'

The 1989 car crash happened when Howard was on his way to deliver a subpoena.

'When he died it took me a couple of years to get over. That was absolutely horrendous,' said Joe. 'His wife, Marie, called us at two in the morning on the night Howard died and said, "I don't know what to do." It was pretty bad. He'd just got his life going, he'd broken away from his mother and the brothers, he'd gotten his own place and a great job with the government, and it all came to an end. It's like one of those frozen-in-time things that day for me.'

He said the family has a wealth of information about William Patrick's pre-war life. 'They don't know who to trust,' he said. 'They have a wealth of photographic information because I've seen it. It really should be in a museum. There are personal Third Reich pictures. This stuff should be out there. They are part of our history, like it or not.

'I saw the letter that Willie wrote to FDR. I saw the original of that. That's part of the books that have all the wonderful information that nobody's seen. Howard showed it to me. There were pictures of Adolf and Willie together – family shots.'

CHAPTER EIGHTEEN

HITLER STREET

JULY 1936. YAPHANK, LONG ISLAND

I t's about a fifteen-minute drive east from the small town on
the south shore of eastern Long Island where the Hitler sons
were raised to a rural backwater with a secret Nazi past that its
older residents would also rather forget.

Today in Yaphank, Suffolk County, parents mow meticulously
kept lawns and children play on their bikes in the unremarkable
community with anonymous street names like Park Boulevard
and Private Road. Many families have lived here for generations
and take pride in owning their own homes.

But in the 1930s, a decade before William Patrick, Phyllis and
Brigid moved out to Long Island to escape their heritage, this
same neighbourhood had a much more sinister reputation as the
American heartland of German Nazism.

And those same streets weren't called Park Boulevard and
Private Road – they were Hitler Street and Goebbels Street.

Incredibly, as many as 40,000 swastika-waving Americans,
many of them with German roots, would converge on a park

in Yaphank every Sunday in the summer of 1936 to celebrate Nazism as a movement and Adolf Hitler as its architect. Wearing grey shirts and black ties and black breeches and boots – the uniform of the US fascist group, the German-American Bund – many headed out from New York City, catching a special train that left at 8 a.m. every Sunday morning from Penn Station. They would then march through the Long Island village to their destination, a bucolic lakefront park they had renamed Camp Siegfried after a mythical dragon-slaying German hero who was adopted by the Nazis.

It looked like any other family camp with cabins, playgrounds, and barbecues – except everywhere you looked, there was a swastika. Tellingly, a German flag flew higher than the American banner above the camp. While some neighbours may have regarded the newcomers with suspicion and disdain, there was a strong Germanic influence in the area from immigrant families that remains to this day.

Camp Siegfried marches – including on 4 July, America's Independence Day – would include adults and children, all of them white, showing off stiff-armed Hitler salutes and singing the Nazi anthem, the *Horst Wessel.*

Out in front of the Camp Siegfried Inn, flowers were planted in the shape of a giant swastika and a two-foot-high photograph of Hitler adorned the wall inside. Along with swimming, sports games and sunbathing, there were sessions spent listening to Wagner, Hitler's favourite composer, and anti-Semitic lectures.

Marvin Miller, a former schoolteacher and author of a book, *Wunderlich's Salute,* about the camp, wrote: 'At Camp Siegfried and its like, the Bundists and the Young Siegfrieds heiled, paraded in uniform, sang the *Horst Wessel* and openly propagandized Nazism amid its insignia. Fanatically, some trained for soldierhood, bludgeoned other German-Americans, utilised patriotic American organisations for their purposes and conspired to commit espionage and sabotage.'

Suffolk County and New York residents paid a total of $3,000 into a collection for Germany's Winter Relief Fund and seventy-one signed their names into a 'Golden Book', which was presented to Adolf Hitler by the leader of the Bund, Fritz Kuhn, when he visited Germany for the 1936 Olympics.

Kuhn was photographed with Hitler who apparently urged him to keep up the 'struggle' in America, says Miller.

David Behrens, a reporter with the Long Island newspaper, *Newsday*, wrote in a 1983 article that the beginning of the end for the camp came in 1938 when six camp officials were accused of breaking the state's civil rights laws by being involved in an organisation that required members to take an oath of allegiance to Adolf Hitler.

One of them, Willie Brandt, testified he had taken the oath – 'I pledge faith to my leader, Adolf Hitler. I promise Adolf Hitler and those put in charge by him . . . loyalty and obedience and oblige myself to execute all commands carefully and without personal regard . . .'

Behrens writes about Miller's research of the case and the testimony of another Bundist, shipping clerk Martin Wunderlich, who was quizzed in court about the Nazi salutes given by members to the America flag.

He quotes the exchange as follows:

Q. How do you salute the American flag?

A. A greeting of the white race.

Q. How do you hold your arm when you salute the American flag at Camp Siegfried?

A. You have seen so many pictures.

Q. The jury would like to see. You are on the stand to tell us.

A. I refuse to.

Q. You refuse to do that?

JUDGE. Stand up and show us how you salute the flag over Camp Siegfried.

A. (Standing and raising his right arm in a stiff Nazi salute) I salute the American flag as a member and a proud member of the white race.

Q. That is an American salute?

A. It will be.

Q. It will be? That is what you want to put over on the United States, you and your crowd, make us all salute that way. That is enough from you. That is all.

The camp lost its alcohol licence the following year and was disbanded as Germany invaded Poland in 1939 and the war in Europe steadily loomed closer to home in the United States. Kuhn was convicted of fraudulently using the Bund's money and spent the war in a detention camp along with another forty leading camp members before he was deported to West Germany in 1945.

But the shadow of Camp Siegfried refused to die.

Three former Siegfrieders were captured in June 1942 after being dropped off by German submarine off the coast of Long Island with a mission to sabotage some of America's biggest targets. The mission was a shambles and six of the eight would-be saboteurs were given the death penalty, but it illustrated the sinister edge to the supposedly idyllic Yaphank campground.

The swastikas were removed, and the street names were changed decades ago, but the strong German influence in the community has never really gone away. That may be a reason why families with German heritage are still attracted to the area.

Yet still the past haunts the town and suggests the pro-German sentiment did not disappear with the pre-war visitors in their grey and black fascist uniforms.

The Camp Siegfried land was seized by the US authorities after the Second World War broke out, but it was later won back by the owner of the site, a homeowner group called the German-American Settlement League, and renamed German Gardens and Siegfried Park.

According to a lawsuit brought by a couple of residents who lived in the neighbourhood for years, the landowners were still picky about the types of people who live in the community.

Philip Kneer and Patricia Flynn-Kneer accused the league of 'racially divisive housing policies', saying it prevented anyone who wasn't of German heritage or white from living in the forty-home suburb. They claimed the group's constitution says residents must be of 'German extraction, and of good character and reputation'.

The league, and many residents, denied there was any profiling involved in deciding who was allowed to live there, but in 2017, according to the Associated Press, the GASL settled an anti-discrimination case brought by New York State.

There has never been any suggestion that the decision by

William Patrick, Phyllis and Brigid to move to the same area had anything to do with the heavy German contingent, but it is intriguing to think that the secret histories of Yaphank and the family were so closely aligned to Hitler's Germany.

If they were aware of the town's Nazi past, it would have been all the more imperative for the Hitlers to remain secretive about their own.

CHAPTER NINETEEN

WHAT'S IN A NAME?

9 JANUARY 1927. BAYREUTH, GERMANY

The winter funeral for Houston Stewart Chamberlain in Bayreuth, Bavaria, on 9 January 1927 was a very Wagnerian affair and it was no surprise that a burgeoning political figure in Germany, Adolf Hitler, was among the high-ranking Nazi Party members who attended.

The seventy-one-year-old who died was born in Southsea, Hampshire, but had long ago forsaken the country of his birth for a new life in Germany. Initially, the move was motivated by his devotion to the composer Richard Wagner but, in time, he came to adore everything about his new country and eventually became a naturalised citizen.

A weak, sickly youth, Chamberlain grew up with an antipathy towards England that never really left him, and he took a very different path than that expected of him. His father, an admiral in the Royal Navy, wanted his son to follow in his footsteps. Instead, his anti-Semitic ideology would inspire the worst genocide the world has ever seen. He believed the Germans to be a cultural master race and the Jews to be dangerously inferior. He was Hitler's racist mentor.

And it appears possible that Chamberlain's name, in part, may have been adopted by William Patrick Hitler to hide his identity as the late German leader's nephew. I don't know for certain if he selected the racist English writer and philosopher for his double-barrelled surname, but the coincidence seems remarkable.

A family source would say only that the name derived from a relative in County Cork and an author that William Patrick admired. The brothers would offer no further comment. But it bears some further examination, not least because it once again illustrates the power of a name and the inference it can have, both good and bad.

In the feature documentary *Meet the Hitlers*, Oscar-nominated director Matt Ogens explores how identities are influenced by a name, in this case, the most hated one in history. Those who were born with the name, and were no relation to Adolf, appeared to live fairly normal lives without changing it, although one man's daughter was heckled off stage when she ran for class president and there had clearly been obstacles for them along the way.

The ones who chose the name, in particular a neo-Nazi from America called Heath Campbell, who named his son Adolf Hitler and has now changed his own name to Hitler, are way more disturbing. He also named his other children JoyceLynn Aryan Nation, Honszlynn Hinler Jeannie, Heinrich Hons, and Eva Lynn Patricia Braun. Campbell settled on these names to shock, and none is more shocking than Hitler.

Chamberlain's views on the role of the Aryan race in the history of the world had already captured the interest of Germany's Kaiser Wilhelm II before the English writer first met Hitler in 1923.

Later, according to the *Nazi Germany Sourcebook*, he would write to Hitler, saying:

> Most respected and dear Hitler,
> It is hardly surprising that a man like that can give peace to a poor suffering spirit! Especially when he is dedicated to the service of the Fatherland. My faith in Germandom has not wavered for a moment, though my hopes were – I confess – at a low ebb. With one stroke you have transformed the state of my soul. That Germany, in the hour of her greatest need, brings forth a Hitler – that is proof of her vitality.

His rambling tome espousing his views on Aryan racial superiority was later described as 'the gospel of the National Socialist movement'.

The avowed Germanophile became a part of Wagner's inner circle and ended up marrying the composer's daughter, Eva, in 1905. Needless to say, he didn't live to see Hitler's attempt to carry out his hateful philosophy, but many of his racial science theories lived on through his Nazi disciples.

'What we must fight for is to safeguard the existence and reproduction of our race and our people, the sustenance of our children and the purity of our blood, the freedom and independence of the Fatherland, so that our people may mature for the fulfilment of the mission allotted it by the creator of the universe,' Adolf Hitler wrote in *Mein Kampf*, very much reflecting his British mentor's ideas.

But while Chamberlain was an academic and a man of ideas and ideology, in Hitler he found a driven manipulator who would not only support and promote these twisted ideals to a vulnerable public, but he would also do everything in his considerable power to make them happen.

Between 1933, when the Nazi Party came to power, and the end of the war in 1945, Hitler led a state-sponsored, systematic attempt to wipe out the Jewish people he regarded as inferior and a threat to German culture. The persecution grew steadily from discriminatory laws and violence against Jews, excluding them from the country's political, economic and cultural life, to what Nazi leaders termed the 'Final Solution to the Jewish Question'.

This 'Final Solution' was the organised mass execution of Jews from Germany and across Europe in concentration camps between 1941 and 1945. Most of the victims died in one of two ways, although there were many other brutal, merciless methods that were employed. One was through mass shootings that took place in more than 1,500 cities, towns and villages in Europe after forcing Jewish men, women and children to dig their own graves. Another was in extermination camps such as those in Chelmno, Belzec, Sobibor, Treblinka and Auschwitz-Birkenau, where the victims would be shipped in and asphyxiated in gas chambers or put to work at hard labour before they, too, were often gassed. Nearly 2.7 million Jews were killed in this way.

In 1934, the Jewish population in Europe numbered 9 million.

WHAT'S IN A NAME?

By the end of 1945, it had dwindled to just 3 million. The other 6 million had been murdered by the Nazis and their collaborators.

These atrocities were graphically detailed at the Nuremberg Trials after the war, when nineteen military and political leaders of the Third Reich were convicted of war crimes. Twelve of them, including Hitler's right-hand man Hermann Goering, Nazi lawyer Hans Frank, and Alfred Rosenberg, a devotee of the English philosopher, were sentenced to execution, although Goering killed himself the night before his hanging.

It is a feature of my search that after so long, some key questions remain. This is another one I have failed to find an answer to despite all my efforts. If William Patrick was aware of the connotations attached to one of the most prominent racist writers of the nineteenth and twentieth centuries, why on earth would he choose his name? At the very least, if he was, indeed, aware of Chamberlain's role as one of the architects of the Holocaust, why didn't he avoid that name like the plague and opt for another, less distinctive surname.

Like Smith.

The Long Island Hitlers had no choice about the family they were born into and no interest in exploring a past they had no control over, but in a rare public comment, the eldest son, Alex, said that he was not a supporter of Donald Trump.

When Germany's *Bild* newspaper tracked down Alex to his home in 2018, he refused to discuss his family in any detail, just as he had with me in our various meetings over the years. But the patriot, who hadn't missed a US vote in decades, did reveal his views towards then President Donald Trump – and he definitely wasn't a fan of the maverick Republican.

'I always vote for the person who does the best work,' he told *Bild*. 'The last person I would say I admire is Donald Trump. He is definitely not one of my favourites.

'Some things that Trump says are all right. It's his manner that annoys me. And I just don't like liars.'

He was more supportive of former German Chancellor Angela Merkel, saying: 'I like her. She's good. She seems to be an intelligent and smart person.'

It is inconceivable to most reasonable-minded people – in Germany as much as anywhere else – that a monster like Adolf Hitler could have risen to a position of such power. While I am in no way comparing the two men, it is equally bemusing that a nation of wonderful, enquiring, energetic people such as those in the United States could vote Donald Trump into the White House. I don't profess to understand what drives such decisions, but I do understand the power of words…and the importance of names. Sticks and stones can, indeed, break your bones but words can also hurt you. Calling someone a Hitler is never going to be good, even when it really is your name. That's why it is so hard to understand why William Patrick would allow the possibility that a racist such as Chamberlain would taint the new life he had created so successfully for his family.

CONCLUSION

After it became clear the family were not going to collaborate, I continued to research the life of William Patrick Hitler. As you will know by reading up to this point, other doors opened to help bring him alive, to colour in the cardboard outline offered in footnotes and asides by most previous books. I discovered never-before published FBI reports and secret service records that offer a fascinating insight into William Patrick's thoughts and actions at the time. Not only that, but they provide a unique glimpse into a rarely explored side of his uncle, the most evil man of modern times – that of the family man, albeit an extremely antagonistic one.

The discovery of the FBI file on William Patrick was one of my most important breakthroughs in piecing together the truths and half-truths of his life. The bulky, once top secret, file found in a forgotten corner of the FBI archives in Washington,

D.C. contained a wealth of never-before published information about both William Patrick and Brigid.

Aided by America's Freedom of Information Act and the FBI's helpful staff, I managed to obtain a copy of the 112-page report, which has now been unclassified, and reading through the documents was like a Wellsian ride back in time with names like Roosevelt, Hoover and, of course, Hitler standing out from the sometimes-stilted texts. Crucially, the file provided independent confirmation of stories from less concrete sources. While the papers were no use in discovering what became of William Patrick and his family – the file was listed under the surname of Hitler – they included a detailed report of Special Agent White's 1942 interview with the Führer's nephew.

Much of the information William Patrick gave to the FBI mirrored that contained in his mother's mysterious memoirs. In the past, many Hitler biographers have tended to quote from Brigid's manuscript while, at the same time, knocking its authenticity. To my mind, the contents of the FBI file meant that, at the very least, Brigid's memoirs should be taken seriously. While some passages in the book are overly dramatic, the prose rather florid at times and some of the facts clearly fudged, most of the key episodes – Brigid's meeting with Alois and her early years in Liverpool and London, Alois's bigamy, William Patrick's stormy 'blackmail' meeting with Adolf, and William Patrick's arrest during the 'blood purge' – are all verified in either the FBI file or newspaper accounts from William Patrick's US lectures.

Although the post-war William Patrick would have never thanked me for the comparison, there are some intriguing parallels he shared with his uncle. Their fathers were certainly cut from the same cloth. Alois Hitler Sr was an unrepentant womaniser and an arrogant bully who was married three times and always insisted on being addressed with his full title as a middle-ranking Austrian customs official. Alois Jr was his father's son, a bigamist and heavy drinker who beat his wife and son and revelled in acting above his social station. Both had the cunning to successfully navigate their way through potentially disastrous situations: Alois Sr by protecting his professional reputation despite the recurrent scandals of his romantic adventures; his son by evading jail for bigamy and surviving the fall of his brother's Third Reich relatively unscathed.

As children, Adolf and William Patrick were adored and spoilt by doting mothers and, perhaps as a result of that attention, both were dreamers as young men, so much so that they were seen as lazy and unfocused.

The infant deaths within weeks of each other of Klara Hitler's first three children between 1887 and 1888 and the subsequent death of her fifth child, Edmund, in 1900 were perhaps the reason she clung all the tighter to Adolf and Paula, the two children who did survive. In turn, the children loved her with an intense loyalty, particularly Adolf. In his Hitler biography, Ian Kershaw quotes the Hitler family's Jewish doctor, Eduard Bloch, as saying of Adolf: 'Outwardly, his love for his mother was his most striking feature. While he was not a "mother's boy" in the usual sense, I have never witnessed a closer attachment.'

In one of the very isolated passages showing any sign of sentiment in *Mein Kampf*, Hitler wrote: 'I had honoured my father, but loved my mother.'

Kershaw said that Hitler carried Klara's picture with him everywhere, right through to his last days in the bunker. 'Her portrait stood in his rooms in Munich, in Berlin, and at the Obersalzberg (his alpine residence near Berchtesgaden). His mother may well, in fact, have been the only person he genuinely loved in his entire life.'

It was often up to his mother to try and protect the young Adolf from the thrashings and beatings his father would dole out in sudden violent rages. When she died in 1907, aged forty-seven, Adolf was devastated. 'I have never seen anyone so prostrate with grief as Adolf Hitler,' wrote Dr Bloch.

It is impossible to underestimate Brigid Hitler's importance in William Patrick's life. One of his sons recalled the first time he had ever seen his father cry was after his mother's death in 1969. Before finally parting from her husband, Brigid left him three or four times because he had lifted a hand to her baby and from those earliest times the fates of mother and son were inextricably linked. They moved from Liverpool to London together and even when William Patrick was old enough to work, he went home to his mother. When both were fired from their jobs because of their name, they went searching for work together. 'Week after week, coming home after a day spent in fruitless searching, we compared notes,' Brigid wrote in her unpublished memoirs. 'Our daily adventures ran in parallel . . . Our quest became more and more hopeless. At first, we had supposed that after a few months people would forget us and we could sink into the quiet and unsensational obscurity of the average humdrum London experience, but ours was a special case.'

CONCLUSION

When William Patrick went to work in Germany in the 1930s his mother, left behind for once, felt 'hot tears blurring my eyes. The way home had never seemed so lonesome and gloomy before.' It was over his mother that William Patrick aroused his uncle's wrath. Hitler, evidently choosing to forget his own maternal attachment, excoriated his nephew for his repeated requests for a better-paying job so he could send some money home to Brigid.

When William Patrick won a contract for his US lecture tour in 1939, Brigid crossed the Atlantic with him, and on his release from the navy in 1946, the dutiful son's first remark to a reporter was that he was heading home to see his mother. She remained by his side even when he was married, living right next door, and she lies beside him still, sharing the same grave in Long Island.

Although the vast differences in the ways their lives played out make meaningful comparisons difficult, there are undoubtedly some shared family traits.

It is interesting that Hitler used the name Wolff at various times in his life and William Patrick himself later chose an alias to hide from the consequences of his real name. Neither was easily intimidated, be that in the small-town life of a family phlebotomist or as a powerful statesman on the world stage.

But the real key to this book is the way these two men, for different reasons, tried so hard to distance themselves from their roots.

Hitler was fanatically secretive about his background, a fact that helps explain the continuing fascination with it today. Only the dimmest outline of his parents emerges from the biographical chapters of *Mein Kampf*. He falsified his father's occupation, changing him from a customs official to a postal official, and made no mention of his sister Paula or of his two half-siblings Alois and Angela.

In reality, Hitler recognised his relatives, but only when pushed and never in public. He barely tolerated his older half-brother, allowing him to keep his Berlin restaurant open during the war but never visiting it; he let Angela work as his housekeeper for nearly eight years but insisted she remain in the background; and he so feared any public link with his sister Paula that he ordered her to assume the name Frau Wolff so no one would know who she really was. As we have seen, William Patrick and Brigid he considered simply 'loathsome'.

With the immense power he wielded, Hitler was able to take his abhorrence of his family and his disavowal of his roots to extremes. In 1956, Austrian archivist Franz Jetzinger, author of *Hitler's Youth*, wrote:

Not two months after Hitler invaded Austria, in May 1938, an order was issued to the Land Registries concerned to carry out a survey of Dollersheim (Alois Hitler's birthplace) and neighbourhood with a view to their suitability as a battle-training area for the Wehrmacht. In the following year the inhabitants of Dollersheim were forcibly evacuated and the village together with the surrounding countryside was blasted and withered by German artillery and infantry weapons. The birthplace of Hitler's father and the site of his grandmother's grave were alike rendered unrecognisable, and today this whole tract of what was once fertile and flourishing country is an arid desert sown with unexploded shells. But an area so closely associated with Hitler's family could not have been used for battle training without his knowledge and permission. Then why did he give it? Or did Hitler himself initiate the order for the destruction of Dollersheim out of insane hatred of his father and the desire to erase all evidence of his Jewish blood?'

When he was informed in 1942 that a plaque had been set up for him in the village of Spital, where he had spent some time as a youth, he flew into a rage and had it torn down.

Whether his obsessive secrecy over his family was simply the strategy of a master propagandist creating a mystery around his past and bolstering his ideology of belonging only to the Fatherland, or he was worried his hazy genealogy would automatically exempt him from his exclusive Aryan club, it is one of the areas most overlooked by historians and academics seeking to unlock Hitler's mind.

There was no great mystery behind William Patrick's determination to hide his family background after the unimaginable scale of his uncle's barbarism became clear after the Second World War. The name had been a hindrance to him even before the war when a Hitler in London was about as welcome as a Vladimir Putin in Kyiv. He had tried to profit from it with varying success in Germany and the United States. But after the Holocaust he knew that even denouncing the Nazis in countless lecture halls and fighting for the Allies against his uncle was not going to protect him from the possible consequences of such a direct and personal connection to the man responsible.

The families of six million people had good reason to hate the name Hitler.

William Patrick was raised with the name and Brigid had long ago learned to live with the folly of her marriage. Perhaps left alone they would have dealt with the shame. During his first visits to Germany in the 1930s to visit his father, William Patrick sought out his other relatives and enthusiastically urged them to pass on the family stories, not because he was seeking to blackmail his uncle but because he had grown up with the Hitler name albeit without the father and the history that should have come with it.

After the war, the family history had changed so terribly that it was unthinkable to try and raise a family called Hitler in America. William Patrick was determined not to leave future generations facing the inevitable questions and looking forever over their shoulders. In the tradition of Adolf destroying his ancestral home with a brutal efficiency, the English Hitler dropped utterly and completely out of sight and never looked back.

It is curious to note that his OSS interviewer Walter Langer, and others examining what they knew of William Patrick's life, came to the conclusion that he had not 'amounted to much' as if his uncle's ascension to the pinnacle of infamy was somehow to be admired. The fact that his accomplishments are compared to Adolf Hitler's and found to be wanting is absurd. I suspect many of those who had pondered William Patrick's fate believed he had probably died in obscurity a broken man. The fact that when he died he was loved and treasured by his wife and four sons made William Patrick the only twentieth-century Hitler to have made a conventional success of his life as a father and family man.

If, in hindsight, he did try and exploit his family connection to win favour with an uncle who just happened to be the idolised leader of Nazi Germany, then he certainly was not the first or last person to try and benefit from a blood relationship. By the time the grotesque degree of Hitler's villainy became clear, William Patrick had long ago distanced himself thoroughly from his uncle, so much so that he went to war himself and toured the US giving lectures and radio broadcasts warning the public about the excesses of the Reich.

There is some evidence to suggest that William Patrick had already been actively working against his uncle even before he moved to the United States by spying for the British intelligence services during his years in Germany. In her disputed memoir, Brigid describes her son meeting with a mysterious man called 'Fenton' in London before returning to Germany in 1938 and hints that William Patrick was sent on a spying mission. 'All the other sons could wait quietly for their turn to fight, my son had to wage his war secretly,' she wrote. On the last page of the unfinished manuscript, William Patrick tells how he escaped from Germany after rejecting Hitler's offer of German citizenship, saying: 'I'm sure you won't believe it when I tell you it was a magician – Bunny Aulden – who smuggled me out of the country, but that is the plain truth. You know, mother, it is very difficult for agents to get into Germany, so the interested parties have had to adopt all sorts of unlikely characters to do their work. Many of them are actors or barbarians.'

When the FBI was investigating William Patrick's

background in 1942, it was given assurances from the British authorities that the Führer's nephew was 'one of ours'. A number of pages referring to liaison between the FBI and British intelligence are missing from William Patrick's file. All my efforts to get any information from intelligence sources in the UK were fruitless, but in author William Stevenson's book, *A Man Called Intrepid*, about Sir William Stephenson, who set up British Security Co-ordination, a wartime body linking secret services in the US and Britain, William Patrick was said to have been known in the BSC as 'Pearl'.

Although the historical credibility of *A Man Called Intrepid* has been questioned, it also claims BSC records allude to the disputed visit by Adolf Hitler to Liverpool before the First World War that was described in Brigid Hitler's book. A footnote written by Stevenson reads: 'BSC records suggest that Adolf Hitler spent much of his time watching the flow of sea traffic through Liverpool to the four corners of the British Empire, undoubtedly impressed by this evidence of maritime power.'

Ernst Hanfstaengl also wrote of his leader's fascination with England: 'I tried to fire his enthusiasm by talking about Windsor Castle and the National Gallery and the Houses of Parliament . . . Hitler was quite carried away and started sketching on the back of a menu card from memory a drawing of the Palace of Westminster. This was the sort of parlour trick he could pull at a moment's notice and the drawing was perfectly accurate.'

Hanfstaengl pointed out that Hitler could easily have seen the building in an encyclopaedia, and that he never mentioned the trip to any of his confidantes. But the obsessively secretive manipulator may well have had very good reasons for not wanting anyone to know about it. Hitler's version of his own past, as we have seen, was often far from the truth.

Historians question the story of Adolf Hitler's trip to Liverpool but there is no proof either way. He was living as a tramp in Vienna as a young man and the only witnesses to this time have proved unreliable. There is this intriguing missing period in his life. Checks of passenger lists of ships leaving Hamburg for Britain at around that time did not show any Hitlers or anyone else by any of the names he assumed, and passenger records from the other possible port of departure, Bremen, were destroyed by fire. It has been claimed that during the 1930s the Nazis attempted to reconstruct the Bremen lists. We can only wonder why.

As I was nearing the end of my inquiries into the lives of the English Hitler and his American heirs, I decided to make one last trip to Long Island to try and answer some of the nagging questions that remained. By now I was convinced that William Patrick's widow and his eldest son misled me by continuing to claim the Brigid memoirs were bogus and I went back to see a key family source who had helped me before in return for anonymity.

Our previous meetings had built up a trust and it was suggested that I read the first and last pages of the memoir out aloud. They were clearly written in different styles and, I quickly deduced, by different people. One was flowery and descriptive, the other more matter-of-fact. 'The apple doesn't fall far from the tree,' I was told, cryptically.

'Are you trying to tell me that they both wrote it – that the memoir was written by William Patrick and his mother?' I asked.

A smile and a nod of the head told me I was right. And I got a similar response when I suggested the missing second half of the manuscript may still exist.

'The memoirs are factual. Some of the stories may have been dramatised a little, just as any storyteller might do, but they are basically true,' said the source.

'Does that mean Adolf Hitler did go to Liverpool then?' I asked.

'Not only did he go to Liverpool, but he also went to Ireland to visit relatives. They had family there,' I was told. 'Hitler was a much more well-travelled young man than people realise. Just because people can't prove he made the trip, that doesn't mean that he didn't make it.'

'So how did the manuscript get to be in the New York Public Library?' I continued.

'How do things get to the Smithsonian or any major museum? To be kept for posterity. It is not usually an accident that they are there,' came the answer. I was also given the strong impression that there is more to the memoirs, but that the second half of the book was being withheld, possibly because it contained clues to the family's post-war plight.

To the other question that haunted my investigation – Did William Patrick call his first son Adolf after his uncle? – the answer was much more direct. He did.

In trying to understand William Patrick's bizarre decision to willingly confer the name Adolf Hitler on his son I was given the strong guide that while shocked and repulsed by many of his uncle's actions, he was, nevertheless, proud of his close links to events of such worldly magnitude, even if he had decided to keep them secret. 'What good is a secret if nobody ever gets to hear about it?' I was asked.

Notwithstanding the note he left me on my earlier visit to his home suggesting I contacted his lawyer, I called several more times at Alex's house. I wanted to ask him, as the family's appointed spokesman, whether he had reconsidered an offer to consult on the television programme being made about his father by David Howard and Madoc Roberts for Britain's Channel 5 and if they would consider a request for an interview with Oprah Winfrey. I also wanted to ask him one more time about the origins of his grandmother's memoirs.

The first time I returned was just after 9/11 and an American flag hung proudly from the front of the house. Alex was in the garden planting trees. But he appeared more tense than I'd seen him before.

'I spoke to my mum and my brothers about it,' he said. 'We had a long conversation and we decided there is nothing in it for us. We don't want to talk about it, especially after what has just happened in the United States. Who cares about us?'

I tried to say that the emergence of a new bogeyman like Bin Laden only increased interest in the likes of Adolf Hitler.

'It really makes me aggravated when people talk about Hitler and Bin Laden. Where I work today they had an anthrax scare. The stuff you are talking about is something I don't want to deal with. We all sat down, and we all talked about it. To us, the last thing we need to do is anything that brings us nearer to someone like Bin Laden.

'I said to my brothers that maybe after mum is dead, maybe then we will do something. All of this is ancient history to us.

It just happens to be that we have a similar name, that is all. But to me, that is not my name anyway. Maybe after my mum passes away then we will have a different attitude.'

Unnerved by the questions but either too polite or too intrigued to go inside and shut the door, he played down the story told to me by another family member that the brothers had a blood pact not to have children. 'That's just the way life was,' he said. 'We never made a pact or a plan or anything like that. All of us have dated people and have had long-term relationships with people. It's just something that hasn't come about.'

Then he added: 'Maybe my other two brothers did, but I never did.'

On the memoirs, he was sticking to his story: 'As far as I know it was all made up,' he said. 'Everybody in my family who has read it says it's full of fantasy stories – and we should know.'

But Alex accepted that his parents did, indeed, call him Adolf. 'So, there are lots of people who have that name,' he said defensively. 'I don't know why they chose it. I wasn't there when that was decided.

'Come back and see me in ten years,' he continued as he finally made for the door. 'By then my mother won't be around anymore.'

Several years after his mother's death, in 2004, I did, indeed, return to ask Alex if he had any change in heart in telling his father's story in full.

'I don't really know that much,' said Alex, who by then had retired from his job as a veteran's counsellor. 'When I was a kid, I would ask my father all about it and say, "Why don't you tell us?"

'He would say, "What do you want to know for? It is not going to do anything to help you."'

'When he came to the United States, he said that life is over, this is my new life. He did everything in his former life and then he had us and he became a dad.

'I have spoken about this with my brothers, and we will not be talking about this. Not now or ever.'

With that, Alex Adolf Hitler slammed the door on the past.

On that same trip, I paid an emotional visit to Holocaust survivor Reich Werner, who lived just a few towns away from the Hitlers on Long Island. Mr Werner's family fled to the then Yugoslavia in 1933 when the Nazis rose to power in Germany and was hidden with his sister, Renate, by a family in the resistance movement for two years after the country was invaded in 1941, but he was eventually rounded up by the Gestapo. He was separated from his mother when he was taken to Auschwitz concentration camp and never saw her again.

'I was born in Germany. We lived a perfectly normal life. One morning, there was a knock on the door and a bunch of guys in long black coats turned up,' he told me. 'It was the Gestapo, the German secret police, and they found me. At that time, I knew absolutely nothing about the Nazis. And I went to Auschwitz. We knew that we wouldn't be there for very long. I had thirteen Jewish friends before the war and, when the war was over, I was the only one still alive. They were all killed.'

While at Auschwitz, he learned how to do magic from another prisoner, Herbert Lewin, who was known as Nivelli the Magician before the war, and he credited the distraction of performing tricks in the camp for helping him to survive.

Other ways he was able to survive proved more traumatising. He remembered being forced to run naked past Mengele, who would later escape the Allied troops and the almost certain execution he would have faced for the inhuman experiments he carried out on inmates. Mengele then decided who was fit for work and who would go to the gas chambers. 'We were literally running for our lives,' said Werner. 'We would smile, try to look bigger and stronger – anything for him to believe we were well enough to work.'

When he was finally liberated by US troops on 5 May 1945, he was still only seventeen and weighed just sixty-four pounds.

Werner immigrated to England – meeting his future wife, Eva – and moved to the United States in 1955. This gentle, thoughtful man was neither shocked nor disturbed when I told him descendants of Hitler lived just a short drive away from the peaceful cabin home where he lived in retirement. If anything, he said he blamed the German people for allowing Hitler and his cronies to wreak such havoc.

Werner, who died in 2022 aged ninety-four, said he bore no ill will towards the Long Island Hitlers. 'I feel that by me persecuting these people, by me expressing hatred, I'm not one little bit better,' he said.

'I'm not going to blame you for the deeds of your parents, nor do I want to be blamed for what my ancestors did or didn't do.

'If you had asked me twenty years ago or fifty years ago, maybe my attitudes would have been different, maybe I would have said, "Give me a machine gun and I'll go over there and wipe them out," but that's not me anymore. Life to me is beautiful.'

CONCLUSION

I am not a historian, nor do I pretend to be. The details of William Patrick Hitler's life have largely been presented in this book as I discovered them. They do not show William Patrick in a consistent light. He is, by turn, described as exceedingly lazy, loathsome, repulsive, blackmailing, disreputable, brave, loving, caring, hard-working and funny. But real life is like that; we do not all fit into neat little categories and maybe there are a little of all these things in us all. Some of the details and scenarios I have reported do conflict with each other and others may lead to confusion. Many of the pieces are now in place but the jigsaw of William Patrick Hitler's life is far from complete. Did Adolf Hitler visit England? I believe he did. Is the manuscript of Brigid Hitler's memoirs in the New York Public Library authentic? Again, I believe it is. But what of the other questions that will continue to taunt historians. Did William Patrick leave Germany because he was horrified at what he saw? Or was it because his uncle wouldn't give him a decent job? Why did William Patrick go to such lengths to change his identity and still choose an alias that is tainted by Nazism? And why on earth would he name his eldest son after Adolf Hitler?

If William Patrick or Brigid were alive today, they could perhaps answer some of these questions. It is more likely they would say that it was all too long ago to matter. The most important thing to them was to protect the Hitlers they left behind.

William Patrick spent a great deal more than half of his life living a lie because that was the most effective legacy that he could give to the sons who inherited the world's least wanted genes.

They have no reason to believe the demons that lurked behind their great-uncle's twisted psyche were fingerprinted on the DNA they share.

But they do not want to take any chances. Writing this update, I should add that none of the brothers were married in 2022. Neither did they have any children.

And that is why they will forever be the Last of the Hitlers.

IMPORTANT DATES

7 June 1837: Birth of Alois Schicklgruber, father of Adolf, Alois, Angela and Paula, in Strones, Austria. He is the illegitimate son of Maria Anna Schicklgruber

1873: Alois Schicklgruber marries Anna Glassl

6 June 1876: Alois Schicklgruber changes his name to Hitler

1880: Alois and Anna divorce

January 1882: Birth of Alois Hitler Jr in Braunau, Austria. He is the illegitimate child of Alois and Franziska Matzelsberger

22 May 1883: Alois Sr marries Franziska

28 July 1883: Birth of Angela Hitler in Braunau

1884: Franziska dies

7 January 1885: Alois Sr marries Klara Pölzl

20 April 1889: Birth of Adolf Hitler in Braunau. He is the child of Alois and Klara Pölzl

3 July 1891: Birth of Brigid Dowling in Dublin, Ireland

21 January 1896: Birth of Paula Hitler in Hafeld, Austria

3 January 1903: Alois Hitler Sr dies

1909: Brigid meets Alois Hitler at the Dublin Horse Show

3 June 1910: Brigid marries Alois Hitler at the Marylebone Register Office in London

12 March 1911: William Patrick Hitler is born in Toxteth, Liverpool

November 1912–April 1913: Adolf Hitler stayed with his brother's family in Liverpool, according to unverified account in Brigid Hitler's memoir

May 1914: Alois leaves Brigid and William Patrick to live in Germany

28 July 1914: First World War begins; Britain declares war on 4 August

11 November 1918: First World War ends

1923: Alois charged with bigamy for marrying German wife while still wed to Brigid

August 1929: William Patrick makes first visit to Germany to see his father

1930: William Patrick's second trip to Germany and his first meeting with Adolf Hitler

1930: According to Hans Frank, the Nazi 'Butcher of Poland', William Patrick was attacked as a 'loathsome relative' by Hitler who gave his nephew an angry dressing down for talking to the press. Frank claimed he was sent off to investigate Hitler's possible Jewish ancestry because of a blackmail threat from William Patrick

18 September 1931: Adolf Hitler's niece Geli Raubal found shot dead in his Berlin apartment

30 January 1933: Hindenburg invites Hitler to be German Chancellor

1933: William Patrick leaves England to live and work in Germany

1938: William Patrick is summoned to Berchtesgaden, Hitler's alpine retreat, and asked to give up his British nationality and take a prominent role in the Third Reich. He refuses and has to leave Germany for his own safety

20 January 1939: Brigid Hitler in court in Highgate, London for non-payment of rates

30 March 1939: William Patrick Hitler and his mother arrive in New York on the French liner SS *Normandie*

1 September 1939: Second World War begins; Britain declares war on 3 September

3 March 1942: William Patrick writes to President Franklin D. Roosevelt asking for help to be enlisted in the US military so he can fight against his uncle

30 March 1942: William Patrick interviewed by the FBI over his links to Adolf Hitler

10 September 1943: William Patrick interviewed by Walter Langer of the Office of Strategic Studies, forerunner to the CIA, for information about his uncle

6 March 1944: William Patrick called up into the US Navy

30 April 1945: Hitler commits suicide as Russians close in on his bunker

8 May 1945: Germany surrenders unconditionally

2 September 1945: Second World War ends

February 1946: William Patrick discharged from the navy

2 October 1946: William Patrick applies for a social-security card in the name of William Hiller

1947: William Patrick marries Phyllis in New York, USA. They adopt an alias

1949: Alex Hitler is born in New York, USA. Angela Hitler dies

1951: Louis Hitler is born in New York, USA

1956: Alois Hitler dies

1957: Howard Hitler is born in New York, USA

1960: Paula Hitler dies

1965: Brian Hitler born in New York, USA

18 November 1969: Brigid Hitler dies in New York, USA

1979: *The Memoirs of Bridget Hitler*, edited by Michael Unger, published in the UK by Gerald Duckworth and Co.

14 July 1987: William Patrick Hitler dies in New York, USA

1989: Howard Hitler dies

2004: Phyllis Hitler dies

ACKNOWLEDGEMENTS

Firstly, I would like to thank Tim Miles, my friend and former partner in New York. We started work together on the story that would provide the basis for this book and I will be forever grateful for sharing the most enjoyable years of my career in our little office at the junction of Spring and Lafayette in SoHo in the 1990s.

I had the pleasure to work with some good people on several documentaries about the Long Island Hitlers, most notably with director Matt Ogens and with David Howard and Madoc Roberts. I also owe a debt of thanks to Randall Northam, publisher of *The Last of the Hitlers*.

As always, it has been a dream working with Toby Buchan and Ciara Lloyd at John Blake Publishing.

I dedicate this book to my wife Michelle and our children, Mickey, Jazmin and Savannah.